Victor Lippit's *Capitalism* taps the vast literatures of both radical and Marxian political economy to produce a provocative new assessment of contemporary capitalism as a global system.

This is first-rate work—sophisticated in its scholarship yet also clear, direct, and generally accessible in its message. It teaches as well as persuades. It provokes in the best sense of rousing readers to think urgently—and without the currently fashionable self-delusions of capitalist triumphalism—about one of the central problems of our times. Professionals, lay readers, and college students can all benefit from this fine new contribution.

Richard D. Wolff, *Professor of Economics, University of Massachusetts*

In *Capitalism* Victor Lippit provides us with a wide-ranging and thought-provoking analysis of the long-term trajectory of the global capitalist economic system. His concluding chapter on future scenarios is must reading for everyone concerned about building an alternative economic system that will be both viable and humane.

Thomas E. Weisskopf, *Professor of Economics, University of Michigan*

The capitalist economic system is a dominant force shaping the lives of all of us on the planet, as well as the ecological life of the planet itself. Victor Lippit presents an eloquent, sweeping, and insightful perspective on the capitalist system today and its likely evolution over the coming historical epoch. *Capitalism*, the book, offers a much-needed jolt of reality about capitalism, the system, as it proceeds through the twenty-first century.

Robert Pollin, *Professor of Economics and Co-Director, Political Economy Research Institute (PERI), University of Massachusetts Amherst*

Capitalism

Capitalism is the dominant mode of production, distribution, and exchange in the world today. Since its true emergence in the sixteenth century, capitalism has contributed to a rapid acceleration of living standards in the industrialized world. As it spreads to China and other less-developed countries, it appears likely to play a comparable role elsewhere as well. Its impact, however, is not entirely beneficent, as growing prosperity has been accompanied by various manifestations of acute social injustice and environmental degradation.

This book explores the contradictions of capitalism, its internal dynamics, and the forces that have shaped its evolution over time. In doing so, it considers the principal forms that capitalism has assumed—the Anglo-American free-market kind that has reached its apogee in the United States; state-directed capitalism as exemplified in such countries as Japan and South Korea; and the welfare-state capitalism that has characterized capitalist development in continental Europe. The contemporary forces of globalization and technological change affect each of these forms of capitalism differently. Whatever form it assumes, the capitalist system is shown to have survived by overcoming its inherent contradictions and repeatedly reinventing itself. Its ability to continue doing so in the long run is open to question, however, since some contradictions may well be insurmountable.

This impressive, scholarly volume will appeal across many disciplines, including economics, political science, sociology, and history.

Victor D. Lippit is Professor of Economics at the University of California, Riverside.

Routledge frontiers of political economy

1 **Equilibrium Versus Understanding**
Towards the rehumanization of economics within social theory
Mark Addleson

2 **Evolution, Order and Complexity**
Edited by Elias L. Khalil and Kenneth E. Boulding

3 **Interactions in Political Economy**
Malvern after ten years
Edited by Steven Pressman

4 **The End of Economics**
Michael Perelman

5 **Probability in Economics**
Omar F. Hamouda and Robin Rowley

6 **Capital Controversy, Post-Keynesian Economics and the History of Economics**
Essays in honour of Geoff Harcourt, volume one
Edited by Philip Arestis, Gabriel Palma and Malcolm Sawyer

7 **Markets, Unemployment and Economic Policy**
Essays in honour of Geoff Harcourt, volume two
Edited by Philip Arestis, Gabriel Palma and Malcolm Sawyer

8 **Social Economy**
The logic of capitalist development
Clark Everling

9 **New Keynesian Economics/Post Keynesian Alternatives**
Edited by Roy J. Rotheim

10 **The Representative Agent in Macroeconomics**
James E. Hartley

11 **Borderlands of Economics**
Essays in honour of Daniel R. Fusfeld
Edited by Nahid Aslanbeigui and Young Back Choi

12 **Value, Distribution and Capital**
Essays in honour of Pierangelo Garegnani
Edited by Gary Mongiovi and Fabio Petri

13 **The Economics of Science**
Methodology and epistemology as if economics really mattered
James R. Wible

14 **Competitiveness, Localised Learning and Regional Development**
Specialisation and prosperity in small open economies
Peter Maskell, Heikki Eskelinen, Ingjaldur Hannibalsson, Anders Malmberg and Eirik Vatne

15 **Labour Market Theory**
A constructive reassessment
Ben J. Fine

16 **Women and European Employment**
Jill Rubery, Mark Smith, Colette Fagan, Damian Grimshaw

17 **Explorations in Economic Methodology**
From Lakatos to empirical philosophy of science
Roger Backhouse

18 **Subjectivity in Political Economy**
Essays on wanting and choosing
David P. Levine

19 **The Political Economy of Middle East Peace**
The impact of competing trade agendas
Edited by J. W. Wright, Jnr

20 **The Active Consumer**
Novelty and surprise in consumer choice
Edited by Marina Bianchi

21 **Subjectivism and Economic Analysis**
Essays in memory of Ludwig Lachmann
Edited by Roger Koppl and Gary Mongiovi

22 **Themes in Post-Keynesian Economics**
Essays in honour of Geoff Harcourt, volume three
Edited by Claudio Sardoni and Peter Kriesler

23 **The Dynamics of Technological Knowledge**
Cristiano Antonelli

24 **The Political Economy of Diet, Health and Food Policy**
Ben J. Fine

25 **The End of Finance**
Capital market inflation, financial derivatives and pension fund capitalism
Jan Toporowski

26 **Political Economy and the New Capitalism**
Edited by Jan Toporowski

27 **Growth Theory**
A philosophical perspective
Patricia Northover

28 **The Political Economy of the Small Firm**
Edited by Charlie Dannreuther

29 **Hahn and Economic Methodology**
Edited by Thomas Boylan and Paschal F. O'Gorman

30 **Gender, Growth and Trade**
The miracle economies of the postwar years
David Kucera

31 **Normative Political Economy**
Subjective freedom, the market and the state
David Levine

32 **Economist with a Public Purpose**
Essays in honour of John Kenneth Galbraith
Edited by Michael Keaney

33 **Involuntary Unemployment**
The elusive quest for a theory
Michel De Vroey

34 **The Fundamental Institutions of Capitalism**
Ernesto Screpanti

35 **Transcending Transaction**
The search for self-generating markets
Alan Shipman

36 **Power in Business and the State**
An historical analysis of its concentration
Frank Bealey

37 **Editing Economics**
Essays in honour of Mark Perlman
Hank Lim, Ungsuh K. Park and Geoff Harcourt

38 **Money, Macroeconomics and Keynes**
Essays in honour of Victoria Chick, volume one
Philip Arestis, Meghnad Desai and Sheila Dow

39 **Methodology, Microeconomics and Keynes**
Essays in honour of Victoria Chick, volume two
Philip Arestis, Meghnad Desai and Sheila Dow

40 **Market Drive and Governance**
Reexamining the rules for economic and commercial contest
Ralf Boscheck

41 **The Value of Marx**
Political economy for contemporary capitalism
Alfredo Saad-Filho

42 **Issues in Positive Political Economy**
S. Mansoob Murshed

43 **The Enigma of Globalisation**
A journey to a new stage of capitalism
Robert Went

44 **The Market**
Equilibrium, stability, mythology
S. N. Afriat

45 **The Political Economy of Rule Evasion and Policy Reform**
Jim Leitzel

46 **Unpaid Work and the Economy**
Edited by Antonella Picchio

47 **Distributional Justice**
Theory and measurement
Hilde Bojer

48 **Cognitive Developments in Economics**
Edited by Salvatore Rizzello

49 **Social Foundations of Markets, Money and Credit**
Costas Lapavitsas

50 **Rethinking Capitalist Development**
Essays on the economics of Josef Steindl
Edited by Tracy Mott and Nina Shapiro

51 **An Evolutionary Approach to Social Welfare**
Christian Sartorius

52 **Kalecki's Economics Today**
Edited by Zdzislaw L. Sadowski and Adam Szeworski

53 **Fiscal Policy from Reagan to Blair**
The left veers right
Ravi K. Roy and Arthur T. Denzau

54 **The Cognitive Mechanics of Economic Development and Institutional Change**
Bertin Martens

55 **Individualism and the Social Order**
The social element in liberal thought
Charles R. McCann Jnr.

56 **Affirmative Action in the United States and India**
A comparative perspective
Thomas E. Weisskopf

57 **Global Political Economy and the Wealth of Nations**
Performance, institutions, problems and policies
Edited by Phillip Anthony O'Hara

58 **Structural Economics**
Thijs ten Raa

59 **Macroeconomic Theory and Economic Policy**
Essays in honour of Jean-Paul Fitoussi
Edited by K. Vela Velupillai

60 **The Struggle Over Work**
The 'end of work' and employment alternatives in post-industrial societies
Shaun Wilson

61 **The Political Economy of Global Sporting Organisations**
John Forster and Nigel Pope

62 **The Flawed Foundations of General Equilibrium**
Critical essays on economic theory
Frank Ackerman and Alejandro Nadal

63 **Uncertainty in Economic Theory**
Essays in honor of David Schmeidler's 65th birthday
Edited by Itzhak Gilboa

64 **The New Institutional Economics of Corruption**
Edited by Johann Graf Lambsdorff, Markus Taube and Matthias Schramm

65 **The Price Index and its Extension**
A chapter in economic measurement
S. N. Afriat

66 **Reduction, Rationality and Game Theory in Marxian Economics**
Bruce Philp

67 **Culture and Politics in Economic Development**
Volker Bornschier

68 **Modern Applications of Austrian Thought**
Edited by Jürgen G. Backhaus

69 **Original Choices**
Individuals, incommensurability, and democracy
Robert Urquhart

70 **Labour Theory of Value**
Peter C. Dooley

71 **Capitalism**
Victor D. Lippit

Capitalism

Victor D. Lippit

Routledge
Taylor & Francis Group
LONDON AND NEW YORK

First published 2005
by Routledge
2 Park Square, Milton Park, Abingdon, Oxon OX14 4RN

Simultaneously published in the USA and Canada
by Routledge
270 Madison Ave, New York, NY 10016

Transferred to Digital Print 2006

Routledge is an imprint of the Taylor & Francis Group, an informa business

Typeset in Times by Wearset Ltd, Boldon, Tyne and Wear
Printed and bound in Great Britain by MPG Books Ltd, Bodmin

British Library Cataloguing in Publication Data
A catalogue record for this book is available from the British Library

Library of Congress Cataloging in Publication Data
A catalog record for this book has been requested

ISBN 10: 0–415–27394–3
ISBN 13: 978–0–415–27394–7

This book is dedicated to all those who have contributed to the rich scholarly tradition of radical political economy, seeking to make the world a better place—and hopefully to preserve it.

Contents

Tables

Preface

As the reader may have observed, this book is about capitalism. It reflects both an appreciation of the role capitalism has played in raising living standards in much of the world, and concerns with the great social injustices and suffering that the capitalist system has generated. The thrust of the book, however, is not with a normative evaluation of the capitalist system but with a positive analysis of the system: the types of capitalism, its main contradictions, and the forces that shape its evolution over time. My own conclusion is that the capitalist system is not compatible with the continuation of human life as we have experienced it, and in the extreme case may not be compatible with the continuation of human life at all. I realize that this will be highly controversial, and while I would be delighted to be able to persuade all of my readers that strong action is called for to prevent this coming about, I will feel my purpose fulfilled if the book succeeds in generating serious debate over the issues it raises.

Since the 1960s, a serious and growing environmental literature has emerged. With a number of exceptions, this literature has not placed the issue of environmental destruction within the context of the dominant economic system associated with it: the capitalist economic system. Yet as I argue in the text, the issue of environmental destruction is intimately bound up with the capitalist system, and with the emphasis it places on the growth in throughputs—on ever-increasing production, consumption and the generation of wastes. To my mind, this is the core contradiction of capitalism, one of such seriousness that it threatens not only the continuity of the system but the future of the human tenure on earth as well.

I approach my analysis within the tradition of radical political economy. My own use of the word "radical" combines some traditional meanings: something is radical if it gets at the root of things, is marked by considerable departure from the usual or traditional, and looks toward social change as a necessary means of improving the human condition. The workings of the capitalist system have long been a principal concern of those writing within the radical political economy tradition, and my book is in the first instance addressed to them, and to the debates in the field. At the same time, however, I believe the issues it addresses are of importance to all those concerned with the future of the planet and of humankind, and have deliberately written it in such a way as to make it accessible to the general reader. There are portions of the book, I realize, that address issues mainly of concern to others working within the radical political economy tradition, and I envision general readers with their eyes glazing over when they come upon such sections. I would like to encourage these readers merely to skim through the more arcane sections when they encounter them rather than to give up on the book as a whole, for the issues it raises will presumably be of concern to all thinking people rather than to a narrow subset of specialists.

Given the enormous scope of the subject matter, there has been no way to avoid leaving out vast amounts of relevant material, so I beg the reader's forgiveness if particular issues of concern have failed to find their way into the text. I have been working on this manuscript for six years, and while additional time may have improved the result, I believe that I have reached a point where a coherent analysis emerges. I also recognize that there is a special challenge in attempting a work that crosses the boundaries of many disciplines. I cannot of course claim the specialist's competence in the vast majority of these, but I do believe that there are many important issues that cannot be addressed within the boundaries of a single discipline. I beg the pardon of those with far greater specialized knowledge of the areas I touch upon, and hope that the flaws they discover will not forestall serious consideration of the issues I raise.

My own pathway to the writing of this book has been a winding one. My own training in economics at Harvard (undergraduate) and Yale (graduate) was a conventional one. Between college and graduate school—decades ago—I worked in the research department of Merrill Lynch, Pierce, Fenner and Smith for a year and a half. Since that time I have retained an interest in the financial press—which I follow almost as much as the baseball news—and about eight years ago I introduced the course on the stock market at the University of California, Riverside, where I have been teaching since 1971. Since my own training in economics was conventional, most of my knowledge of radical political economy is self-taught, acquired through an avid exploration of the literature, and through countless discussions and arguments with friends.

From the time of my graduate studies I was particularly interested in the economy of China under Mao, a subject on which I wrote my dissertation and numerous articles. For me this reflected, in part, a combination of my interests in comparative economic systems and in economic development. My interest in China at that time had deeper roots as well, however. I believe it is often the case that when people immerse themselves in a foreign culture they do so as a means of learning something more deeply about their own; this was certainly true in my own case. Concerned with the existence of poverty, racism, sexism and various other forms of social injustice in my own society, I became interested in exploring the possibility of organizing society in a way that did not take self-interest as its starting point. Under Mao, China made an attempt to do so.

Soon after Mao died (in 1976) I became aware of the serious injustices embodied in the Maoist model and in Maoist practice. My own interests shifted increasingly to an exploration of market socialism, an important branch of the radical political economy literature. During the 1980s it appeared at first that China was moving in this direction, expanding the use of market forces and permitting a mixture of public and private ownership. Over the course of the decade, however, it became apparent that for all his shortcomings Mao's apprehension that the unleashing of market forces would inevitably lead to capitalism was firmly grounded. At first China tried to limit the size of capitalist enterprises, but given the vast underemployment that existed both in cities and in the countryside the government could not reasonably limit the number of employees that private enterprises could hire. Further, as foreign private enterprises sought entry into China, offering jobs, technology and export prowess, no government concerned with the welfare of its own citizenry could reasonably resist.

By the 1990s, following the collapse of the Soviet Union, it became clear that capitalism was the only game in town—not only in China but worldwide. The field of comparative economic systems, which was initially focused on comparing the economies of the Soviet Union as a prototype of socialism (although I myself always considered it a form of statism rather than socialism) and that of the United States as a prototype of capitalism, appeared to have reached a dead end. This was not really the case, however, since the scope of the field merely required a redefinition. By the end of the twentieth century it became increasingly apparent that what the field of comparative economic systems needed to explore was the different types of capitalism, the core contradictions of the system, and the dynamic forces driving its evolution.

This book emerges from a personal attempt to think through these issues. I owe an immense personal debt to all of the writers in the radical political economy tradition. This includes numerous friends, colleagues and countless others whom I have never met, people who in their discourse and writings have challenged my thinking and forced me to think yet again—numerous times. Although many—perhaps most—of these will disagree with the conclusions of this book, we share a deep concern with social injustice and a desire to contribute to the formation of more humane societies, both in our home countries and throughout the world.

I owe a special debt to the late David Gordon, who laid the groundwork for social structure of accumulation theory, and to the subsequent developers of that theory, including, among others, Michael Reich, Sam Bowles, Tom Weisskopf, David Kotz, and Phillip O'Hara. Five of my present and former colleagues at the University of California, Riverside read a late draft of the manuscript and provided me with valuable feedback and encouragement. They include David Fairris, Bob Pollin, Aziz Khan, Steve Cullenberg, and Howard Sherman. David Fairris and Bob Pollin especially provided me with detailed comments that proved invaluable. My colleagues and neighbors, Susan Carter and Richard Sutch, were also kind enough to provide me with relevant sections of their forthcoming edited book, *Historical Statistics of the United States: Millennial Edition,* which will be published in 2005 by Cambridge University Press.

Directly or indirectly, through extended conversations or through the medium of their writings, I have also learned greatly from friends and scholars throughout the world, including Ron Chilcote, Haider Khan, and Rick Wolff in the United States, Zhang Yunling in China, Akmal Hussain in Pakistan, Jomo in Malaysia, and You Jong-Il in South Korea. I must also acknowledge my indebtedness to the late Paul Baran, whose path-breaking work on the surplus stimulated my own thinking immeasurably; to the late Alec Nove, whose work on market socialism also opened doors to my own thinking; and to the late Kenneth Boulding, whose essay on "The Economics of the Coming Spaceship Earth" made me aware both of the dangers of an open-ended commitment to economic growth and of the possibilities of an alternative approach to economics, an approach founded on concerns with the quality of the capital stock, including that embodied in human beings.

I am also indebted to my editors at Routledge, who have borne with me through the extended period it has taken to complete this manuscript, and especially to Rob Langham, who pushed me to focus on this project in the first place. Closer to home, I must acknowledge how much I have learned from many of my graduate students, including especially Hashem Kardevani, who completed his dissertation on regulation theory with me, and Anirban Dasgupta and Lopamudra Banerjee, both of whom made great contributions as my research assistants during my work on the manuscript. The University of California also contributed through sabbatical leaves, and its Academic Senate through research support.

My fiercest critics have always been my (adult) children—Aki, Seiji, Kio, Tami, and Taku—and they too have contributed greatly by forcing me to rethink my approach to various portions of the manuscript; Aki and Tami especially made specific critiques that led to significant revisions in the text. I owe a special debt of gratitude to my wife Joyce, who made numerous suggestions to improve the writing and whose unfailing support through a difficult six years made the completion of this book possible. In the last analysis, while recognizing the contributions of so many people without whom this book would not have been possible, I am well aware that it will be a controversial work, and must take upon myself responsibility for the final product and all its shortcomings.

Riverside, California
October 2004

1 The capitalist system

It is only natural for people to take for granted the economic and social institutions within which they carry out their daily activities. In industrialized countries we think of educational institutions, the job market, career opportunities and so forth as creating a set of choices or possibilities that we navigate to achieve our chosen ends. We are, of course, aware of marginal changes in institutions, but to envision an entirely different set of institutions is almost akin to envisioning an alternative universe. In the usual course of events, then, we do not think of capitalism as a distinctive means of organizing human existence, even though capitalism has a history, a future, and immense consequences for the human condition. My intention here is to explore a set of issues related to capitalism—its nature, forms, history, contradictions, and future. I do so not with the hope of providing definitive answers, but with the hope of spurring thought that will enhance our ability to understand the forces shaping our behavior, to control our economic and social environment, and to consider countermeasures for some of the serious threats that capitalism poses to human existence.

Capitalism first appeared as the dominant economic system during the course of the "long" sixteenth century, and it is no accident that the rapid acceleration in living standards in the portion of the world that is now industrialized can be traced to the same era. As Adam Smith perceived in his *An Inquiry into the Nature and Causes of the Wealth of Nations* (1776), individuals' efforts to pursue their own material benefit can generate positive social and economic consequences for the entire community. Smith's insight continues to provide a core theoretical justification for the capitalist system, especially for the proponents of free enterprise and the market system. The enormous increases in income and wealth that have materialized in the industrialized countries are currently in the process of spreading to other parts of the world, with the Asian tigers—South Korea, Taiwan, Hong Kong, and Singapore—already enjoying living standards comparable to those of the West, and large regions like China apparently in the midst of similar transformations. If capitalism persists for several more centuries, as seems to be highly likely, then from the vantage point of the future, capitalism may be seen as the system responsible for the transformation of the human condition from one of mass subsistence to mass prosperity.

The consequences of capitalism, however, are not entirely positive. As many economists have recognized, the widespread benefits of the market system are accompanied by pervasive market failures. When people buy houses or drive cars, for example, they are unlikely to be focused on their personal contributions to global deforestation or warming. Moreover, even if some enlightened individuals are conscious of these consequences of their behavior, the global trends will hardly be altered if they refrain from pursuing their personal ends. In cases like these, the common good that Adam Smith envisioned resulting from individuals' pursuit of their own benefit will not materialize. Thus the capitalist system calls into question the future sustainability of the human habitat. Further, history is filled with instances in which the pursuit of individual benefit under the capitalist system has contributed to social injustice on a gargantuan scale. One need only consider the history of the slave trade, or the fact that Liverpool, the first great industrial city in England, owed much of its prosperity in the eighteenth century to that trade and the building of ships for it.[1]

Further, if we think of the world as being in the midst of an extended period of capitalist transformation, perhaps extending forward as long as the four and a half centuries capitalism has already existed, then it would be well to keep in mind the fact that the majority of the world's population has not yet benefited from the promise of material prosperity that the capitalist system appears to make. To the contrary, the early stages of capitalist development have typically been accompanied by vast immiserization and exploitation. During the Industrial Revolution in England, children as young as seven had to work in factories for twelve or more hours per day (Mantoux 1961: 410–412; Ashton 1962: 113); the widespread exploitation of child labor remains commonplace in countries like China and India today, countries just starting out on the path of capitalist development.

In response to the transparent injustices of capitalist development, socialist and communist movements have attempted to define an alternative path. These have invariably foundered, most notably with the collapse and disintegration of the Soviet Union. This collapse can be attributed to many factors (including of course the hostility of the capitalist world), but two especially noteworthy ones include a series of internal contradictions and a failure to develop a workable basis for economic calculation and action. If socialism is in some measure a system meant to overcome the inequality (of income, wealth and power) and alienation that characterize capitalism, it is difficult to see how a system of central planning, which concentrates authority in unprecedented fashion and leaves ordinary working people with little control over their own work and lives, is compatible with socialism. Moreover, in the Soviet Union, as a consequence of the inefficiencies inherent in central planning, an ever-growing share of national product had to be allocated to capital formation for each incremental rouble of consumer goods production, pushing aspirations for popular prosperity ever further out into the future (Nove 1986: 155; Gregory and Stuart 1995: 316, 326).

While my focus here is on the capitalist system, I mention the case of the Soviet Union simply to make the point that there is in fact no viable alternative to capitalism at this stage in world history. One would certainly hope that when and if the entire world has been incorporated as developed entities within the capitalist world system—that is, when capitalism has completed its transformative "task"—an alternative system will emerge that focuses on the development of the human potential rather than the unlimited increase in the quantity of goods and services that capitalism promises. I will develop the case for this position more fully below, but here I would like to focus on just two points.

First, as John Kenneth Galbraith (1984: 119–133) has pointed out, when wants are created by the system and then satisfied, there may be no net gain in satisfaction. In fact, for those unable to satisfy those wants, a more or less severe sense of deprivation may be engendered. More significantly, the cumulative environmental destruction associated with a virtually open-ended increase in production and consumption threatens the capacity of human beings to carry on life as we have known it—and in the extreme case threatens the continuity of human life itself. Thus, for example, with practically all countries treating the oceans as sewers—depositories for the ever-growing quantities of waste associated with expanding production and consumption—it may not require a stretch of the imagination to envision a time, perhaps a few centuries from now, when the oceans become vast dead seas in which nothing can live.

Already, extensive "dead zones" have appeared in various places, including one of around 7,000 square miles that appears every spring and summer in the Gulf of Mexico (Bungo 2004). In the dead zones, marine life has essentially vanished in response to sharp drops in the oxygen levels. According to the United Nations Environment Programme, the dead zones will soon reduce fish stocks more than over-fishing. The main cause of dead zones is thought to be excessive nitrogen from fertilizers and other human sources washing into the sea. These result in algae blooms; when the algae then die and decompose they absorb the oxygen in the water. Since the 1960s the number of dead zones in the world's oceans has doubled every decade and is now nearing 150 (Kirby 2004).

In addition to endangering the world's oceans, human activity has placed the atmosphere increasingly at risk, with the ongoing destruction of the ozone layer in the upper atmosphere having made exposure to the sun increasingly hazardous in recent decades. It is also not beyond the realm of imagination to envision a time when exposure to the sun has become so hazardous that outdoor activities are, in the main, restricted to the night or human civilization simply moves underground. Although these scenarios represent extreme cases, and actual environmental deterioration may well fall short of the extreme, it is nevertheless useful to consider the direction in which our unchecked actions are leading. Even if environmental deterioration merely involves significant expansion of the current oceanic dead zones, and merely calls for significant curtailment of daylight activities, dramatic changes in the way human life is carried out are likely to be required. This expectation is reinforced when all of the other aspects of environmental deterioration are taken into account.

The relationship between these threats to human existence and the capitalist system warrants close consideration. Capitalism is defined above all by the accumulation process and the ongoing search for expanded profitability. Enterprises can increase their profits by reducing costs or expanding sales; both of course play a role. There is, however, a limit to cost reduction; in the extreme case costs cannot be pushed below zero. On the other hand, there is no limit to the potential expansion of sales. Thus capital accumulation and the expansion of sales are at the core of the capitalist process. A fundamental contradiction exists, however, between an environment with given resources (the earth) and limited pollution absorption capacity on the one hand, and a system that requires ever-increasing throughputs of production and consumption on the other. In this sense, capitalism is ultimately incompatible with the continuity of human life as we have known it.

My purpose in this book, then, is to explore the dynamics, contradictions, and implications of capitalism as a distinctive economic system. My intention is to introduce a number of perspectives that will facilitate the understanding of capitalism and its consequences. I believe it should be recognized that the capitalist system has both positive and negative implications for the character of human life. The chief positive element is the great improvement in living standards that capitalism has made possible for a sizable (if minority) portion of the earth's population, and the promise it holds for those who have not yet been its beneficiaries. Table 1.1 indicates the change in living standards that took place in selected countries between 1820 and 1989.

Even while generating considerable prosperity in parts of the world, capitalism remains rife with negative features, ranging from inequality and social injustice to the crassness of commercial culture. Above all, however, its environmental contradiction, which threatens serious disruptions to human life on earth and in the extreme case its very continuity, must be a cause for concern. Since there is no viable alternative to capitalism, however, and since the capitalist system is likely to be with us for several more centuries at least (assuming that we do not destroy ourselves in the interim), my analysis of capitalism is meant to promote thinking about the dynamics and contradictions of the system with a view to enhancing its positive features and ameliorating its most destructive and socially reprehensible ones.

Table 1.1 Levels of gross domestic product per head of population, 1820–1989 (US$ at 1985 prices)

	1820	*1870*	*1913*	*1950*	*1989*
Denmark	988	1,555	3,037	5,224	13,514
France	1,052	1,571	2,734	4,149	13,837
Germany	937	1,300	2,606	3,339	13,989
Japan	588	618	1,114	1,563	15,101
Sweden	947	1,316	2,450	5,331	15,406
UK	1,405	2,610	4,024	5,651	13,468
USA	1,048	2,247	4,854	8,611	18,317

Source: Angus Maddison, *Dynamic Forces in Capitalist Development: A Long-Run Comparative View* (New York: Oxford University Press, 1991), pp. 6–7.

Types of capitalism

In the contemporary world, we can distinguish three primary types or models of capitalism. First, there is the Anglo-American type, a form of capitalism that emphasizes the role of markets and consequently tends to be extremely harsh in terms of its consequences for human welfare. Second, there is the continental European type of capitalism, with its emphasis on the welfare state and social democracy. Third, there is the East Asian model of state-led capitalism, exemplified especially by the form capitalism has assumed in Japan and South Korea. While no country fits these models perfectly, it is nevertheless useful to think of these different prototypes. I will argue below that the state-led model is no longer viable in its historic form, although in modified form it is likely to remain extremely important as the states of developing countries in particular take advantage of the opportunities provided by globalization and technological change to accelerate their growth trajectories. I will argue as well that both state-led capitalism and welfare-state capitalism are under severe pressure to emulate their American cousin.

The Anglo-American form of capitalism, which reaches a more extreme form in the United States than in the United Kingdom, is the harshest form. This is a consequence of its extreme reliance on markets, and a widespread conviction that market prices have some normative value. Thus if a person's value in the labor market is insufficient to provide a living wage for himself (herself) and his (her) family, that is simply regarded as unfortunate, but not a cause for social action. In fact, it is argued conventionally that efforts to bring the minimum wage up to the subsistence level will deprive people of employment opportunities and the ability to improve their status over time by learning on the job. In effect, this argument has prevailed in American public policy since, over many decades, the minimum wage has been set below the subsistence level.[2]

Although the United States is the most prosperous nation in the history of humankind, 43.6 million of its citizens lacked health insurance in 2002, while 16.3 percent of its children lived in poverty (US Department of Commerce 2003). In 2004,

> [m]ore than 28 million people [in the US], about a quarter of the work force between the ages of 18 and 64, earn less than $9.04 an hour, which translates into a full-time salary of $18,800 a year—the income that marks the federal poverty line for a family of four.
>
> (*Business Week*, 5/31/04: 61)

While it is certainly true that many people have benefited from the relatively unconstrained free market in the United States, there are clearly numerous people as well who have failed to gain from the beneficence of Adam Smith's "invisible hand." These issues are above and beyond those raised by the prevalence of commercial culture and the destruction of the environment.

In the United States, someone who loses his job is likely to lose his health coverage as well. If that person is unfortunate enough to fall ill, there are a number of patchwork palliatives, but there is no formal safety net to provide succor. Since, moreover, the United States tends to have the fewest job protections among the industrialized nations, it is not an exaggeration to characterize its form of capitalism as "harsh."

This is not to argue that the American form of capitalism lacks significant advantages. The rewards to innovation, hard work, and commercial success are substantial, generating incentives that support economic growth and a rising standard of living. Moreover, despite the prevalence of imperfect forms of competition, competitive pressures tend to compel improvements in efficiency on an ongoing basis, and encourage investment, research, and development. This is the part of the story that the market "faithful" emphasize, just as the critics tend to emphasize the harshness and injustice that are embodied in the same model. An accurate picture must recognize the existence of both parts of this duality.

In continental Europe, an alternative form of capitalism has evolved, one in which the potential injustices and inhumanity of the system are more fully recognized. In Europe, it is more difficult to close plants or fire workers. Health-care systems operated by the state cover the entire population, pensions tend to be relatively generous, a high proportion of wages is provided during illness (with payments coming from the employer, the state, or both), and generous benefits (and leave arrangements) are provided for childbirth and childcare.

The downside to the European system is the high level of taxation and other forces that discourage innovation, employment, and effort. In Germany, for example, as of 2002 there was a 41 percent payroll tax (split between employer and employee) to cover health care, unemployment insurance, and pension requirements.[3] Given the difficulty of firing workers, a European employer contemplating hiring a worker in his/her twenties must think about the possibility of a forty-year commitment; the worker becomes, in effect, a fixed cost. There is a high risk in making such commitments since firms are unlikely to have a clear picture of their business outlooks for more than a few years, if that much. The result is that firms tend to prefer to minimize new employment by automating production as much as possible, by establishing new facilities abroad, or by outsourcing as much production as possible. As a consequence, high levels of unemployment, especially among young people, tend to characterize the continental economies.

Moreover, in certain areas, the European economies are able to piggyback on the more dynamic American economy. By limiting pharmaceutical prices, European governments have achieved the laudable result of making prescription drugs more affordable. Since the cost of developing new drugs, however, can reach as high as $802 million (including the costs of developing drugs that fail to work),[4] drug research and development would fall sharply if all countries followed the price control practices common on the continent. Thus for a number of reasons, the European model of capitalism, while more humane than its American counterpart, is also less dynamic. Although it is possible to envision forms of capitalism that combine the best features of each, albeit in modified form, substantive changes in the capitalist system (explored more fully in Chapter 8) will be required in other directions as well.

The issue of systemic change has added significance since both American and European capitalism are subject to a process of dynamic evolution, and the European system in particular is under enormous pressure to become more like the harsh, market-driven American form. As a part of the ongoing process of globalization, competition is becoming increasingly international in scope. Firms in countries with high levels of taxation and laws that limit labor mobility find it difficult to compete with firms in countries that create a more favorable business environment. Some of the European countries—such as the Netherlands—have introduced more flexible labor laws (especially by easing restrictions on part-time and temporary work), while others—such as Germany—have lowered taxes. The problem posed by such measures, however, is that they tend to undermine the job security and welfare-state expenditures that most of the European population regard as the foundation of a civilized society.

In thinking about the pressures for change in the various capitalist systems, it is also important to keep in mind the development of capitalism in new areas as some of the less developed economies industrialize and as the former "communist" countries take on an increasingly capitalist hue. The institutions in these developing and/or transitional economies are in a much greater state of flux, and whether the type of capitalism that emerges will be closer to the American or European model is still an open question, although it is important to recognize that these societies face the same pressures as their European counterparts to move closer to the American model. In addition they lack the fiscal resources of the Europeans that have been used to underpin the welfare state.

Many of the developing and transitional economies have tended to follow the East Asian model of state-led development, a consequence of past success (of export-led development especially), and, in the case of the transitional economies, the heritage provided by central planning and state-owned enterprises. South Korea provides an example of the success that at one time could be achieved by following the Japanese model. In South Korea, state-owned banks "rewarded" firms that achieved state-determined export goals with low-cost loans, and the state created a growth environment that enabled highly leveraged firms to prosper (Kim 1997: 82–83).

The Asian financial crisis of 1997–98, however, revealed serious deficiencies in the state-led development model. By managing exchange rates to keep them stable and favorable, the state in effect encouraged firms to borrow short term from abroad at low interest rates to fund long-term domestic investments. When the local currencies dropped sharply in value, the viability of the domestic firms was placed in question.

The problem with the state-led model, however, extends far beyond exchange rate policy, for that (in principle) can be fixed. Here we might focus on just two problems that are deeper and more critical in nature. First, the nature of technological development has changed, and the possibilities for state action have changed accordingly. It is quite possible for the state to establish a world-class steel industry. That in fact has been done in Japan, South Korea, China, and elsewhere. The shift in the frontiers of technology to fields like information technology and biotechnology, however, has made it impossible for the state to play a comparable role. The state, for example, cannot be expected to establish a viable software industry (although it can of course help to provide necessary conditions for such an industry). The point worth emphasizing is that in the new industries success cannot be based largely on simply replicating (and improving upon) what was done elsewhere.

In the area of macroeconomic policy too, the state has become more constrained than it once was. In the case of Japan, for example, the social consensus that supported "lifetime" employment encouraged the government to pressure the banks to maintain and renew loans to companies with excessive debt and excessive numbers of employees. The result was a banking system with massive bad loans and an inability to extend credit to firms with more favorable prospects. Dealing with the bad loans and other economic problems has taken well over a decade in Japan, and, following the bursting of the stock market and real estate bubbles at the end of 1989, it took Japan almost a decade and a half to once again display signs of sustainable economic growth.

In parallel fashion, in China, the state-owned enterprises are often kept in business through governmental support and pressure on the (state-owned) banks to extend loans that cannot and will not be repaid. In both Japan and China, a primary objective of public policy has been to alleviate the social pressures that high levels of unemployment would generate.

This objective is certainly understandable, but it violates one of the core mechanisms that enable the capitalist system to remain viable. By falling periodically into slumps, capitalist economies bring down asset prices, renew the attractiveness of investment, and ensure the movement of capital to more productive uses. By thwarting this self-corrective process, state-led development, despite its past successes, appears likely to remain viable in the future only by assuming new forms in which control is more indirect. If one should point to the rapid growth of the Chinese economy as belying this assertion, it should be kept in mind that the dynamic sectors of the Chinese economy are the foreign, private, and township enterprises, with the state-owned enterprises declining in importance over time.[5]

Any attempt to focus on the three major types of contemporary capitalism, as I have done here, obviously does violence to the very real differences and singularities that characterize the various capitalist states. I do not mean to assert that any state fits one of the three prototypes precisely, nor do I mean to minimize the differences among states. It is useful, nevertheless, to recognize some of the broad distinctions among types of capitalism that can be made, and a necessary part of analyzing the possible future trajectory of the capitalist system.

The central features and history of capitalism

In the late 1970s and early 1980s, a great debate was waged between Robert Brenner and Immanuel Wallerstein concerning the essential nature of capitalism.[6] Brenner, hewing closely to the analysis provided by Karl Marx, saw the essence of capitalism in the relationship between the capitalist owner of the means of production and the worker, forced to sell his or her labor power in order to subsist. The capitalist buys that labor power and uses it to create commodities with a value greater than that of the equipment, raw materials, and labor power used to produce them. This surplus value is the source of the capitalist's profit.

Wallerstein, by contrast, saw the essence of capitalism in the capitalist's production of commodities for sale on the world market. Wallerstein recognized a wide variety of methods of labor control as consistent with capitalism. Thus, in addition to capitalists hiring workers, capitalism also encompassed slaves producing cotton for sale on the world market and serfs producing grain for the same purpose. The methods of labor control differed, but the common objective of producing goods for sale on the world market brought all of these activities under the rubric of capitalism. In contrast to Brenner, who focused on a single owner–producer relationship (that between the capitalist and worker), Wallerstein saw capitalism as a world system capable of encompassing multiple such relationships. The market system plays a central role in both conceptions of capitalism, but sales on the world market play the defining role in Wallerstein's.

Clearly, there are elements of truth in both conceptions. Despite his argument that "the relations of production that define a system are the relations of production of the whole system," Wallerstein (1976: 88) can be criticized for defining capitalism in terms of product markets exclusively, while neglecting modes of production. At the same time, Brenner's exclusive focus on one set of relations of production as the defining characteristic of capitalism may draw attention away from the thrust of globalization and the existence of hybrid systems.

While the capitalist system does indeed differ from previous modes of production in the prevalence of workers "freely" selling their labor power to capitalists as a norm, hybrid modes of production have often appeared over the centuries. Consider the following advertisement published in 1784:

> "To Let, The Labor of 260 Children
>
> With Rooms and Every Convenience for carrying on the Cotton Business. For particulars, enquire of Mr. Richard Clough, Common Street, Manchester."
>
> (quoted in Marglin 1996: 44)

The labor of pauper children leased by local government (to minimize the local tax burden) hardly conforms to the prototype sale of labor power by free workers. Even so, it would be difficult to consider the firms that utilized such labor anything but capitalist. The point here concerns the legitimacy of Wallerstein's insight into the differing methods of labor control that capitalist firms may employ; it should be recognized that hybrid modes of production have often been a part of the capitalist process. Thus the use of unpaid child labor in factories or, historically, of slave labor in the American South to produce cotton for sale on the world market provides instances of hybrid modes of production, modes that are encountered especially often in the earlier stages of capitalist development.

Markets are at the core of the capitalist system, and a fully developed capitalism requires a labor market in the production process as well as a product market at its conclusion. Nevertheless, in the early stages of capitalist development, differing methods of labor control have been used. We need only recognize that the modes of production in use at such times include some that have been hybrid rather than purely capitalist. Under fully developed capitalism, then, the market system is characteristically used in a search for maximum ongoing profit, where the concept of maximum profit is subject to the constraints of what is socially or culturally acceptable (this of course is the source of a major difference between the European and American forms of capitalism discussed above).

Although we can find examples of capitalism in the ancient world and limited regions where capitalism flourished in the later Middle Ages, the continuous development of the capitalist system began in the sixteenth century (Dillard 1984: 79–86). Long-distance trade was at the forefront of the early development of capitalism. Increasingly, the economic surplus of society took the form of merchant profits:

> Productive use of the "social surplus" was the special virtue that enabled capitalism to outstrip all prior economic systems. Instead of building pyramids and cathedrals, those in command of the social surplus chose to invest in ships, warehouses, raw materials, finished goods and other material forms of wealth. The social surplus was thus converted into enlarged productive capacity.
>
> (Dillard 1984: 80)

The dynamics of capitalism include an unending search for expanded markets on the one hand, and for securing sources of supply and minimizing their cost on the other. Thus merchants, discerning which goods had value in trade, had an incentive to increase their sources of supply at reduced costs. Initially, this spurred colonialism, but in time it gave rise to an ongoing effort to improve production processes, eventually leading into the Industrial Revolution. Somewhat arbitrarily, merchant capitalism can be said to have held sway in the period from 1500 to 1750, after which the Industrial Revolution shifted the focus of the system to production activities. From late in the twentieth century, terms like "postindustrial society" found increasing usage, signifying a shift in advanced capitalism away from the production of material objects (which were increasingly produced in the less-developed countries) and increasingly toward the production of services, which dominated the provision of employment in America by the start of the twenty-first century (Bureau of Economic Analysis 2004).

The rise of the nation-state played a critical role in the sustained development of capitalism from the sixteenth century, but in accordance with its internal logic, capitalism has in certain respects superseded national boundaries, especially from the second half of the twentieth century. In its early stages, the capitalist system benefited from the security, stability, and larger market size that nation-states could offer. In addition, capitalist enterprises were able to gain from colonial and imperialist expansion, which provided raw materials, markets, and the benefits of state procurement. Ultimately, however, the drive for profit maximization implies production for the world market (in this Wallerstein is certainly correct) wherever in the world costs can be minimized. As technology (especially information technology and transport) increasingly permitted, multinational or transnational corporations (MNCs or TNCs) came to dominate large-scale enterprise.

Social structures of accumulation

Throughout its history, capitalist development has not been linear. Rather, in each country, extended periods of vigorous growth have alternated with extended periods of sluggish growth or stagnation. The long waves generated by these alternating periods have varied considerably in duration, but a common pattern would include several decades of relatively vigorous expansion followed by a lengthy period of sluggish growth or stagnation. Each period of expansion has been associated with a specific, supportive social structure of accumulation (SSA), a set of institutions that facilitates the accumulation process.

While Chapters 2 and 3 will examine the concept of social structures of accumulation more systematically, they play such a central role in the capitalist accumulation process that an introductory discussion may be in order here. When capitalists or firms invest, they naturally are concerned with maximizing their profits. However, an entire set of supporting institutional arrangements is typically required as well if the investment is to be undertaken. If, for example, firms refuse to pay back money they have borrowed or to pay for equipment they have purchased, there must be a system of laws and courts in place to secure redress. Or the institutions may take the form of facilitating long-term leasing arrangements or collective bargaining, so that firms can have reasonable certainty of the level of their costs over an extended period. The full set of institutions that give capitalists the confidence to invest is the SSA.

It should be noted at the outset that the institutions of an SSA are distinct from the profit opportunities that capitalist enterprises may perceive; they cannot substitute for such opportunities. If perceived opportunities are present, however, that is not sufficient to encourage investment. The institutions of an SSA create a context within which the prospective investor feels confident of a supportive environment. The extremely rapid growth of the South Korean economy from the 1960s, for example, took place in the context of extremely high leverage (the ratio of debt to equity) on the part of the Korean industrial groups or *chaebol*.[7] The government support for their business activities gave them the confidence to borrow heavily—and provided them with the funds needed to pursue their investment activities vigorously.

While an SSA can support decades of relatively vigorous economic growth, no SSA can endure indefinitely. Inevitably, internal contradictions, interacting with changes in the external environment, bring about the collapse of every SSA. In postwar Japan, for example, the state played a leading role in industrial policy. This can work well when the issue is primarily one of copying the best practices developed abroad and making marginal improvements on them. Thus with an able administration it is quite feasible to establish a steel industry, whether in the private or public sector. As noted, this indeed has been done under quite disparate regimes in Japan, South Korea, and China. It is much more difficult, however, for the state to develop a viable software industry in a highly competitive international environment.

Necessary conditions for the development of a software industry are apt to include a high degree of decentralization, a venture capital industry, exceptionally high rewards for successful innovation, and so forth. A strong, meritocratic educational system is also necessary and can of course be provided by the state, but this alone is insufficient. Thus as the cutting edge of economic activity shifts from conventional industrial production to areas like information technology and biotechnology, an economic model which requires the state to take a leading role becomes increasingly problematic.[8] This example is simply meant to show how an institution that contributes to a successful SSA under certain circumstances may have precisely the opposite effect under others; part of Chapter 2 will explore in somewhat greater detail the factors that helped to create and then to destroy Japan's postwar SSA.

The long waves that characterize capitalist economies do far more than help to explain the extended, alternating periods of vigorous growth and stagnation. Each new period of vigorous growth, as I have already noted, is marked by a distinctive set of supporting institutions; that is, it is marked by a distinctive social structure of accumulation or SSA. For this reason, each new SSA marks a distinctive phase in the development of capitalism in each country. Thus, for example, the post-World War II SSA in the US is quite different from the one that was formed at the turn of the twenty-first century. Stated somewhat differently, contemporary American capitalism is quite different from the capitalism that existed in America in the 1950s. In essence, capitalism survives by repeatedly reinventing itself.

An understanding of this process helps us to understand the way in which the capitalist system has been able to overcome severe contradictions and repeated crises. This is not meant to maintain that past success offers any guarantees for the future. When a given SSA has crumbled in response to internal contradictions and a changing external environment, an indeterminate period of time is required before a new one can be constructed, and this period of time may stretch out indefinitely. When and if a new SSA is constructed, it emerges by indirection—as a by-product of the interaction between capital seeking investment opportunities, "exogenous" changes taking place, and the wide variety of social conflicts taking place at any given time. Class conflict plays a major role in this regard, but that is only one of numerous conflicts that can play a role.

Among such conflicts we may consider, for example, intergenerational conflicts (will more funds be allocated to subsidizing the aging or to education?), conflicts between rural and urban areas (who will obtain the water necessary to sustain population and production growth?), the conflict between men and women, the conflict between the beneficiaries of rapid economic growth and those concerned primarily with protecting the environment, and so forth. Class conflict does play an important role in this regard, but the Marxian tendency to elevate it to a determinant role ignores the multiple factors that always play a part in bringing about social change.

Writings on capitalism

Although the capitalist system is typically taken for granted by contemporary economists, this was not the case in the era of classical political economy—from Smith to Marx. And during the course of the twentieth century, both inside and outside the Marxian tradition, a fairly substantial number of authors (including a few economists) concerned with broader social issues have written on the capitalist system and its consequences, including such economists as Joseph Schumpeter, Robert Heilbroner, Paul Sweezy, and Paul Baran. I have learned a great deal from the insights of these writers and many others, but I continue to believe that a coherent and convincing analysis of the contemporary capitalist system remains to be done. Moreover, the need for such an analysis has become more pressing as the systemic contradictions of capitalism have grown more threatening. Fortunately, the additional information provided by the evolution of capitalism into the contemporary era of globalization and accelerated technological change enhances the possibilities for undertaking such an analysis on a more informed basis.

My purpose in this section is not to provide an exhaustive analysis and critique of existing writings on capitalism (an impossible task in a single volume in any event), but just to touch on some of the high points as a way of introducing the distinctive vision that informs this book. In this regard I would like to comment briefly on some of the core contributions and limitations of Adam Smith, Karl Marx, Paul Baran, and Paul Sweezy.

Adam Smith, generally recognized as the founder of modern economics, is above all seen as the author who understood that self-centered behavior (later given the gentler term of "utility maximization") can contribute powerfully to the social good.[9] During earlier periods, businessmen or merchants did not have high social standing; Smith provided an ideological justification for upgrading their social status. In pursuing maximum profits they were not only benefiting themselves but benefiting the entire community as well. Moreover, as a corollary to the benefits of the unfettered market system, Smith argued in favor of minimizing government interventions in the economy. His views helped to create an environment within which the capitalist market system could flourish.

Smith did recognize that the division of labor—both product and cause of the expansion of the market system via its contribution to the growth of labor productivity—had the capacity to make human beings "as stupid and ignorant as it is possible for a human creature to become" (1937: 734), a consequence of the repetitive, mindless activity to which it reduced ordinary workers. The emphasis of his writings, however, was overwhelmingly on the benefits of the unfettered market system; he paid little attention to the internal contradictions and cruelties of that system. The focus of Karl Marx, by contrast, was just the opposite.

Marx, of course, became the foremost critic of the capitalist system and made numerous contributions to our understanding of its core contradictions. Among these we may first take special note of his grasp of capitalism as a distinctive mode of production and social formation, one which emerged in the process of social evolution and which would eventually be replaced, just like all other social formations. That is, he recognized that history does not end with capitalism. Marx was also among the first to apply extensively the concept of internal contradictions to the analysis of capitalism, and to focus on the role of class conflict in bringing about historical change.

The two core classes in the capitalist mode of production, according to Marx, are the capitalists and the workers. Although they need one another, their interests are diametrically opposed in various respects. According to Marx's argument, the capitalist starts with a sum of money (M), acquires means of production including labor power, capital goods and raw material (C), converts those means of production into a product with greater value (C′), and then sells the product for a greater sum of money than he started with (M′); the process then starts all over again with a larger initial sum of money capital (M′).[10] The key to ending up with a greater value, for Marx, lies in the fact that the worker in a competitive market receives a subsistence wage, but produces output with a value greater than that. The value of the extra output produced by the worker, whether it is "absolute surplus value" created when the worker is required to work longer hours than needed for subsistence, or "relative surplus value" created when enhanced labor productivity reduces the hours required to produce the worker's subsistence, is the source of the capitalist's profit. The most basic contradictions in capitalism, according to Marx, stem from his labor theory of value.

Here it might be helpful to focus on just two of the main ones: one at the enterprise level and one at the (capitalist) systemic level. At the enterprise level, since the worker's surplus labor is the source of the capitalist's profit, harsh working conditions and growing inequality (in power, wealth, and income) are built into the capitalist–worker relationship. At the systemic level, Marx envisioned several ways in which the capitalist production process would prove unsustainable, leading to depressions and eventually crisis. At the realization stage in the cycle of capital, when the products created (C′) must be sold for a greater sum (M′) than the capitalist began with, thus providing both the profit and the source of a renewed round of investment on a larger scale, sales must be based on popular purchasing power. But if the wages of labor are held down to subsistence levels, then purchasing power will be inadequate; firms will cut back on production and recession or depression will ensue.[11]

At the same time, Marx's view that value could be created only by live labor (not by machinery or raw materials) suggested to him that as the proportion of raw materials and capital goods relative to labor power rose in the production process, the profit rate would have to fall. Competition among firms would assure that this took place, since when one introduced labor-saving (productivity-enhancing) equipment, others would have to follow suit. Prices would then be forced down through competitive pressure, so the initial innovator's profit advantage would soon disappear. The result would be an industry-wide production process that increased the amount of capital relative to live labor, thereby forcing down the rate of profit. This in turn would diminish the incentives for investment, ultimately leading to a crisis of the system. In Marx's system, internal contradictions such as these would ultimately lead to the demise of capitalism.

One can disagree with certain elements of Marx's analysis and vision while still appreciating his contributions to our understanding of the capitalist system. Neither the labor theory of value nor the falling rate of profit theory is convincing. The former, for example, ascribes no value contribution to innovation or product usefulness, while the latter ignores the role technological progress or innovation may play in enhancing profitability—and there is no logical reason for assuming that the rate of such progress or innovation must diminish over time. At the same time, it is also appropriate to take note of the fact that Marx underestimated the capitalist system's capacity for improving living standards and for self-renewal when confronted by crisis.

Even while recognizing these limitations, we must acknowledge Marx's central place among the analysts of capitalism. He was the first major thinker—or among the first—to perceive and explore deeply the system's tendency to recession, depression, and crisis; to focus on the central role of accumulation within the capitalist process; to bring to the fore the concept of surplus labor or surplus value; to recognize the central role of class conflict within the system (even if many of his followers tended to place it on a pedestal while ignoring other major conflicts); to focus our attention on the significance of internal contradictions within the system and their latent potential for systemic change; to explore the process of "primitive accumulation," in which a labor force was created by divesting small producers of the means to sustain their own production independently and in which capital was initially accumulated through the slave trade, theft from indigenous peoples, colonial exploitation, and other unsavory means; and to recognize capitalism as a distinct stage in social evolution rather than the end of history.

I have focused on these particular contributions for a purpose. In some sense, many of the issues I take up in this book are meant to respond to or build upon them. In Chapters 2 and 3, I focus on social structures of accumulation (SSAs), accepting Marx's focus on the accumulation process as lying at the core of the capitalist system, while moving beyond his analysis in clarifying the way in which capitalism has been able to overcome repeated crises by creating new SSAs in the wake of the collapse of their predecessors and thereby, in effect, to reinvent itself. Chapter 2's analysis of SSA theory is followed by the presentation (in Chapters 2 and 3) of three distinct case studies: the rise and demise of Japan's postwar SSA, the SSA in postwar America, and the SSA that was created in America at the end of the twentieth century and which remains in place today (2004). These three case studies are of interest in themselves, but they also have implications for other countries (there are important parallels between Germany and Japan, for example) and cast light on broader issues, such as the manner in which capitalism evolves over time by continually reinventing itself.

In Chapter 4, I turn to a consideration of the role of globalization and accelerated technological change in contemporary capitalism. In one sense these forces can be treated as exogenous to the nature of capitalism *per se*. In another sense, nothing is truly exogenous, since capitalism is continuously shaping the course of globalization and technological change, and the interactions among them are unceasing. Thus when I treat the two as exogenous, I am simply employing an analytical device that enables me to address each of them independently; to focus on the forces driving their development and the ways in which they in turn react back on the capitalist system and the other forces shaping that system.

In the contemporary world, globalization and technological change are in themselves closely connected. The share of global output involved in foreign trade, for example, was not very different toward the end of the twentieth century than it was early in the century (Maddison 1991: 149, 326). The nature of globalization, however, was quite different in the two periods. More recently, the advances in information technology have made possible international supply chains and patterns of outsourcing that would have been inconceivable a century earlier. Automobile parts can be made at lowest-cost sites anywhere in the world to support assembly on another continent, for example, or Fortune 500 firms routinely and increasingly outsource their software development needs to Indian firms, taking advantage of the far lower labor costs available. Moreover, instantaneous communications and (often) high-speed transport make just-in-time inventory management increasingly possible. This means on the one hand that firms can minimize inventory costs and reduce the leading role that inventory investment has often played in traditional business cycles, even while making individual firms and indeed the system as a whole increasingly vulnerable to shocks that may disrupt the supply system.

Globalization has many other implications for the capitalist system. There are numerous implications stemming from the fact, for example, that it has become much easier to outsource production to low labor-cost sites anywhere in the world. To select just three examples—but all of great significance—consider the impact on capital–labor relations, the welfare-state system of capitalism, and price stability in the already-industrialized countries. Since outsourcing has become so easy to implement in a wide range of industries, the bargaining power of labor relative to capital has diminished markedly—with evident consequences for income, benefits, and job security. At the same time, the welfare-state system of capitalism relies upon heavy taxation of individuals and enterprises. Since it has become much easier for both to move their activities offshore, the result is that the tax revenues necessary to provide the benefits of the welfare state have been threatened. The problems created by this are intensified by the aging populations in the industrialized countries (and their common pay-as-you-go pension systems), and the revolutionary changes in medical practice and the pharmaceutical industry (including the development of biotechnology), which have contributed to lengthened lifespans and sharply higher medical costs.

As yet another example of the effects of globalization, its impact on the macroeconomic conditions in the developed countries—and indeed in the less-developed ones as well—may also be considered. The growing shift of manufacturing to low-cost sites in China and elsewhere has contributed to a disinflationary environment in the West, a deflationary environment in the manufacturing sector, and even actual (Japan) or potential deflation in various national economies. In the US, over the one-and-a-half centuries to World War II, periods of deflation and periods of inflation were roughly comparable in the aggregate (Hanes 2005), but in the second half of the twentieth century inflation was the dreaded demon in the West, with consumer prices in the US rising 516 percent between January 1950 and December 1999 (http://inflationdata.com). The appearance of deflation in Japan during the 1990s raised awareness that deflation remained possible, that the systemic forces associated with globalization and technological change (including enhanced global competition as well as global outsourcing) were increasing its likelihood, and that the economic consequences of deflation could be much more severe than those of inflation, especially in countries with high levels of debt in the private and public sectors.

As for the less-developed countries, increased globalization meant increased dependency on foreign investment, both real and financial. Given the weaker economic and institutional conditions in such countries compared to their more developed counterparts, they became increasingly vulnerable to economic or financial shocks emanating from other parts of the world. A more complete consideration of the impact of globalization and technological change on the capitalist system will be provided in Chapter 4, but my purpose here is merely to indicate the rationale for including a discussion of these forces in this book.

In Chapter 5, I examine the ways in which the concept of the surplus has been used in the Marxian tradition, finding fault with all of them and proposing an alternative means of thinking about the surplus. This in turn provides a distinctive perspective for analyzing the capitalist system and its central contradictions. When Marx wrote in the middle of the nineteenth century, most enterprises were relatively small and competition was the norm. By the middle of the twentieth century, oligopoly had become the primary form of industrial organization, with a few firms dominating most of the major industries and able to exercise considerable pricing power, a power that firms in competitive industries lack. Paul Baran and Paul Sweezy argued in *Monopoly Capital* (1966) that under the new conditions the core contradiction of capitalism was the tendency of the surplus to rise and the inability of capitalist societies to absorb that surplus in productive fashion, with stagnation and crisis avoided only through military expenditure, marketing, and waste. Although I believe (and will attempt to demonstrate that) their analysis is incorrect, it has been quite influential among the critics of capitalism, and an understanding of the surplus provides insights into the functioning of the capitalist system that would otherwise be unavailable.

In Chapter 6, I turn to the vexing question of capitalism and class. Early in the nineteenth century, David Ricardo, one of the giants of classical economics, analyzed the process of economic growth using a model with three principal classes: capitalists, landlords, and workers. As Ricardo believed that workers would always tend toward a subsistence income (any temporary increase in their incomes above subsistence would lead to an increase in their numbers and a return to subsistence income), the principal classes contending for the economic surplus were the capitalists and the landlords.[12] Since the capitalists would invest the surplus while the landlords would use it for luxury consumption (think of the country estate weekends for which the British gentry are so famous), economic growth and the progress of society depended, in Ricardo's view, on the capitalists winning out over the landlords.

Although he switched his focus to the capitalists and workers, Marx retained the classical economists' focus on class relationships. After all, as Marx noted, previous social formations usually had been differentiated by their core class relationships, with a dominant class appropriating the surplus above subsistence generated by a class of producers. Thus lords had lived off the surplus created by serfs, slave-owners off the surplus produced by slaves, and so forth. In Marx's own time, during the nineteenth century, the image of capitalists as captains of industry confronting a mass of unskilled or low-skilled workers as laborers and living off the surplus they generated simply marked a continuation of this duality in new form.

By the twentieth century, however, the question of how to deal with the so-called "intermediate" classes, and the growing prevalence of multiple class roles performed by single individuals, made the classical dualities increasingly irrelevant. Accountants and teachers are neither capitalists nor workers in the classical nineteenth-century sense of the words. Airline pilots and senior software engineers are workers, but certainly not in the traditional sense. A small business owner may work full time alongside his employees; is he both a capitalist and a worker? The pathbreaking class analysis undertaken by Stephen Resnick and Richard Wolff (1987 and 1996) helps considerably in addressing questions such as these, and their work will play a central part in the discussion that appears in Chapter 6. In addition, however, several other class theories will be addressed briefly and tentative hypotheses advanced concerning ways in which class analysis may remain relevant to an understanding of contemporary capitalism.

Chapter 7 will focus on capitalism and the environment. If one posits that the purpose of material production is to meet human needs, then a rational system of economic organization will expand production until those needs are met. This would imply eventually reaching a (modified) stationary state. The conception of a modified stationary state (MSS) will be developed at some length in Chapters 7 and 8. Suffice it to say here that it suggests a stable world population offering a comfortable livelihood to all. Increases in output will not be mandated by the imperatives of the (capitalist) economic system, but may occur if they improve the quality of human life without harming the environment.

Capitalism, it will be evident, is inconsistent with a stationary state. Profit maximization requires ongoing accumulation and expanding sales. As I have noted, firms can maximize their profits by reducing costs or by increasing sales. There is a limit to reducing costs, however, which cannot be reduced below zero in the extreme case. There is no limit to the potential increase in sales, however, and if people are content with what they have, then new product development and marketing (interacting with peer envy) can create new desires effectively without limit.

The problem posed by never-ending expansion, however, is most serious. In an environment with effectively fixed resources and limited pollution absorption capacity, an economic system focused on maximizing throughputs (output and consumption) will at some point come into catastrophic conflict with the constraints of its fixed environment. This is already becoming evident in global warming, holes in the upper-ozone layer of the atmosphere leading to an increase in skin cancer hazards, deforestation, desertification, and the loss of species, among other manifestations of environmental deterioration. As I have mentioned before, it is not difficult to imagine a world in which the oceans will become vast dead seas, and in which people will start living underground to avoid the deadly rays of the sun.[13] Even if the outcome proves somewhat less extreme, the environmental contradiction posed by capitalism, a system that requires ever-growing throughputs in a constrained environment, is likely in the long run to prove the most serious contradiction in the capitalist system. This is an argument that I will develop more fully in Chapter 7.

The eighth and final chapter addresses the future of capitalism. Its purpose is not to provide an outlook separable from the earlier chapters and their analyses but to weave these analyses into a coherent whole. Ultimately, dividing the treatment of capitalism into separate components introduces an element of artificiality into the analysis, since each element interacts with and shapes or "overdetermines" each of the others. Dividing this work into multiple chapters and multiple sub-themes within the chapters is purely for the convenience of making each of the topics manageable. In the last analysis, however, each of the themes addressed affects the others and is in turn affected by them.

The ability of capitalism to renew itself on new institutional foundations, for example, is analyzed in some detail in the discussion (in Chapters 2 and 3) of social structures of accumulation. The discussion of the surplus in Chapter 5 will reveal both constraints and opportunities bearing on the renewal process. Technological progress, globalization, environmental degradation, the interrelationships that mark the capitalist world economy, and class and other social conflicts are all among the forces that play a role in the ongoing evolution of the capitalist system. Analyzing the core contradictions in capitalism and the "external" forces with which they interact will provide the basis for understanding the systemic tendencies most likely to emerge.

I would like to emphasize that this is not meant to represent idle speculation concerning the future of capitalism. The analysis is informed by a particular vision. Capitalism has been a powerful force in raising the average living standards in the currently industrialized countries. Since no alternative to capitalism appears likely to emerge in the foreseeable future, it may well persist for several more centuries at least, possibly for as long as the four-and-a-half centuries it has already been the predominant social formation. During this time, it is reasonable to expect that much if not all of the less-developed world will industrialize, thereby raising living standards, eliminating the curse of underdevelopment, and paving the way for the transition to post-capitalist social formations. That is the favorable part of the vision.

There is also, unfortunately, an unfavorable part. The more humane forms of capitalism, represented by its social democratic form in continental Europe, are likely to be systematically undermined by the growing forces of globalization and global competition. The degradation of the environment brought on by capitalism's focus on maximizing throughputs will certainly continue, leading to the extinction of many species, possibly including human beings. Even if we are able to survive, it may be in an environment that would be unrecognizable to those of us living today. Finally, the unevenness of capitalist development and the ideological celebration of self-seeking behavior that supports the system make probable the indefinite perpetuation of vast social injustice and misery, both within and among countries. These in turn magnify greatly the probability of war and terrorism, rendering questionable—especially in an era of increasingly accessible weapons of mass destruction—whether human beings will survive into the post-capitalist era.

For better or for worse, the capitalist system is likely to be with us for an indeterminate period of time, stretching over future centuries. By understanding the tendencies in and the consequences of capitalist development, we may put ourselves in a position to forestall or modify some of the most pernicious among them. It is with that hope that I have approached the writing of this book.

2 Social structures of accumulation

The theoretical issues

With appropriate adjustments for risk, capitalists or firms are normally concerned with maximizing their profits when they undertake investment activities. Other factors enter into the decision-making process as well, however. In particular, a set of institutions that supports the investment activity and generates confidence in the investors plays a key role. Such institutions may range from a labor market that functions in such a way that assures investors that they will be able to hire (at reasonable cost) employees with the requisite skills to a legal system capable of enforcing contracts and a system of international trade relations that assures access to raw materials, intermediate goods, and export markets. The full range of institutions that favors investment activity—in the economists' sense of new capital goods and the technology embodied in them rather than in the financial sense—is the social structure of accumulation (SSA).

Accumulation is at the core of the capitalist process. It involves the reinvestment of profits by capitalists or firms as part of an ongoing effort to expand their capital. For the most part, conventional economic theory focuses on prospective returns as motivating investment decisions. This is correct as far as it goes, but it does not go far enough. In addition to high expected rates of profit, firms must typically gain confidence from a set of supportive institutions before undertaking investments. A slightly different way of conceptualizing an SSA is as this set of supportive institutions.

Under ordinary circumstances we would expect that the returns to investment would be greatest in countries with the least capital. If maximizing returns were a sufficient condition for investment, then funds would be flowing rapidly into the less developed countries from the capital-rich regions of the world. With a few notable exceptions, this is not happening, and it does not happen for a good reason. In most of the less-developed countries the institutional support and protection that investors or firms in the industrialized world expect are not present.

In Indonesia, for example, firms that are unable to repay their debts are able to continue to operate with few constraints for an extended period of many years. In the United States, by contrast, firms seeking protection from their creditors are forced to seek bankruptcy protection, and their creditors have a claim on their assets. The minimal protections afforded by contracts and commercial law in Indonesia, therefore, discourage investment from taking place.[1]

To provide another example, "robber baron" capitalism characterized Russia in its early post-Soviet period. In one case, BP (the former British Petroleum), one of the largest oil companies in the world, invested $484 million to acquire a 10 percent share of Sidanco, a Russian oil company, essentially because BP wished to have an ownership stake in one of Sidanco's subsidiaries (which owned a valuable oilfield). Sidanco's management insiders, however, sold the subsidiary to another company, one that was fully owned by themselves, for a nominal price (*Business Week*, 2/24/03: 56). In seeking to block the sale or recover its investment, BP found that it had no recourse in the Russian legal system. Eventually, BP was able to reach an accommodation with the Russians who had fleeced it, since the latter were able to receive some billions of dollars in cash as well as benefit from BP's expertise in the industry (*Wall Street Journal*, 2/27/03: A1). It is not the final outcome that is of interest here, but the fact that institutional safeguards often taken for granted in the West are not in fact universal. And the presence or absence of such safeguards plays a critical role in giving investors the confidence to place their capital at risk.

These examples may help to clarify the reasons for which investors will usually hesitate before committing funds to ventures which, however high their potential returns, lack essential institutional safeguards. But the role of supportive institutions is much broader than protection against theft. For example, if collective bargaining is established in labor relations, companies may be able to gain three or more years of labor-cost "certainty," before committing funds to new ventures. In similar fashion, a well-established bond market or financially strong banking system may provide reasonable assurance concerning the availability and cost of the necessary funds. For firms that require specialized skills, an educational system that provides these and a well-functioning labor market that facilitates the recruitment of employees who have the requisite skills also provide part of the institutional framework that is needed to encourage investment.

In essence, then, a social environment that favors investment is a necessary accompaniment to the microeconomic inducement of high prospective returns. The institutions that provide this environment comprise the social structure of accumulation or SSA. An SSA is not simply shorthand for "the rest of society," for it focuses on those institutions that, while external to the prospective investment activity itself, affect it most directly. Thus the financial institutions of a country would ordinarily comprise a key component of its SSA, while the nature of its wedding ceremonies would not.[2]

There are several reasons for which the concept of the social structure of accumulation provides essential insights into the nature of capitalism. I would like to focus here on three major issues. First, capitalist countries are characterized by extended, alternating periods of vigorous growth and relative stagnation; the full cycle may stretch over fifty or sixty years, some ten times the length of the average business cycle. Thus the United States grew rapidly in the quarter century following World War II, but then entered a period, especially from 1973 to 1995, when the growth of productivity and gross domestic product slumped sharply. Between 1948 and 1973, output per hour worked grew at an average rate of 2.9 percent per year, but then collapsed to an average rate of 1.4 percent per year between 1973 and 1995 (Baumol and Blinder 2003: 114–115). The strong growth in the earlier period can be tied to the SSA that prevailed at that time, and the subsequent stagnation to its collapse. In general, a series of long waves have characterized American economic history.[3]

These waves appear in other capitalist countries as well. In Japan, for example, national income grew at a rate of 9.7 percent between 1955 and 1970, and at a still-respectable 4–5 percent between 1970 and 1990, after which the growth rate collapsed to 1.3 percent between 1990 and 2001 (Hirata 1995: 41; Statistics Bureau 2004: 8). Stated somewhat differently, the social structure of accumulation that supported vigorous economic growth between 1955 and 1990 collapsed subsequently, ushering in an era of relative stagnation.

If we understand the institutional framework that comprises a given SSA, then we can understand the dynamics of the accumulation process as it proceeds within a given country at a particular point in time. Moreover, we can gain insights into the process by which any given SSA, over a period of time, becomes subject to stresses and strains brought on by its internal contradictions and changes in the external environment, and ultimately collapses, bringing on the subsequent era of stagnation. SSA analysis, accordingly, provides a key to understanding the economic tribulations that have replaced the postwar economic "miracles" in contemporary Germany and Japan. When sluggish growth or stagnation appears, it is accompanied by a wide range of social struggles; the resolution of which can, in time, lead to the creation of a new SSA. Thus the analysis of SSAs enables us to understand the dynamics of change within the capitalist system.

Among countries with differing institutional structures, it goes without saying that SSAs will differ. Of equal interest, however, is the fact that within any given country each SSA formed over time will be different from its predecessor. Thus, in a sense, we can say that capitalism continually renews and reinvents itself. This helps us to understand the fact that despite its severe internal contradictions, contradictions that Marx anticipated would bring about the ultimate collapse of capitalism, the capitalist system has managed to remain vibrant over the centuries. The capitalism that exists in the United States today (2004) is quite unlike the capitalism that existed in the 1950s. A grasp of social structures of accumulation enables us to understand the power of the capitalist system to overcome its contradictions and to renew itself.

This is not to say that it will retain this power indefinitely, for capitalism, like all socioeconomic systems that preceded it, will one day disappear. What SSA analysis helps us to do is to differentiate between the "lesser" contradictions that characterize each SSA and the more deeply embedded, systemic contradictions. Some of the former may be overcome, while others may contribute to the collapse of the SSA in question, leading into a period of stagnation and ultimately the creation of a new SSA. The latter, by contrast, have the potential to lead, ultimately, to the demise of the capitalist system.

Finally, it is of interest to note that each SSA represents a new stage in the development of capitalism. This is a consequence of the fact that new institutions are required to sustain the accumulation process at different historical junctures, reflecting the fact that the external conditions and the other institutions with which they interact have changed. Consider, for example, the capital–labor relations that prevailed in the United States in the 1950s and those which prevail today. During the postwar period there existed what Gordon, Weisskopf, and Bowles (1996) refer to as a "capital–labor accord." Under this tacit agreement, collective bargaining assured a relatively high degree of labor peace, with workers receiving job protection, rising real wages, pensions, seniority rights, and so forth. Management, in exchange, received control over the workplace, the ability to introduce productivity-enhancing equipment, and stable labor relations.

This trade-off was possible because firms found it to their advantage. With the US assuming the role of dominant economic power after World War II, and other countries unable to compete effectively for an extended period of postwar reconstruction, peaceful labor relations could assure high and increasing profits despite rising real wages. If we compare the current era, the early twenty-first century, with that period, however, dramatic differences in external conditions immediately become apparent. Intense, increasingly global competition is forcing companies to do all in their power to limit their labor and other costs. Under such circumstances, the class conflict between capital and labor cannot be resolved along the lines of the accommodation that characterized the postwar period. Rather, capital has sought successfully to dominate labor.[4]

The power of capital and weakness of labor that mark the current period are one of its primary distinguishing institutional features. The relative power of capital is reflected in the sharp drop in labor union membership (in the private sector membership fell from 16.5 percent of the labor force in 1983 to 9 percent in 2000 (US Department of Commerce 1996: 436; 2001: 411)), the stagnation in real wages between 1973 and 1995, and the decrease in major strikes; Chapter 3's discussion of America's new SSA presents the supporting data. Increasing globalization, fostered by international trade agreements and changes in information technology especially, made it possible to move production overseas or outsource component manufacture. This greatly weakened the bargaining position of labor. At the same time, the growth of markets abroad made US producers less dependent on the domestic market, thereby avoiding the potential contradiction posed by limited wage payments leading to limited purchasing power and sales at home. In sum, the differing conditions that prevailed in the early twenty-first century called for a set of institutions that in some respects at least differed dramatically from those that supported the accumulation process half a century earlier. It is for this reason that each SSA represents a new stage in the development of capitalism.

Theoretical issues surrounding the concept of social structures of accumulation

The significance of SSA analysis to an understanding of capitalism can best be demonstrated by presenting a variety of examples. The cases selected here will include the rise and demise of Japan's postwar social structure of accumulation, and, in Chapter 3, the postwar social structure of accumulation in the United States (Gordon, Weisskopf, and Bowles 1996), and the development of a new SSA in the United States over the course of the 1980s and 1990s (Lippit 1997). In the course of discussing these cases, a number of important theoretical issues will be addressed and, hopefully, clarified. A brief discussion of these issues first should help to facilitate an understanding of both the general concept of social structures of accumulation and the specific case studies that follow.

The theoretical issues to be addressed are as follows. (1) In what sense can we talk of a social *structure* of accumulation? That is, if an SSA is more than simply a listing of distinct institutions that happen to impinge upon the accumulation process, they must be related to one another in such a way that they create a distinctive *structure*. Only by understanding the structural integrity of each SSA can we understand the forces leading to its formation, endurance, and ultimate collapse. (2) Why does it take a long time for SSAs to form, and, once formed, why do they tend to endure for a long time? (3) What causes SSAs to collapse? What forces lead to the formation of new SSAs?[5]

The discussion that follows will suggest that all of these theoretical issues are related. It will take the form, primarily, of assertions rather than proofs; in the last analysis, whether these assertions are found convincing will depend on the extent to which they help to make sense of the case studies that follow. Before turning to a brief discussion of these theoretical issues, an explanation of the way in which I am using the term "institution" may prove helpful.

We can think of an institution in two principal ways. The first is essentially as an organization, like the World Bank or a university. The broader sense of an institution refers to the habits, customs and expectations that prevail in a particular society. While both senses of the term are used in SSA analysis, it is this second usage that is emphasized. The second usage, moreover, can be employed narrowly or broadly, and it is the broader form that is usually more helpful. A union, for example, is an institution in the first sense. Collective bargaining would be an example of an institution in the second sense, employed narrowly. A national system of labor relations would also be an example of an institution in the second sense, but one employed broadly. It might include collective bargaining, but also might include a set of expectations concerning health and pension benefits, working conditions, the circumstances that would warrant employment termination, the role that seniority would be expected to play in salary, promotions and job security, the role of government in mediating between the interests of employers and those of employees, and so forth. The case studies of SSAs below will generally be employing this broadest concept of an institution.

What accounts for the structural integrity of an SSA?

This example of an "institution" leads right into the first of the theoretical questions posed above: what accounts for the structural integrity of an SSA? If we think of the system of labor relations that exists in any given country we must start with the historical legacy, which gives people an initial set of expectations. But class struggles between capital and labor are one of the enduring characteristics of capitalism, so those expectations will be subject to change over time as the struggle proceeds. And the struggle itself will be subject to a host of factors that contribute more broadly to shaping the relations that emerge between capital and labor.

If workers have skills that are difficult or costly to replicate, then they are likely to be able to gain more favorable terms of employment. If a political party more favorable to employers (usually the Republicans in the United States) is in power, then laws governing the terms of employment are apt to be less favorable to labor, as are administrative and judicial decisions. New technologies may facilitate the outsourcing of production, and in the current era of globalization that increasingly includes nonmaterial work (like the creation of software) as well as material goods. Ideological beliefs such as belief in the unfailing beneficence of the free market can also play a role in labor–management relations by determining the level of public support when conflicts become open.

It would be possible to add to this list indefinitely. That is because the system of labor relations in any country is *overdetermined*, generated by all of the other institutions and external forces with which it interacts.[6] Moreover, the system of labor relations in its turn influences the full array of institutions and social processes with which it interacts, contributing in its turn to *their* overdetermination. For example, expectations concerning the nature of the jobs likely to be available affect the educational system, the jobs themselves affect family life, and employee feelings about health care and retirement benefits are likely to affect voting behavior and therefore political institutions. In other words, the various institutions of a society are mutually determinative; each one contributes to overdetermining the others. Moreover, since institutions are also subject to the effects of the full array of social processes and of "exogenous" events or conditions, there are numerous forces contributing to the overdetermination of any particular institution, and any particular institution contributes to shaping the rest of society and influencing exogenous events or conditions. Of course this means that in the last analysis such events or conditions are not fully "exogenous," and their treatment as such is largely for reasons of analytical convenience.

The logic of overdetermination provides the key to understanding the first theoretical issue posed—what accounts for the structural integrity of an SSA? Since each institutional component of a given SSA is shaped in part by all of the other institutional components (and in its turn contributes to shaping each of them), they join together to form a more or less integrated structure. This means that when we think of a social structure of accumulation supporting an extended period of vigorous economic expansion, we must keep in mind the importance of the entire structure, a structure that is sustained by the interrelationships among its component parts. If we understand SSAs in this way, then it will be readily evident why isolated events or institutional changes will not in themselves bring about the collapse of an SSA. At the same time, we can understand why such changes will tend to reverberate throughout the SSA over time, undermining it to a greater or lesser degree unless countervailing forces are able to offset them.

Why do SSAs take a long time to form and, once formed, why do they tend to persist?

The answer to the first theoretical question posed leads directly to the answer to the second: why do SSAs take a long time to form and, once formed, why do they tend to endure for a long time? I would like to note at the outset that there is no particular length of time it takes an SSA to form or for which it will endure. The intensity of the internal contradictions, the strength of the impact of exogenous events, and the interactions among the component parts of the SSA will all have a bearing on its durability. And it should be kept in mind as well that there will always be an element of arbitrariness in dating SSAs, since the process of institutional formation and change is extended and always ongoing.

If we think of institutions as formed by a set of habits, customs, and expectations, then it is quite natural for them to change only slowly. As I have mentioned, America's postwar SSA included a "capital–labor accord" (Gordon, Weisskopf, and Bowles 1996), under which labor received, largely through a collective bargaining process, rising real wages, pensions and health care, seniority protections against lay-offs, and other benefits. In exchange, management received considerable latitude in organizing the work process, the ability to introduce labor-saving equipment, and labor peace. We can think of the capital–labor accord as a truce in the ongoing struggles between capital and labor, one that was possible because both sides gained real benefits.

Since both sides were beneficiaries there were strong incentives to maintain the accord, which prevailed through most of the 1950s and 1960s. Over time, however, economic conditions changed, and capital in particular found the capital–labor accord increasingly unsatisfactory. There were many reasons for this. Productivity gains during the postwar period had been relatively rapid, so that rising real wages did not cut into profits to any significant degree.[7] But productivity gains are never automatic, and when the rate of productivity growth slowed sharply in the 1970s rising real wages could come only at the expense of profits. As I have noted above, the growth rate of US labor productivity fell from 2.9 percent per year in the quarter century to 1973 to 1.4 percent in the 1973–1995 period.

Further, following a quarter century of postwar reconstruction, Europe and Japan had rebuilt their economies to an extent where they could pose a serious competitive threat to American business. This threat was magnified by the fixed exchange rates agreed upon at Bretton Woods in 1944; the fixed rates increasingly undervalued the currencies of America's trading partners as their economies recovered, allowing them to undersell their American competitors. In addition, with stagflation coming to characterize the US economy in the 1970s, labor's expectation of and insistence on rising real wages posed a threat to the competitiveness and even survival of many US firms.

Under these conditions firms felt it imperative to rein in their labor costs. But this feeling came in the face of labor's *expectations* of rising wages and benefits, and labor's sense that management was no longer playing according to the agreed-upon rules. This in turn paved the way to an era of extended conflict, one marked by deep bitterness and numerous strikes. In 1981, President Reagan demonstrated that the power of the state would be brought to bear on the side of capital when he fired the air traffic controllers, who had gone on strike. The importance of Reagan's action was later acknowledged (in a speech) by Federal Reserve Board chairman Alan Greenspan:

> [T]here was a growing recognition, both in the United States and among many of our trading partners, that a market economy could best withstand and recover from shocks when provided maximum flexibility.
>
> Developments that enhanced flexibility ranged far beyond regulatory or statutory change. For example, employers have long been able to legally discharge employees at modest cost. But in the early postwar years, profitable large corporations were dissuaded from

> wholesale job reduction. Contractual inhibitions, to be sure, were then decidedly more prevalent than today, but of far greater importance, our culture in the aftermath of depression frowned on such action. Only when bankruptcy threatened was it perceived to be acceptable.
>
> But as the depression receded into history, attitudes toward job security and tenure changed. The change was first evidenced by the eventual acceptance by the American public of President Reagan's discharge of federally employed air traffic controllers in 1981 when they engaged in an illegal strike. Job security, not a major concern of the average worker in earlier years, became a significant issue in labor negotiations. By the early 1990s, the climate had so changed that laying off workers to facilitate cost reduction had become a prevalent practice.[8]

In his speech, Greenspan recognized the institutional change—in the form of a change in the public's expectations—to which Reagan contributed. After the Great Depression and World War II, US culture "frowned" on mass firings ("wholesale job reductions"). Reagan's action, however, ushered in an era in which "the climate had so changed that laying off workers to facilitate cost reduction had become a prevalent practice." Institutional change typically involves struggles over an extended period of time and on many fronts, however, and direct struggles between capital and labor also played a major role; the ultimate ascendancy of capital was marked most definitively, perhaps, by the collapse of the Caterpillar strike in the mid-1990s.

The Caterpillar conflict stretched on and off over more than half a decade.[9] The central issue was one of "pattern bargaining," according to which a major union would select one firm in a small oligopoly grouping for initial bargaining; that firm would be subject to a strike if the union found itself dissatisfied with the results of the negotiations, putting it at a competitive disadvantage within its industry. Once agreement had been reached with the firm, however, the other firms in the industry were expected to follow the same pattern, agreeing to broadly similar terms. In the case of the Caterpillar strike, the automobile workers' union (the UAW) had reached agreement with John Deere, also a producer of construction equipment, and expected Caterpillar to agree to similar terms.

Caterpillar, however, viewed the world differently. Its corporate strategy was to concentrate production within the US for sale on the world market. It saw John Deere as primarily a producer of agricultural equipment, and felt that its primary competitor in the worldwide construction equipment market was Japan's Komatsu. Agreeing to the terms the UAW had worked out with John Deere, in Caterpillar's view, would have rendered it incapable of competing effectively with Komatsu. From the standpoint of the UAW, which had used the pattern bargaining system to its advantage for decades in the automobile and other industries, allowing

Caterpillar to settle on more favorable terms would have undermined the entire institution of pattern bargaining.

The Caterpillar strike began in October 1991. After twenty-one weeks, management threatened to replace the strikers permanently (*Los Angeles Times* 5/14/95: A14). The workers went back, but sought to slow down production as a means of continuing their protest; some were fired and others suspended. The UAW complained to the National Labor Relations Board, which filed dozens of charges against the company. The workers resumed their strike. In 1995 replacement workers were brought in and the strike collapsed. In March 1998, the two sides finally agreed on a new contract, which was broadly similar to the contract offered in 1991 (*Wall Street Journal* 3/23/98: B10). The victory of management in the Caterpillar strike can be thought of as signifying the victory of capital over labor, a hallmark of the new SSA that has been formed in the United States.

On the one hand, then, the capital–labor accord lasted for decades because it was to the advantage of both sides, and because the other conditions and institutions existing in the domestic and world economies supported it. When it collapsed, however, there could not be any quick transition to an alternative set of institutional arrangements. First of all, the expectations of workers would not allow that. Second, and of comparable importance, a wide range of other conditions had to be met before the dominance of capital could be assured. For example, the ability of firms to move production abroad depended on finding production sites with adequate institutional guarantees, the progress of technology and transportation, foreign firms capable of filling outsourcing orders to acceptable standards, and so forth. Intensifying international competition made firms more assertive in standing up to union demands, and unions more accommodative as they found themselves risking total job loss if firms were forced under (and indeed during the 1980s the industrial Midwest in the United States was often referred to as the "rust belt").

New institutions are typically formed through processes of intense social conflict interacting with changing external conditions, and this example is meant to demonstrate that that process is inevitably a drawn-out affair. Thus, once established, an SSA is apt to last for a prolonged period of time, but when it collapses the reconstruction of a new one is also apt to require an extended period.

At the risk of belaboring the obvious, one more example from the postwar SSA in the US should help to clarify the reasons for which established SSAs tend to endure for prolonged periods. After World War II, the US was the dominant country in the capitalist world, benefiting from the fact that the economies of its principal competitors had been devastated by the war and its currency had become the *de facto* reserve currency for the entire capitalist world, allowing it to import real resources (or acquire foreign assets) while printing up and exporting its own paper currency in exchange. These conditions could change only when postwar reconstruction allowed the other major industrialized countries to recover to a point at which they could become viable competitors; that was a process that could take place only over decades.

Why SSAs collapse and how new ones are formed

The third theoretical question raised concerns the causes of SSA collapse and the ways in which new SSAs are created. Each SSA is composed of a set of institutions that are related to other institutions and social processes, as well as to external conditions and events. In addition, they are subject to internal contradictions that can undermine them over time. Consider, for example, the seniority system and lifetime employment in Japan. These practices were firmly institutionalized only in the larger, more established firms (since marginal firms were not in a position to offer the assurances they implied). The two labor practices suggest that once new employees have passed a trial period (usually about two years), they will not be fired or laid off and their salaries will increase each year, regardless of their work performance or productivity.

There are real benefits to the employers in this system. Workers tend to identify with their employers, working readily with greater intensity or for longer hours, and pay extra attention to the quality of the products they are making. The costs of recruiting and training new employees are reduced with the limited turnover that firms experience. Furthermore, firms can spend to develop particular skills in selected employees without worrying that those same employees will take their new skills to a competitor. In addition, what the seniority system does in effect is to underpay new employees relative to their productivity, and to overpay older employees who are close to retirement. One way of thinking about this system is to regard young employees as making long-term loans on favorable terms to their employers.

For reasons such as those enumerated, the seniority/lifetime employment system gave a considerable boost to the Japanese economy over a prolonged period of time. If we consider the development of internal contradictions and external changes, however, it becomes possible to understand the ways in which an institution that contributed to the accumulation process under one set of circumstances could have the opposite impact under another set.

First of all, when Japan experienced its period of most rapid GDP growth, 9.7 percent annually between 1955 and 1970 (Hirata 1995: 41), companies were hiring many new workers, skewing the age distribution of their labor forces heavily in favor of quite young workers, reducing average costs for the firms involved. By the 1990s, however, the reverse situation prevailed, with the average age quite high and the labor costs per unit of output increased accordingly. If one considers Japan's working age population only (15–64 years of age), then in 1965 26.1 percent of it was in its twenties and 12.9 percent was in its fifties, whereas in 1990 the corresponding proportions were 19.6 percent and 18.4 percent (Statistics Bureau 2004: 46). Reflecting in part the seniority system and the aging of the work force, the average labor cost per employee (in firms with thirty or more employees) rose from 294,476 yen per month in 1980 to 459,986 yen in 1991 (Statistics Bureau 2004: 538). This outcome is simply the result of a major internal contradiction in the employment system, and would exist with or without changes in external conditions. Such changes did occur as well, however, intensifying the effects of this internal contradiction.

With global competition increasing sharply during the last two decades of the twentieth century, especially from producers enjoying lower labor costs and sufficiently skilled workforces in the rest of Asia, Japanese firms felt themselves compelled to establish their own production facilities abroad. This limited employment opportunities within Japan, weakening the Japanese economy and, given the seniority/lifetime employment system, diminished new job creation, increased the average age and wage of existing employees, and made Japanese firms producing at home even less competitive.

At the same time, the shift in the frontiers of technology to information technology, a field whose frontiers are often driven by venture capital and entrepreneurship and whose emergence diminishes the efficacy of state-led development, further weakened the Japanese model, putting more pressure on firms to change. The old *keiretsu*, or industrial group system, another key institution in Japan's period of prosperity, also became an increasing liability under the changing global economic conditions. Banks were at the heart of the *keiretsu*, and would often hold shares in the group members as a way of cementing their alliance. This was so deeply embedded in the Japanese system that the regulators allowed the banks to count the value of the shares they held as part of their capital requirements. Common stock, however, is subject to severe fluctuations, and with the collapse of the Japanese stock market, starting at the end of 1989 and continuing until 2003 (when a bottom appears to have been reached), the banks' reserve position became precarious. In addition to that, the *keiretsu* system encouraged the banks to roll over loans rather than calling them in even when the borrowers' financial position became precarious, basically shifting the risk of insolvency to the banks themselves and inhibiting new lending.

A fuller description of the rise and demise of Japan's postwar SSA will be presented below (see pp. 37–41), but the point to be emphasized here is that a set of institutions that support the accumulation process by mutually supporting one another under a given set of external conditions, can lose that ability over time as external condition change and internal contradictions emerge. In this way, all social structures of accumulation are subject to collapse.

New social structures of accumulation emerge out of a mix of contending social forces, shaped to a greater or lesser extent by the drive of capital (that is, of capitalists or firms) to accumulate—to find profitable outlets for reinvestment and to secure the necessary conditions for doing so with a high degree of confidence that their capital will be protected. An understanding of the way in which this entire process is *overdetermined*—that is, complexly shaped by a myriad of contending forces interacting with externally given conditions—may be facilitated by considering the way in which a new SSA was constructed in the United States following the collapse of its postwar SSA. A more complete description of this process will follow in Chapter 3; the focus here is on clarifying the theoretical issue concerning the manner in which new SSAs are formed.

In the United States, the 1970s was a decade of "stagflation," a combination of high inflation and sluggish economic growth, with conditions worsened for business by growing international competition, intense capital–labor conflict, high taxation, and heavy governmental regulation. President Reagan's willingness to come down heavily on the side of capital in the struggles between capital and labor (symbolized by his 1981 firing of the air traffic controllers), his administration's support for lower taxes and reduced regulation, and its pursuit of a "free trade" agenda were all intended to help create conditions favorable for the accumulation process. It is important to realize as well, however, that society is the site of a multitude of conflicts, and the way in which these play out often bears on creating favorable conditions for accumulation without specifically seeking that objective.

Consider, for example, the struggles for racial and gender equality. In 2003, the US Supreme Court was considering the legality of the University of Michigan's racial preferences in admissions. The University indicated that such preferences play a limited role in the admissions process, with the major objective being a diverse student body. Preferences have long been given, at Michigan and elsewhere, to the children of alumni, to athletes, to people with special talents, to people from diverse geographic regions, and so forth; racial preferences are simply part of this mix. Nevertheless, President George W. Bush authorized the Justice Department to intervene in the case against Michigan (cnn.com/inside politics, 1/16/03). What is of interest here, however, is the fact that a large group of retired military leaders, including former superintendents of the US military and air force academies, and (separately) twenty of the Fortune 500 companies, intervened on behalf of the University of Michigan, maintaining that affirmative action helps them to achieve their objectives.[10] That is to say, they find it desirable to have a racially diverse student body (in the case of the military academies) in order to have a diverse officers' group, and the business firms find it desirable to have a racially diverse pool of college graduates from which they can select their own employees, something they find beneficial in a global economy with diverse ethnic and racial groups.

From the time of the civil rights movement in the 1960s, struggles for racial and gender equality have been ongoing in the United States. As opportunities opened for women and for minorities, the US economy benefited from a larger pool of qualified personnel. In addition, with two-wage-earner households increasingly common, living standards could readily be maintained and improved even without materially higher real wage rates. Under these circumstances, companies could limit their wage bills and improve their profit rates even while mass purchasing power was sustained. Thus, conditions that contributed to the emergence of a new SSA were established through indirection.

At the same time, prior to the 1980s, the US had—compared to other countries—well-established venture capital and investment banking industries. When the frontiers of technology shifted to information technology in the 1980s, this meant that sources of financing for the technological revolution under way in the new industry were readily available, giving the US a great advantage over the other industrialized nations. If we think of technological change as exogenously driven by invention and innovation (this of course is not strictly true since like all other social processes these are overdetermined), then we can think of the US economy as benefiting fortuitously from the fact that the new industrial frontiers were established in fields that could be supported by its existing economic strengths. If we think of a counterfactual possibility, supposing that the new industrial frontiers had been established in industries demanding primarily a high degree of precision engineering and precise workmanship, then we can see that Japan or Germany might have been the primary beneficiaries.

The key point here is that over the course of the 1980s and 1990s, the US economy benefited from what might be considered a matter of historical contingency—the fact that the new industrial frontiers were better suited to its existing economic strengths than to those of its potential competitor states. In this way, the emergence of the new SSA in the US by about the mid-1990s can be thought of as shaped by the drive of capital (that is, of capitalists and firms) to establish favorable conditions for accumulation, by a wide variety of social struggles that incidentally contributed to the formation of the new SSA, by changes in exogenous conditions that also proved favorable on balance, and by historical contingency. With all of these forces playing a role in the formation of the new SSA, we can think in general of each SSA as being overdetermined.

A social structure of accumulation, then, is a set of institutions that supports the accumulation process over an extended period of time, usually a matter of decades. The existence of SSAs accounts for extended periods of relative prosperity alternating with extended periods of relative stagnation in capitalist countries. Since institutions by their very nature are slow to change, since SSAs (or their constituent institutions) generate strong support from their beneficiaries, and since SSAs are overdetermined by changes in exogenous circumstances, by historical contingency, and by the other institutions and social processes with which they interact, their durability is readily understandable. But just as each SSA represents a structure that is supported by all of the elements that contribute to overdetermining it, changes in any of those elements can contribute to undermining it, and since each institution is subject to its own internal contradictions all SSAs are subject to progressive weakening and ultimate collapse.

When an SSA does collapse, a widely diverse set of social struggles tends to intensify. These struggles typically interact with the drive of capital to reestablish favorable conditions for accumulation, changes in exogenous conditions and circumstances shaped by historical contingency to create a new SSA. There is no guarantee that a new SSA will emerge from this process (consider the case of Argentina over the course of the twentieth century), but in nations where the power of capital is reasonably strong, that will usually be the outcome. When a new SSA is established, that marks a new stage in the development of capitalism in the country in question. Thus capitalism overcomes its internal contradictions by repeatedly reinventing itself. American capitalism today differs markedly from the American capitalism that existed in the middle of the twentieth century, which in turn differed markedly from that which existed at the end of the nineteenth century; each period reflects the existence of a distinctive SSA, and represents a distinctive phase in the development of American capitalism. This can be understood more clearly by considering in somewhat further detail two of the stages in question; this will be the subject matter of Chapter 3. First, however, the broad applicability of the SSA concept can be clarified by considering the case of Japan.

The rise and demise of Japan's postwar SSA

A good example of a social structure of accumulation can be found in postwar Japan, in which growth averaged 9.7 percent per year between 1955 and 1970, falling to a still-respectable 4–5 percent per year between 1970 and 1990 (Hirata 1995: 41). The institutions especially deserving of our attention include the leading role of the state in the economy, the *keiretsu* (corporate group) system, "lifetime" employment and the seniority system, the educational/career path system, and the family system. A brief clarification of the way in which these institutions contributed to economic growth and in which internal contradictions, interacting with changed external circumstances, ultimately arose to bring the postwar growth era to a close may help to clarify in general the nature and significance of an SSA.

It should be noted at the outset that the institutions of an SSA are distinct from the profit opportunities that capitalist enterprises may perceive; they cannot substitute for such opportunities. If perceived opportunities are present, however, that is not sufficient to encourage investment. The institutions of an SSA create a context within which the prospective investor feels confident of a supportive environment. With regard to the role of the state, for example, the Ministry of International Trade and Industry (MITI) established industrial bureaux for the major industries that, in addition to their limited regulatory duties, tended to focus on the health and growth of each one.[11] Thus, for example, when MITI was overseeing the expansion of the steel industry in postwar Japan, either directly or via other government agencies, it saw to it that tariffs on needed equipment were eliminated, financing was made available for the development and construction of large, ore-carrying ships (to compensate for Japan's poor domestic resource base), port facilities and the related land infrastructure were created to facilitate the import of the raw materials and the distribution of finished steel products from newly built factories along the coast, and took other steps to aid the industry. In other cases, when an industry was hit by problems of oversupply and falling prices, MITI would organize cartels to limit the economic damage and, where necessary, carry out an orderly downsizing in capacity of the entire industry.

The *keiretsu* are the Japanese industrial groups that were either the descendants of the old *zaibatsu*, which were abolished by the Occupation at the end of World War II, or organized around lead banks; in both cases, the banks were at the core of the *keiretsu*. These groups were marked by interlocking shareholding, joint ventures, preferential business relationships, and periodic meetings of their CEOs. Industrial members were sure they would have access to financing on favorable terms, the banks would have deep knowledge of the business conditions of the member firms and assured lending business, the trading companies (typically among the leading firms in each group) would be able to secure imported inputs on favorable terms and facilitate the exports of the group members. In such ways, the various enterprises realized substantial benefits from their membership in the group.

The "lifetime" employment and seniority systems assured the companies of the loyalty, experience, and dedication of their employees. While only the large firms could provide such security, the employees of such firms tended to identify their own status and well-being with that of their employer, making them willing to work longer hours with greater conscientiousness, and frequently to skip holidays to which they were entitled. Moreover, companies could invest in the education and training of their employees without fear that they would wind up using their enhanced skills in the employ of a competitor.

Finally, it is worth noting here that employees were typically hired directly out of high school or college. They were, characteristically, severely underpaid relative to their productivity when newly hired, but were compensated for this by the prospect of being overpaid in the years preceding their retirement. This is not quite the even trade-off it may appear, since in effect the employees are making long-term loans to their employers on terms quite favorable to the latter. Moreover, when companies are expanding rapidly, as was the case during the initial burst of growth in the postwar period, the vast majority of their employees are relatively young, keeping their average wage payments at very low levels.

The education/career path system also played a central role in Japan's postwar SSA. Japan is world-famous for the "examination hell" through which it puts its children. Examinations can start with pre-school, but become increasingly serious by the time the student reaches middle school. Entry into academically rigorous middle and high schools facilitates entry into one of the leading universities. Admission to one of these, in turn, often determines an individual's career opportunity, since movement among firms is uncommon; it is discouraged by the seniority system, and employers traditionally do their hiring out of high school or college as part of the "lifetime" employment system.

The students with the strongest academic credentials typically seek jobs in one of the government ministries. This reflects, in part, the power of government officials and the exceptionally high esteem in which they are held. It reflects also, however, the extremely favorable career opportunities that follow government service. When officials retire in their early to mid-fifties, they take jobs as heads of or senior advisers to companies in industries they had provided with "administrative guidance." If wealthy enough, many had the alternative opportunity to pursue political careers; a large number of Liberal-Democratic Party senators had previously served in various government ministries. The move from bureaucrat to company head or senator is known as *amakudari*, which literally means descending from heaven.

By preparing its most able students for this career path, and the much larger stratum right behind them for lifetime employment in the leading firms, the educational system in Japan provided a critical foundation for the government–business nexus widely known as "Japan Inc." In a sense, the entire educational system can be viewed as providing firm support for state-led development, and as serving the needs of Japanese capitalism in general.

In similar fashion, the family system also provided critical support. Women were not typically treated as permanent employees; they lacked seniority rights, were paid less than men with comparable credentials, and were expected to retire when they had children. The assumption in postwar Japan was that women would become stay-at-home wives, responsible for running the household and supervising their children's education. This in turn meant that men could devote themselves entirely to filling the needs of their employers, working long hours, or entertaining customers at night. It also meant that the mothers could devote themselves to socializing and educating their children to provide the next generation of devoted corporate employees. With its stark division of labor, the family system in Japan provides another example of an institution interacting with other institutions to provide a structure strongly supportive of the accumulation process.

While an SSA can support decades of relatively vigorous economic growth, no SSA can endure indefinitely. Inevitably, internal contradictions, interacting with changes in the external environment, bring about the collapse of every SSA. As I have previously noted, in postwar Japan the state played a leading role in industrial policy. This can work well when the issue is primarily one of copying the best practices developed abroad and making marginal improvements on them. Thus, as I have noted, with an able administration it is quite feasible to establish a steel industry, whether in the private or public sector. This indeed has been done under quite disparate regimes in Japan, South Korea, and China. It is much more difficult, however, for the state to develop a leading-edge software industry in a highly competitive international environment. Necessary conditions for the development of a software industry are apt to include a high degree of decentralization, a venture capital industry, exceptionally high rewards for successful innovation, and so forth. A strong, meritocratic educational system is also necessary and can of course be provided by the state, but this alone is insufficient. Thus as the cutting edge of economic activity shifts from conventional industrial production to areas like information technology and biotechnology, an economic model which requires the state to take a leading role becomes more problematic. The state can still play an important role, but one that is primarily *indirect*; it can finance targeted degree programs, help establish research parks, provide tax advantages to investors in the targeted industries, and so forth, but state-owned enterprises and centrally directed research agendas are unlikely to prove very helpful.

The *keiretsu* and lifetime employment systems, by contrast, find their diminishing effectiveness tied more closely to the development of internal contradictions. I have discussed briefly some of the principal advantages of the *keiretsu* or industrial groups. Note should also be taken of potential disadvantages as well. Capitalism is a system of ongoing change, of "creative destruction" to use Schumpeter's term (1950: 81–86). Unsuccessful firms fail, releasing assets at advantageous prices that further the accumulation process by other firms. If banks feel obliged to continue to support group members that are unable to earn an adequate return on their capital, then this process of purging and renewal is cut short. Conditions are unfavorable for allowing new firms to assume economic leadership, and more profitable firms lose access to capital that is not being returned to the banking system. Ultimately, bad loans come to threaten the viability of the banking system. All of this happened in Japan starting in the 1990s, in addition to which the cross-shareholdings that cemented the ties between the banks and the other group members heightened the banking crisis. This took place as the value of the shares held by the banks, part of the bank capital requirements in Japan, diminished sharply in value with the decline of the stock market.

Internal contradictions posed by the lifetime employment system also came to contribute to the stagnation the Japanese economy experienced from the 1990s. As the need for new employees diminished over time and the average age of employees rose, average wages rose disproportionately, diminishing the competitiveness of Japanese industry at the very time that much of the rest of Asia, following the Japanese model of state-directed development, was increasing its competitiveness. Japanese firms began to shift much of their production to other countries in Asia, reducing still more their need for new (young) workers and further increasing the average age of their workforces.

At the same time, their aging employees often lacked the skills required by the new technologies. As a consequence, Japanese firms were forced to retain "overpaid" employees who lacked the skills they required while cutting back on new hires to minimize their overall wage bills. In this way, the lifetime employment system combined with the seniority wage system was transformed from a competitive advantage for the Japanese economy to its very opposite. This is a clear example of an internal contradiction, even though its consequences were magnified by the growth of international competition, the shifts taking place in technology, and other "external" factors.

Many writers have pointed to the need for a variety of economic reforms as a precondition for reinvigorating the Japanese economy. This is undoubtedly correct, but the perspectives they present are often too narrow. Reform of the banking system alone, for example, will not be sufficient to reinvigorate Japanese capitalism. Rather, a comprehensive set of institutional changes will be required. Such changes emerge over time from a wide range of social struggles, both class and nonclass. There are struggles currently under way in Japan between generations, between the sexes, between rural and urban interests, between small business and big business, between those who favor political reform and those who feel threatened by it, and between the beneficiaries and the victims of the status quo. As these struggles play out over time, in the context of worsening economic problems with an exploding national debt and a rapidly aging population, the pressures for a broad package of reforms are apt to intensify.[12] Resistance from the beneficiaries of the current system has remained fierce, however, so there is no way to know how long it will take Japan to reconstruct a new social structure of accumulation, a structure that will mark a new stage in the development of capitalism in Japan.

The theoretical issues reviewed

The discussion of the Japanese case provides a basis for revisiting the theoretical issues touched on at the outset of this chapter. When the term "Japan Inc." is used, it connotes a complex of mutually supportive institutions. State-led development and the close alliance between business and government have been at the core of the Japanese system. It has been maintained and strengthened by the family system, the educational system, the seniority/lifetime employment system, the *keiretsu* system of corporate alliances, and other distinctive institutional arrangements. Taken together, these various institutions created a structure that contributed to rapid economic growth over many decades—a social structure of accumulation.

Particular institutions are shaped by and emerge from their historical antecedents, external conditions, the other institutions with which they interact and which serve to define their environment, and by the ongoing struggles that define each society. If a society is able to prosper under conditions of rapid accumulation and economic growth, then many beneficiaries will be created, and their support will add to the stasis that tends in any event to characterize institutions. Social structures of accumulation, therefore, tend to persist for lengthy periods once established. Ultimately, however, they are subject to erosion as external conditions change and internal contradictions emerge.

If we think of the case of Japan, then our attention is called to the fact that mothers are accustomed to sacrificing themselves for the good of their children, with educational attainment supposedly leading to a secure future for their offspring. The children too are sacrificed, forced to endure "examination hell" for the sake of their careers. What happens, however, when large companies cut back on their hiring, and people no longer believe that the implied commitment to lifetime employment will be honored? Under these conditions, patterns of behavior can be expected to change, and the changes will be reinforced by other forces reshaping the Japanese economy and society, such as the weakening of the banking and *keiretsu* systems, the growing fiscal crisis of the state, and so forth. Ultimately new institutions will emerge, but no firm time-line can be anticipated, and the process may well drag out for decades.

The long waves that characterize capitalist economies do far more than help to explain the extended, alternating periods of vigorous growth and stagnation. Each new period of vigorous growth, as I have already noted, is marked by a distinctive set of supporting institutions; that is, it is marked by a distinctive social structure of accumulation or SSA. For this reason, each new SSA marks a new phase in the development of capitalism in each country. Thus, for example, the SSA formed in America at the turn of the twenty-first century is quite different from its post-World War II SSA. Stated somewhat differently, contemporary American capitalism is quite different from the capitalism that existed in America in the 1950s. In essence, American capitalism, like capitalism elsewhere, overcomes its recurrent crises by reinventing itself each time.

An understanding of this process helps us to understand the way in which the capitalist system has managed to thrive in the face of severe contradictions and repeated crises. This is not meant to maintain that past success offers any guarantees for the future. When a given SSA has crumbled in response to internal contradictions and a changing external environment, an indeterminate period of time is required before a new one can be constructed, and this period of time may stretch out indefinitely. When and if a new SSA is constructed, it emerges partly in response to the drive of capital to reestablish favorable conditions for accumulation, and partly by indirection—as a by-product of favorable "external" conditions interacting with the wide variety of social conflicts taking place at any given time. Class conflict plays a major role in this regard, but that is only one of numerous conflicts that play a role.

Among such conflicts we may consider, for example, intergenerational conflicts (will more funds be allocated to subsidizing the aging or to education?), conflicts between rural and urban areas (who will obtain the water necessary to sustain population and production growth?), the conflict between men and women, the conflict between the beneficiaries of rapid economic growth and those concerned primarily with protecting the environment, and the conflict between the victims and the beneficiaries of social change. Class conflict does play an important role in this regard, but the Marxian tendency to elevate it to a determining role ignores the multiple factors that always play a part in bringing about social change. The discussion in Chapter 3 of the postwar and contemporary American social structures of accumulation should help to expand upon and further clarify the theoretical issues addressed here and analyzed in the Japanese context.

3 Social structures of accumulation

The reinvention of American capitalism

In the previous chapter, theoretical issues bearing on social structures of accumulation were brought up for consideration and one case study, that of Japan, was introduced as a means of clarifying the argument. This chapter will focus on two additional case studies: the rise and demise of America's postwar SSA, and the rise of America's current SSA during the 1980s and 1990s. Although these cases are of considerable interest in themselves, their presentation here is meant primarily to demonstrate the power of SSA analysis to contribute to an understanding of the general dynamics of the capitalist system. Such analysis, for example, could be equally well employed in evaluating the economic condition and outlook of countries like Germany and China. Some brief observations on SSA conditions in these two countries may help to clarify the broad applicability of SSA analysis and serve as an introduction to the more detailed case studies that follow.

While I have classified Germany with the welfare-state model of continental Europe, it also shares some of the state–business connection of the Japanese model. Moreover, there are interesting parallels in their post-World War II economic performance. Both countries experienced a recovery phase of extremely rapid economic growth, a phase often referred to as an economic "miracle" in discussions of their economic performance. This was followed by decades of strong if more subdued economic growth in which both countries served as economic engines of their respective regions. And then both countries entered into extended periods of economic stagnation, with economic growth in Germany averaging 1.3 percent in the decade to 2002 (*Business Week*, 2/17/03: 44), the same as Japan's growth rate between 1990 and 2001 (Statistics Bureau 2004: 8). Clearly, the institutions that served to promote rapid economic growth in prior years no longer serve that function.

To understand the difficulties confronted by German capitalism, SSA analysis suggests that one can begin by looking at institutions that have become dysfunctional. Without attempting a comprehensive analysis here, I would like to point to a few critical examples. First, the *Kündigungsschutz* is a job-protection law that makes it extremely expensive for employers to lay off workers, whether or not their work is needed. The result, as in Japan, has been that German firms are now reluctant to hire new workers. When companies do invest, they are increasingly likely to do so abroad; German unemployment as of this writing (August 2004) is 10.6 percent (Bloomberg.com, 8/4/04).

A second example is provided by the difficulties confronted by Germany's largest banks—difficulties that weaken its entire financial system. These banks compete with the state-owned banks (the *Landesbanken*) and the municipally owned banks (the *Sparkassen*). Since the public banks seek to promote local business rather than to produce profits, and since they have the credit-backing of their local governments (which enables them to raise funds on more favorable terms), they are able to lend at much lower rates than the major private banks. As a result, the combined market share of the four major private-sector banks (Deutsche Bank AG, HVB Group, Dresdner Bank AG, and Commerzbank AG) is only 14 percent of all loans to individuals, companies and government bodies in Germany.

In the past, these major banks benefited from substantial shareholdings in major German companies. Many of these holdings have been eliminated or have fallen in value in recent years, however, and the banks' income from trading activities and various fees has fallen sharply at the same time. As a result, the major private banks have been sorely weakened, undermining Germany's entire financial system. In short, the low-interest loans available from the state-owned banks increased the availability of credit and promoted Germany's economic boom during one historical juncture, but by undermining the large private banks have become an important source of weakness in the entire economy at present.

A final example of the bearing of institutional change on the German economy is provided by the increasing economic integration of the European Union. In principle, the strengthening of the common market should spur economic growth, and under the proper conditions it would undoubtedly do so. Monetary union, however, has rather complex implications. With the European Central Bank (ECB) setting interest rates for all countries and focused (on German insistence) on minimizing inflation, individual countries lose control over their own interest rates. Even though inflation in Germany is quite low, across the European Union it is higher than the ECB would like, making it hesitant to lower interest rates despite high unemployment and a sluggish economy in Germany. The inability to stimulate its economy by lowering interest rates makes it all the more important for Germany to accelerate its needed institutional reforms.

As in the case of Japan, however, there are strong constituencies behind the status quo. The labor unions, a major political force, are firmly against reforming the *Kündigungsschutz*, the job-protection law. And the numerous businesses and individuals benefiting from the low interest rates offered by the *Landesbanken* and *Sparkassen* are not anxious to see their lending activities curtailed. Under these conditions, stagnation is likely to persist over a more or less prolonged period—until the beneficiaries and advocates of reform are able to gain a decisive advantage.

In the case of China, the fact that the power of the state is behind the institutional reform process helps to explain the dramatic success of the Chinese economy since the reform process was initiated in December of 1978. Over the quarter century to 2004, the Chinese economy averaged growth of 9.4 percent (Zedillo 2004: 43), with "middle-class" lifestyles increasingly becoming the norm in major cities. Basically, by unleashing entrepreneurship in the countryside, by inviting foreign direct investment (FDI) into the country on a massive scale (it reached $53 billion in 2003 alone, passing FDI in the United States; *Wall Street Journal*, 6/28/04: A2), and by instituting a dramatic series of reforms—from encouraging private business to entering the WTO and making employment flexible—the Chinese government was able to transform a Soviet-style economy with sluggish economic growth into the most dynamic economy in the world. Undertaken during the age of globalization and dramatic technological change, the Chinese reforms have contributed to the formation of a new SSA that promises to continue at least as long as the commitment to the reform process remains vigorous.

The (opposing) examples of Germany and China indicate the broad scope within which SSA analysis can be employed to understand the forces shaping contemporary capitalism. The more detailed analysis of the two SSAs created in the United States since World War II should help to serve the same purpose. Moreover, since these case studies are more comprehensive, they may help to provide a more nuanced understanding of SSAs and of the theoretical issues raised in Chapter 2. Ultimately, however, the strongest reason for including them here is the insight they provide into the nature of capitalism, which has been able to overcome its contradictions and to thrive by repeatedly reinventing itself.

The rise of America's postwar social structure of accumulation

Among the clearest case studies of a social structure of accumulation is that presented by David Gordon, Thomas Weisskopf, and Samuel Bowles in their essay, "Power, Accumulation and Crisis: The Rise and Demise of the Postwar Social Structure of Accumulation" (1996). They argue that the relatively rapid growth in productivity and GDP in the American economy over (roughly) the quarter of a century following World War II, a period during which the living standards of the average American household approximately doubled, was underpinned by an SSA with four major components. For the reasons outlined below, I would suggest adding a fifth component. The five include:

1 *A capital–labor accord*, according to which labor received regular

increases in real wages, health and retirement benefits, seniority protections against lay-offs and other benefits in exchange for management control over production and the labor process, together with the right to introduce labor-saving equipment.

2 *Pax Americana*, which refers to America's hegemonic position in the capitalist world economy, including the system of fixed exchange rates determined at Bretton Woods in 1944 that created a high value for the dollar, and the use of the dollar as a reserve currency throughout the capitalist world.
3 *The capital–citizen accord*, according to which citizens accepted the legitimacy and primacy of capital's pursuit of profit in exchange for capital's supporting the economic security of the citizenry (social security, Medicare and unemployment insurance especially) and accepting a measure of responsibility for corporate conduct. This accord was reflected, essentially, in a set of political arrangements.
4 *The moderation of inter-capitalist rivalry*. This had two central components. Domestically, competition was muted due to the emergence of oligopoly as the characteristic industrial structure. With a few large companies dominating most of the major industries, they could all see that price competition was not to their advantage. Internationally, the devastation wrought by World War II on the other advanced industrial countries required a more or less extended period of economic reconstruction, a period during which they were not in position to pose a serious competitive threat to American companies.
5 *A financial structure that supported the accumulation process*. Martin Wolfson (1994) suggests that in addition to the four components noted above, the financial structure in the US economy made a core contribution to the postwar SSA. Wolfson focuses on a number of key elements, most of which emerged during the 1930s in response to the crisis posed by the Great Depression. The fact that these institutions were holdovers from a previous era does not diminish the role they were able to play under the new circumstances that emerged after the war. They included, among other institutional innovations, the separation of commercial and investment banking (which has since been repealed), the prohibition of interest payments on demand deposits (also repealed), the creation of the Federal Deposit Insurance Corporation (FDIC) to insure most bank deposits, and the creation of the Securities and Exchange Commission.

Before turning to an examination of the manner in which this social structure of accumulation functioned, it may prove useful to clarify the institutional character of the component parts. The capital–citizen and capital–labor accords were not, of course, formal accords, and they can be thought of as institutions only in the broadest possible sense. From one perspective, we can think of the capital–labor accord as incorporating more narrowly conceived institutional arrangements, such as collective bargaining. Similarly, the capital–citizen accord can be thought of as incorporating institutions like social security and Medicare. At the same time, however, if we think of institutions in a broad sense as composed of particular habits, customs, and expectations, then the accords can fit within the conceptual framework of institutions. The capital–labor accord, for example, incorporates assumptions on both sides about what types of behavior are legitimate and expected. Labor expected rising real wages and protections against lay-offs for older employees, among other benefits. Management expected to be able to introduce productivity enhancing equipment, to organize the work process to its liking, and so forth. The set of expectations on both sides formed the core of the institution.

In like fashion, the political expectations surrounding the capital–citizen accord can be thought of as its defining feature as an institution. Business or capital expects that the state will not act in such a way as to drive its profits down to unacceptable levels, as it might for example through higher taxation or stricter regulation, but citizens expect that taxation will be maintained at levels sufficient to provide financial security during times of unemployment or retirement. It is this set of implicit expectations held on both sides that mark the capital–citizen accord as an institution.

Presenting *pax Americana* as an institution may appear even more problematic, but here too the concept may be founded on the shared expectations of different parties—although in this case the parties are the world community of nation-states. *Pax Americana* incorporated a set of expectations around the world that accommodated American business's quest for raw materials and intermediate products at low prices, as well as its search for international markets. Over time, the benefits to the rest of the world became obvious as their economies recovered or, in the case of the export-oriented developing countries such as the Asian "tigers," they found themselves able to use American capital or the American market to support their own industrialization. This process was facilitated for both the already-industrialized and the developing countries through the existence of the fixed exchange rates against the American dollar that had been determined at the time of Bretton Woods, for as the other economies grew their currencies could not increase in value commensurately. This in turn made their currencies increasingly undervalued and facilitated their penetration of the American market. Thus American hegemony contributed to the rise of economies capable of competing vigorously with America, one of the core contradictions within the postwar SSA and one that played a major role in its ultimate collapse.

Clarification of the institutional character of America's postwar SSA paves the way to an analysis of why it was so effective in promoting rapid productivity growth, why its different components were mutually supportive (creating a distinctive structure), why it lasted for a long time, and why it ultimately collapsed. The establishment of an SSA is typically associated with high rates of investment, high profit rates, and rapid growth of productivity and real GDP, as well as with rising real wages and living standards; all were present in the postwar SSA (although by the end of the 1960s the postwar SSA was clearly fraying). As discussed in Chapter 2, in the quarter century to 1973 America's productivity growth averaged 2.9 percent per year (after which it fell sharply to a 1.4 percent annual average between 1973 and 1995). Corporate profits as a share of gross domestic profit were 10.2 percent and 10.9 percent in 1953 and 1963 respectively, but fell to 8.9 percent and 7.2 percent in 1973 and 1983 (Sutch 2005). Real per capita gross domestic product rose by 63 percent in the 1948–68 period, but only by 39.6 percent in the 1973–93 period (Ibid.).

America's strong economic performance in the postwar period was sustained by the set of institutions that came to prevail at that time; that is, by its new SSA. Each of the institutional components noted contributed to the long wave upswing experienced by the American economy. More importantly, each of the components contributed to the establishment and maintenance of an overall structure that encouraged the accumulation process.

The 1930s had been a period of intense class conflict, with the rise of militant industrial unions and the Congress of Industrial Organizations (the CIO), their umbrella organization. While the conflict became muted during the war (and largely because of it), the postwar period offered exceptional opportunities for profitable investment. Continued conflict between labor and capital under the conditions that came to prevail in the postwar period would have meant forgoing many of those opportunities.

The postwar period was characterized by large, pent-up demand for consumption goods and housing that the war had made unavailable. In addition, the 1950s and 1960s marked the "suburbanization" of America, with new housing developments and shopping centers springing up throughout the country, the "national defense" highway program spurring road construction, and automobile ownership spreading rapidly. Low interest rates and low inflation facilitated the spread of consumer debt, providing the financing for the new houses, cars, and consumer goods.

With overseas markets spurred by reconstruction, and with little competition from abroad, the market opportunities for American business were considerable. Within this context it was very much in the interest of American capital to secure a "truce" in the ongoing conflict with labor. From the standpoint of labor, all of the new consumption opportunities became attainable with steady employment and real wages rising year after year. With both sides standing to benefit, therefore, the conditions for creating a capital–labor accord were extremely favorable.

The capital–labor accord was also supported by the other institutions that marked the postwar SSA, as well as by exogenous circumstances and historical contingency. As a prime example of historical contingency, we can point to the fact that World War II destroyed most completely the industrial capacity of the two countries that would eventually prove to be the fiercest competitors of the United States in the postwar world, Japan and Germany, with the rest of Europe also damaged severely. That created the basis for American economic hegemony in the postwar world, and contributed to the opportunities for American capital that made the capital–labor accord attractive to it.

Pax Americana refers to this American economic hegemony that was made possible by the outcome of World War II, and thus represents another example of an institution that was aided by historical contingency. It included the widespread use of the American dollar as the primary reserve currency throughout the capitalist world economy. When countries ship goods and services to the US in exchange for paper currency that the US can simply print up, there is a net transfer of real resources to the US. In addition, with the value of the US dollar fixed at a high level—becoming increasingly overvalued as the rest of the world economy recovered and developed—American companies were able to acquire raw materials, intermediate products, real assets, and other companies abroad on favorable terms, increasing their profitability and market opportunities. The strong dollar meant as well that inflationary pressures were muted at home (via lower costs for imported raw materials, intermediate goods, and final products), contributing to the low interest rates that supported the postwar expansion.

The low-inflation, low-interest-rate environment also enhanced the contribution made by the financial system to postwar prosperity. With deposits encouraged by government insurance, the banking system had ready access to low-cost funds to help finance economic expansion. The savings and loans, paying marginally higher interest rates on savings deposits, helped especially to finance the growth of the housing industry. In general, the use of credit was facilitated for both firms and households in the institutional environment that prevailed in the postwar period.

In this environment, the capital–citizen accord also had a distinctive contribution to make. In effect, this accord represents public acceptance of the legitimacy of the corporate pursuit of profits. It may be reflected best in the famous quote from Charles Wilson, secretary of defense under President Eisenhower and former chairman of General Motors. When he was asked during his confirmation hearings whether as secretary of defense "he could make a decision adverse to the interests of General Motors, Wilson answered affirmatively but added that he could not conceive of such a situation 'because for years I thought what was good for the country was good for General Motors and vice versa'" (http://encyclopedia.thefreedictionary.com).

Taxes on corporations were limited (or means provided in the tax code to circumvent some of them), environmental and other regulations were minimal, and in general the state encouraged private business activity. In "exchange," American citizens received a limited range of public welfare benefits, including social security (from the 1930s), Medicare (from the 1960s), and unemployment insurance. Overall, the environment created was one in which the corporate pursuit of profit maximization gained a high degree of social approval, and few political obstacles were placed in the way of this pursuit.

This was true even in the case of the oligopolies, which played a central role in muting domestic competition. Most of the major industries came to be dominated by a handful of very large firms. The intense price competition that had prevailed in an earlier age gave way to varied forms of non-price competition, focusing on advertising and marketing. Although formal price-fixing agreements remained illegal, companies could usually circumvent this through the use of price leadership, in which one of the leading firms would regularly take the lead in making price changes, after which the other firms would follow; they all realized that it was to their advantage to avoid price wars. The beneficent public view of capital facilitated such practices, and the capital–labor accord meant that to some extent the workers at the large firms shared in their prosperity.

The other component of muted competition reflects the inability of foreign firms to compete effectively in the United States, the result of the wartime destruction they had experienced. This factor, a matter of historical contingency, provided de facto protection for the home market of American producers. The muted competition experienced by American firms in the postwar period, then, had both domestic and international sources.

Another element that may be treated as exogenous is the intellectual climate that prevailed with regard to the appropriate role of the state in the economy. In this regard, we may view as especially significant the penetration of Keynesian economic thought, culminating in the famous statement of President Nixon that "We are all Keynesians now" (www.time.com), a statement which came just as major intellectual challenges to Keynesianism were beginning to emerge. The significance of the acceptance of Keynesianism in the postwar period is that it legitimized a major role for the state in the economy, a role that limited the intensity of recessions and facilitated the capital–citizen accord.

While it would be possible to extend this discussion considerably, the principal objectives should already have been attained. The postwar SSA was comprised of a set of institutions that encouraged the accumulation process. These institutions were mutually reinforcing and were supported as well by "exogenous" factors, creating an overall structure that was able to stand for decades. The fact that institutions by their very nature are slow to change, and the fact that the postwar SSA created beneficiaries with a vested interest in seeing it sustained, also worked to promote the endurance of the postwar SSA. As is the case with all SSAs, however, the emergence of internal contradictions interacting with exogenous changes weakened the SSA over time, ultimately leading to its collapse and the introduction of an era of sluggish economic growth.

The demise of America's postwar social structure of accumulation

As I have noted, the muted competition that characterized America's postwar SSA had both domestic and international components. By the late 1960s, international competition intensified as economic reconstruction in the industrialized countries was largely completed and the export-oriented development strategies of the Asian "tigers" made them formidable, low-cost competitors over a range of industries. At the same time, the increasing overvaluation of the dollar, whose exchange rate was initially set in 1944 and which could not be adjusted as economies throughout the world strengthened, heightened the growing competitive disadvantage of American companies.

During the 1970s, rising inflationary pressures intensified the problems of American firms. These pressures were associated with mishandled public finances, the (finally) weakening dollar and the rise of OPEC, among other forces, and served to usher in a decade of stagflation. Under the capital–labor accord, the strong unions had managed to secure cost-of-living allowances and real wage increases regardless of productivity gains. Since inflation was high and rising during the 1970s, the 3 percent real wage gains expected by many union members implied 7–10 percent (or more) money wage increases; these were viewed as unaffordable by the leading firms, which were facing intensified competitive pressures in conjunction with declining productivity gains.

The conditions that had sustained the capital–labor accord disintegrated under these circumstances, ushering in a decade of intensified labor strife in the 1970s, with a large number of strikes taking place and many labor-days of work lost. Thus in 1960 there were 896,000 workers involved in major strikes (involving more than one thousand workers), but in 1970 the figure swelled to 2,468,000 (US Department of Commerce 2002: 411). It should already be possible to see, then, that the collapse of the postwar SSA reflected the interaction of numerous factors—that it was overdetermined by internal contradictions and changes in the exogenous conditions that had sustained it.

The *pax Americana* that had contributed to strong growth at home, for example, also facilitated recovery and growth abroad. Foreign countries were the beneficiaries of aid, capital inflows, and growing market opportunities; as their production capabilities increased, the US economy grew and their fixed exchange rates improved their competitive positions. Rapid economic growth and increased competitiveness abroad undermined directly two of the components of the postwar SSA: *pax Americana* and muted competition. The overvaluation of the dollar could not be sustained indefinitely. Trade imbalances and growing political pressures in the US made a move to floating exchange rates, accompanied by a significant weakening of the dollar, inevitable. The weakened position of American industry ruled out the continuation of the capital–labor accord as an option. Thus the strengthening of foreign economies to which postwar American hegemony had contributed ultimately resulted in the weakening of that hegemony and some of the central institutions that had supported it.

Another internal contradiction of great significance revolved around the capital–citizen accord. With few restrictions placed on the pursuit of profit during the postwar SSA, negative externalities began to mushroom. Several communities, including Love Canal near Niagara Falls, that had been built on top of toxic waste sites, had to be evacuated; in 1969, a river in Cleveland was so filled with chemical contaminants that it caught fire (www.epa.gov). Air and water quality deteriorated substantially in many parts of the country, and public consciousness of environmental deterioration grew significantly. In 1979, the Environmental Protection Agency (EPA) estimated that there were "thousands of inactive and uncontrolled waste sites in the United States that could pose a serious risk to public health" (Ibid.).

The civil rights and anti-war activism of the 1960s paved the way for an environmental movement that sought to block or limit firms' polluting activities. Different levels of government imposed a growing number of environmental restrictions, raising business costs. At the same time, other social goals such as racial and gender equality led to further increases in corporate regulation. However desirable much of this regulatory activity was, it did imply higher business costs, diminishing the attractiveness of investment. By 1992, according to a Washington University study cited in *The Economist* (12/13/97: 52), firms with fewer than twenty employees spent an average of $5,784 per employee to meet federal regulations, with firms employing more than five hundred spending about half that amount. The capital–citizen accord, which had facilitated accumulation in the postwar period by contributing to rising output while minimizing required pollution controls, had also contributed to environmental deterioration. This increased public anger with business behavior and ultimately contributed to the collapse of the accord itself. Once again, an internal contradiction served, over time, to undermine the postwar SSA.

As for the role of the financial system, its various components functioned less effectively in an era of inflation. Savings accounts became less attractive, and financial intermediaries like banks and (especially) savings and loans were damaged by their inability to attract deposits at the low rates fixed by law; banks were also damaged by the increasing ability of large firms to raise money directly from the financial markets (as through the sale of bonds), thereby bypassing the banks.

In addition to the internal contradictions undermining the postwar SSA, "exogenous" events also contributed. As I have indicated earlier, in the last analysis nothing is entirely exogenous since all social affairs and conditions are overdetermined. Even so, in a world in which everything taking place tends to have an impact on other events, treating certain events as "exogenous" makes the analysis more manageable. For example, the rise of OPEC and the Iranian revolution of 1979, both of which pushed up oil prices sharply, had a significant impact on the emergence of stagflation in the 1970s. At one level we can argue that these were essentially external events that had significant domestic economic consequences. At another level of analysis, however, both events were shaped in part by the history of American foreign policy.[1]

The collapse of America's postwar social structure of accumulation was, accordingly, overdetermined by the internal contradictions in its constituent institutions, external changes, and the interaction among the constituent parts and external conditions. With inflation discouraging long-term investment especially, and the institutional supports for strong accumulation undermined, an era of sluggish economic growth was ushered in. The stagflation of the 1970s, however, led to intensified social struggles, including class struggles, as capital sought to reestablish favorable conditions for accumulation. These struggles continued over the 1980s and 1990s, and by the middle of the latter decade a new social structure of accumulation was established (Lippit 1997).

America's new social structure of accumulation

While it is always somewhat arbitrary to provide a fixed date for the start and end of an SSA expansion, a result of the fact that institutional structures and external conditions do not change all at once, the new social structure of accumulation in the United States can be thought of as starting around 1995 and representing the culmination of social struggles and institutional changes that took place during the course of the 1980s and 1990s. After listing and explaining the central components of the new SSA, I would like to turn to a consideration of the forces that gave rise to it and the way in which its various components formed a mutually supportive structure. Then I will turn to an examination of the statistical evidence supporting the proposition that a new SSA has indeed been formed, and place the recession of 2001 and the sluggish recovery that followed in the context of this analysis.

The core elements of America's new SSA are as follows:

1 The strengthening of capital relative to labor.
2 A change in financial institutions favorable to investment.
3 Deregulation.
4 Institutional changes in the nature of the corporation marked by restructuring, downsizing, and reengineering, as well as by ongoing reforms in corporate governance.
5 Limited government.
6 An increase in international agreements to facilitate international trade and investment.
7 Capital markets favorable to small, entrepreneurial companies.

In their essay on America's postwar SSA, Gordon, Weisskopf, and Bowles (1996) argue that it is possible for capital to be too strong relative to labor or too weak. Their logic is based on the observation that if capital is too strong, then real wages will be depressed and the mass purchasing power needed to validate new investment will not be available. Alternatively expressed, capitalists or firms will be able to generate high profits in production, but will be unable to generate sufficient sales at prices high enough to justify new investment. On the other hand, if capital is too weak then high wages will result in lower profits in production, also discouraging new investment. According to their argument, only a balance between the interests of capital and those of labor can result in the interests of both parties being served.

This argument, however, presumes a relatively closed economy; it is undermined by globalization, which was a central feature of the last two decades of the twentieth century. If capitalists as a group must sell to their workers as a group, then the argument of Gordon, Weisskopf, and Bowles remains valid. If, however, capitalists can sell a large portion of their consumer and capital goods abroad, then they do not have to rely so fully on the purchasing power of their own workers (Chapter 4 indicates additional ways in which this problem—the excessive strength of capital—can be resolved). Globalization is one of the central "exogenous" conditions of the new SSA, and it makes a central—and continuing—contribution to one of its defining institutional features, the great strengthening of capital relative to labor. This stands in sharp contrast to the capital–labor accord that marked the postwar SSA.

As I have argued above, the collapse of the capital–labor accord ushered in an era of sharp class struggles, with the period between 1981 (when President Reagan fired the air traffic controllers) and 1995 (when the Caterpillar strike collapsed) of special significance. Both of these strikes failed when President Reagan and the management of Caterpillar proved their readiness to bring in replacement workers. During this period, capital found that globalization created both the incentive and the means to confront labor in a more unyielding fashion. The incentive arose from the intensification of competition; in many industries, firms that were unable to bring their costs down simply failed. The means arose from the possibilities of outsourcing production activities either partially or completely, and the growing foreign markets created by recovery and economic growth abroad.

Tables 3.1–3.4 reflect the growing strength of capital relative to labor. Table 3.1 shows the stagnation in real wages that prevailed in the period between 1973 and 1996; Table 3.2 compares the declining share of wages and salaries in national income to the rising share of corporate profits between 1980 and 1995. It should be kept in mind that corporate profits understate total profits in the national income accounts, since a large share of proprietors' income represents profit. Also, profits understate total returns to capital since they exclude interest income and rental income.

Table 3.1 Trends in real average wages and average hours, 1973–96

Year	*Productivity Per hour (1992=100)*	*Wage levels ($1997)*			*Hours worked*		
		Annual wages ($)	*Weekly wages ($)*	*Hourly wages ($)*	*Annual hours*	*Weeks per year*	*Hours per week*
1973	80.7	25,393	585.22	15.17	1,720	43.4	38.6
1979	86.3	25,580	584.02	15.05	1,745	43.8	38.8
1989	95.7	27,905	614.65	15.64	1,823	45.4	39.3
1992	100.0	27,065	597.47	15.24	1,818	45.3	39.2
1996	102.0	28,222	613.52	15.45	1,868	46.0	39.7
Annual growth rate (%):							
1973–79	1.1	0.1	0.0	–0.1	0.2	0.2	–0.3
1979–89	1.0	0.9	0.5	0.4	0.4	0.4	0.1
1989–96	0.9	0.2	0.0	–0.2	0.3	0.2	0.1

Source: Lawrence Mishel, Jared Bernstein and John Schmitt (1999) *The State of Working America 1998–99*, An Economic Policy Institute book (Ithaca, N.Y.: Cornell University Press), p. 123.

Table 3.2 Wages and salaries, and corporate profits as a share of US national income

Year	*Wages and salaries (%)*	*Corporate profits (%)*
1980	62.2	7.5
1985	59.5	8.4
1990	59.8	8.0
1995	59.0	10.1

Source: US Department of Commerce, Bureau of the Census (1996) *Statistical Abstract of the United States 1996* (Washington, D.C.: US Government Printing Office), p. 449.

Table 3.3 shows the change in major strikes and working time lost between 1960 and 2001, while Table 3.4 shows the decline in union membership between 1983 and 2001, a decline that was concentrated in the private sector of the economy. The decline in union membership and the decline in strikes simply reflect the weakened position of labor. Workers are unlikely to join unions if they fear retaliation and believe that collective action is unlikely to prove fruitful. Further, if strikes are viewed as hopeless or as resulting in the loss of jobs to production sites overseas, then workers are unlikely to commit themselves to strike activity.

Until the late 1970s, the Federal Reserve Board had tended to place considerable weight on both parts of its mandate—to contain inflation and sustain employment. With inflation reaching double digits by the end of the decade, however, Paul Volcker and his successor as chairman of the

Table 3.3 Work stoppages in the US involving more than 1,000 workers, 1960–2001

Year	*No. of stoppages*	*Workers involved (1,000)*	*Working time lost (%)*
1960	222	896	0.09
1970	381	2,468	0.29
1980	187	795	0.09
1990	44	185	0.02
1999–2001 (aver.)	28	189	0.03

Source: US Department of Commerce, Bureau of the Census (2002) *Statistical Abstract of the United States: 2002* (Washington, D.C.: US Government Printing Office), p. 411.

Table 3.4 Union membership in the US as a percentage of the labor force

Year	*Public sector (%)*	*Private sector (%)*	*Total (%)*
1983	36.7	16.5	20.1
1985	35.7	14.3	18.0
1990	36.5	11.9	16.1
1995	37.7	10.3	14.9
1997	37.2	9.7	14.1
1998	37.5	9.5	13.9
2000	37.5	9.0	13.5
2001	37.4	9.0	13.5

Source: US Department of Commerce, Bureau of the Census (2002) *Statistical Abstract of the United States: 2002* (Washington, D.C.: US Government Printing Office), p. 411.

Fed, Alan Greenspan, came to place overwhelming emphasis on the containment of inflation. After briefly raising short-term interest rates above 20 percent in the early 1980s—and seeing inflation begin a secular decline that persisted over the following two decades—Volcker (and Greenspan after him) presided over a corresponding reduction in interest rates. Despite occasional increases reflecting cyclical pressures, the secular decline in interest rates reflected the secular disinflation.

The Federal Reserve Board is not a new institution, of course, but the change in its direction and focus was so extreme as to make it virtually "new." The point to be stressed is that the institutional environment within which economic activity was carried out became much more attractive with relatively stable prices and low interest rates, encouraging investment. Table 3.5 indicates the decline in inflation and in interest rates between 1971 and 2002.

The collapse of the capital–citizen accord had paved the way during the 1970s especially to a significant increase in government regulation. Much of this was in the environmental arena, as the deterioration of American

Table 3.5 US inflation and interest rates, 1971–2002

Year(s)	*Average annual consumer price inflation rate (%)*	*Federal funds rate (%)*
1971–75	9.5	
1976–80	8.9	
1981–85	5.5	11.2
1986–90	4.0	7.7
1991–95	3.1	4.5
1996–2000	2.5	5.5
2001	2.9	3.9
2002	1.4	1.7

Sources: US Department of Commerce, Bureau of the Census (1996) *Statistical Abstract of the United States: 1996* (Washington, D.C.: US Government Printing Office), pp. 483–484, 520; *Economic Report of the President: 2003*. (Washington, D.C.: US Government Printing Office), p. 345.

Note
The federal funds rate is the interest rate banks charge one another on overnight loans made to meet the reserve requirements set by the Federal Reserve Board. The Federal Reserve Board determines the federal funds rate through its open market operations, its most significant tool and one that enables it to influence the entire structure of interest rates in the US.

air, soil, and water reflected the growth in production and consumption in the postwar era—growth that was accompanied by great carelessness in the disposal of waste materials. As the consciousness of smog, water toxicity, and other environmental ills grew, legislation regulating activities that affected the environment began to grow apace. In 1969, the National Environment Policy Act was passed requiring all branches of government to take into account the environmental impact of any significant action. In the 1970s, major environmental acts included, among many others, the Occupational Safety and Health Act of 1970 (which required workplaces to be free of recognized hazards to safety and health), the Clean Air Act of 1970, the Endangered Species Act of 1973, and the Clean Water Act of 1977.[2]

The increase in government regulatory activity extended well beyond environmental and public health issues. The racial/gender equality and anti-war movements of the 1960s had spawned a generation of activists, whose activities resulted in a host of regulations that sought to limit discriminatory treatment of women, racial minorities, and the handicapped. The regulatory movement required a great deal of paperwork, compliance officers, and so forth, adding to business expenses and lowering returns on investment above and beyond the more substantial impact of environmental regulation. According to one study, as I have mentioned, the added cost came to $5,784 per employee for small firms in the early 1990s. The deregulation movement, which got under way in earnest with President Reagan's election in 1980, served in some cases to roll back some of these costs and in others to limit further increases, helping to make investment more attractive.

It is true that some elements of deregulation appeared earlier, as in the abolition of the Civil Aeronautics Board under President Carter (this took place in 1978). The CAB had, among other things, regulated air fares on interstate flights, eliminating price competition. One result was that flying from Los Angeles, California to Phoenix, Arizona cost approximately twice as much as flying from Los Angeles to San Francisco, California. Even though the distances are approximately the same, the latter flights were not subject to CAB regulation.

The Keynesian consensus that had marked the postwar era and provided intellectual cover for the government playing a major role in the economy frayed during the stagflation of the 1970s. This came about in part because the Keynesian model is geared toward explaining inflation that grows out of excess demand rather than out of constrained supply, as was the case during the 1970s. This created an opening for conservative intellectuals—including economists in particular—who sought consistently to maximize the role of the market and minimize the role of the state in addressing social problems. The free-marketeers drove the Reagan revolution in the 1980s, building on the elimination of the CAB and successfully pushing a much more deregulatory agenda than had hitherto prevailed.

Deregulation, of course, covers much more than the elimination of restrictions on business activity or compliance paperwork. It also meant the restructuring of certain industries, such as telecommunications. This usually took the form of finding ways to increase competition in industries that had often been viewed as "natural" monopolies that required regulation. The break-up of AT&T in the early 1980s ushered in an era of competition in the long-distance field, as well as (largely failed) attempts to generate competition in local service. The increased number of firms and competitive opportunities in the telecommunications field expanded investment possibilities, and the effect of this was compounded as the revolution in information and communications technology began to gain traction in the 1980s and 1990s. In addition to reducing business costs, then, deregulation in such fields as telecommunications, transportation, and utilities opened new investment opportunities which new and existing firms sought to exploit.

While this was taking place, the nature of the American firm was also being transformed. Much of the restructuring, reengineering and downsizing that characterized the 1980s was undertaken largely in response to competitive pressures, although financiers seeking to exploit the financial distress of many enterprises were also prominent. To a certain extent, restructuring reflects a shift in management theory that had once favored conglomerates. The justification for conglomerates had been, in part, that firms in many different lines of business could mitigate cyclical problems in some lines through unaffected businesses in other areas, and could allocate capital to those areas with the most promising rates of return. Moreover, the management literature from the 1960s had treated management as a "science," suggesting that capable managers could be successful in any line of endeavor simply by applying the "universal" principles of good management.

In fact, with a few notable exceptions (such as General Electric and Berkshire Hathaway), the conglomerate business model proved to be a failure as managers found that their knowledge and skills were often industry-specific—that success in one field did not assure success in others. As competitive pressures intensified during the 1980s, firms were forced to restructure, divesting themselves of businesses in which they lacked core competency. Gulf and Western, for example, at one point owned over one hundred businesses, ranging from Paramount Pictures to automobile parts, clothing manufacture, zinc mines, and sugar plantations in the Dominican Republic (http://encyclopedia.thefreedictionary.com). When it restructured, it divested itself of most of its businesses, retaining media businesses such as Paramount Pictures and the publisher Simon and Schuster.[3]

Reengineering refers to enterprise efforts to rethink in a fundamental fashion the way in which they conduct their business activities. For example, US automobile companies traditionally used mass production techniques. Toyota, followed by other Japanese companies, introduced an alternative production system, making possible the design and production of higher-quality vehicles, more quickly and at lower cost. The Japanese method, known as "lean production," includes just-in-time delivery of parts, worker empowerment and other distinctive features.[4] In order to remain viable, US and European automobile companies have attempted to emulate lean production, which in fact has been spreading to other industries as well. Lean production provides a crystal-clear example of rethinking how one goes about the production process—of reengineering.

Prior to adopting just-in-time inventory practices, American automobile firms tended to offer many different options (fabric colors, trim, paint colors, etc.) and maintained correspondingly large inventories. This increased the size of factories substantially, slowed production, raised the number of damaged parts, and required additional expense to finance the larger inventories. Japanese firms, by contrast, maintaining close connections with their suppliers, offered far fewer options and requested the delivery of the needed parts just before they were to be used. This just-in-time inventory system became widely followed in the US over the 1980s and 1990s (although the American companies, having a different relationship with their suppliers, could not adopt the complete Japanese system), and became an important part of the reengineering process.

Downsizing often overlapped with restructuring and reengineering, but was sometimes undertaken for distinctive reasons. When competition was limited and conglomerates in fashion, firms tended to grow large without subjecting their various operations to careful profitability considerations.

Downsizing refers essentially to firms bringing financial discipline to their operations, cutting those products and processes that were unable to earn their target rates of return.

Changes in corporate governance actually underwent two distinct stages, one in the 1980s and 1990s, and a second, still under way in 2004, that followed the abuses exposed during the collapse of Enron, World-Com, and other major corporations early in the twenty-first century. In the first stage, companies became much more focused on profitability. Further, to align the interests of managers with those of shareholders, stock options came into widespread use. Whereas IBM, once strongly influenced by the Japanese labor relations model of "lifetime" employment, had approached a "no lay-off policy" for workers performing their jobs well, competitive pressures and the decline of the mainframe computer business led the company to downsizing and widespread lay-offs. The fact that its actions devastated many of the Hudson River Valley communities where these took place, as well as the lives of the workers directly affected, had no place in the new corporate calculus.

In other cases, firms were taken over by buy-out firms or others who were able to raid the pension funds of the acquired firms if these were deemed to be "overfunded" (having more assets than the actuaries deemed necessary to meet their future obligations). Everything was done to maximize profits, no matter the damage to the firms' other stakeholders (employees, communities, suppliers, customers, and service providers).

A new stage in corporate governance reform was spurred by the corporate scandals that emerged in 2001 and 2002, following the collapse of the stock market bubble in 2000, a bubble that was especially concentrated in the information and communications technology field. This stage was essentially a response to the fact that corrupt corporate officials had essentially "hijacked" the earlier reforms, using them not to align their interests with those of the shareholders but to put their personal advantage first. They did so by issuing enormous numbers of stock options, diluting the interests of existing shareholders, and by making the option grants largely independent of performance. Thus, for example, if a firm's share price rose simply with the stock market rather than as a consequence of able management, the options would still vest.

Moreover, managements became adept at using financial data to put themselves in the best possible light, using, for example, pro-forma earnings, GAAP (generally accepted accounting principles) earnings, or various other measures of financial performance; until the early 2000s they also lobbied successfully to prevent option-granting from being treated as a corporate expense—thereby increasing their reported earnings—even though it is clearly a form of employee compensation. Meanwhile, although boards of directors are financial fiduciaries charged with representing the interest of shareholders, the boards of most firms were under the firm control of their managements, with the CEO typically including senior managers on the board and selecting the "outside" board members. The corporate governance reforms under way in the twenty-first century are designed largely to have the firms reflect the interest of their shareholders, while still minimizing any obligation to the other stakeholders.

As a consequence of all these changes, the American corporation today is vastly different from its counterpart of half a century ago. It is increasingly focused on profitability and shareholder interest, with the interests of other stakeholders minimized (except when they coincide with the interest of shareholders). Security of employment is much weaker than it once was, and reciprocal loyalty to employees who have committed themselves to their firms is lacking. At the same time, however, the American corporation is very well suited to compete effectively in a global economy characterized by rapid technological change. If we compare the return on equity (ROE) of American and Japanese firms in 1995, for example, large Japanese firms had a ROE of 3.4 percent while American firms in the Standard and Poor's industrials had a return of 22.4 percent (*The Economist,* "A Survey of Japanese Finance," 6/28/97: 14). The transformation of the American corporation to make it an extremely effective global competitor, then, has played a key role in the establishment of America's new social structure of accumulation.[5]

Limited government refers to the restricted levels of government taxation and expenditure that have characterized the last quarter century (to 2004). Proposition 13, which passed in California in 1978, essentially limited real estate taxes to slightly over 1 percent of purchase prices, with subsequent increases to be kept below 2 percent per year; since these taxes traditionally have funded the public school system, the state made up some of the schools' revenue shortfall, but this in turn limited state spending for other purposes. Nationally, President Reagan pushed through two major tax-cutting measures, one in 1981 and one in 1986, that served especially to reduce marginal income tax rates. Inadequate spending on infrastructure, education, social welfare and other public purposes can, over time, have a seriously negative impact on the economic climate. During the 1980s and 1990s, however, the economic stimulation created by a regime of limited government was predominant. It should be noted, however, that this represents an example of an internal contradiction in the current SSA that may ultimately contribute to its demise; with the negative effects of inadequate public spending reflected in deteriorating schools, traffic gridlock, and so forth, the limitations on government activity appear likely over time to undermine the existing SSA.

The international agreements to facilitate trade and investment flows are another major component of the current social structure of accumulation. These expand investment opportunities directly, but have the added impact of weakening the position of labor in negotiations over wages, benefits, and employment security. The agreements include both broad, multilateral institutions such as the World Trade Organization (WTO), regional arrangements such as NAFTA and APEC, and bilateral ones such as the 2002–03 free trade agreements the US arranged with Chile and Singapore.

The changes in the nature of the US corporation discussed above have made it well-suited to benefit from the expanded business opportunities created by these agreements, even though that was partially undermined by the strength of the US dollar in the 1990s, strength which continued until 2002 (when it began to weaken notably). In constant 1996 dollars, real exports rose from $334.8 billion in 1980 to $1,126.3 billion in 2000, with real imports rising from $324.8 billion to $1,538.7 billion in the same interval; exports plus imports as a share of gross domestic product rose from 13.5 percent to 28.6 percent in this period (US Department of Commerce 2001: 417).

Compared to the capital markets elsewhere in the capitalist world, those in the US are much more favorable to small, entrepreneurial companies. This reflects in part the strength of the US venture capital industry, in part the flexibility of US labor markets, and in part the ease with which relatively new companies can be taken public, with their shares listed on the NASDAQ. In most of the other industrial countries, companies were traditionally required to have a record of three years of profitability before they could be listed on the leading exchanges. In response to the upsurge in innovation in the 1990s, many countries sought to emulate the Silicon Valley model by opening new stock markets to list unprofitable but promising new firms. They did so just prior to the peak of the global stock market bubble in 2000, with consequences that were often disastrous.[6]

During the 1990s, the situation in the US was, accordingly, much more conducive to entrepreneurship and investment than it was in Europe or Japan. Thus, for example, from 1992 through June 1996, 3,000 US companies became public with initial offerings that raised more than $150 billion, whereas from 1990 through June 1996 fewer than 150 European companies became public (*Wall Street Journal*, 9/20/96: A14). The technological revolutions that occurred over the course of the 1980s and 1990s, in such fields as biotechnology and especially information and communications technology, can be thought of as an exogenous factor that greatly enhanced the impact of the favorable capital markets, stimulating new investment and contributing to the strengthening of America's new social structure of accumulation.

The outlook for America's new social structure of accumulation

The argument presented in Chapter 2 suggests that once an SSA is formed, powerful forces tend to sustain it for a lengthy period of time—but not indefinitely. In the aftermath of the collapse of America's stock market bubble and 2001 recession, corporate investment and job creation remained relatively weak for about two years, reflecting three main factors especially: geopolitical concerns, the excessive investment that occurred in telecommunications and information technology during the 1990s, and the extreme caution in corporate boardrooms as companies sought to minimize debt and increase cash holdings after numerous firms failed in the aftermath of the stock market bubble (which began to deflate in 2000). Given the renewed sense of caution in corporate America, the recession of 2001, and a recovery that began to gain traction only toward the end of 2003, there is reason for further consideration of the outlook for America's new SSA.

Although SSAs tend to be enduring (for the reasons I have enumerated), there is of course no specified period for which an SSA may be expected to last, and one can never dismiss the possibility that severe changes in exogenous circumstances will interact with internal contradictions to bring about the collapse of a given SSA sooner than might normally be expected. Before turning to an analysis of the impact of such changes on the current SSA, I would like to take note of how the distinction between financial and real investment affects SSA analysis. The SSA is concerned with real investment, so the secular bear market (one marked by lower highs and lower lows over a prolonged period of time) that began in 2000 does not in itself indicate the collapse of the SSA. Nevertheless, it should be evident that a falling stock market can have serious implications for real investment as well. The question is whether this negative impact is likely to be so great as to undermine the entire SSA. To address this issue it may be helpful to review the outlook for the various constituent elements of the new SSA and to consider the changes that have taken place in the exogenous conditions that contribute to SSA formation and collapse.

First, the strengthening of capital relative to labor shows no sign whatsoever of having diminished. Union membership continues to fall as a percentage of the private labor force, the possibilities for moving production abroad or outsourcing entirely continue to grow, and the shocking collapse or bankruptcy of major companies in telecommunications, the airline industry, and other fields places pressure on the entire labor force in the US. The weakness of labor is reflected in American companies increasing use of a two-tier wage scale (paying new hires less than existing workers [*Wall Street Journal*, 9/1/04: A1]).[7]

Second, the Federal Reserve Board has been largely successful in reducing inflation to a point at which it is not a major factor in most business and household decision-making. The era of disinflation, however, may have come to an end, with two opposing possibilities creating some concern. In recent years, Japan has experienced periods of *deflation* (absolutely falling prices), and in 2003 there were concerns that it might appear in the United States as well. The spread of low-cost production in China especially, but in other less-developed countries as well, creates downward pressure on material goods prices throughout the world. Falling prices are a matter of special concern for two primary reasons. First, both indebted firms and indebted households find it more difficult to meet their financial obligations in an environment of falling prices (and stagnant or falling wages). Second, the ability of central banks to deal with deflation is weaker than their ability to deal with inflation; in the latter case, they can always raise interest rates high enough to stop inflation, but in the former they cannot reduce their interest rates below zero, which, as the Japanese case shows, may not be sufficient to eliminate the problem.

In the United States, however, there are countervailing forces that continue to make deflation an unlikely outcome. The growing size of the Chinese economy has played a major role in the rise of commodity prices throughout the world, with the increase in the prices of oil, steel, and other commodities contributing to inflation globally.[8] In the United States, the service sector of the economy has become much larger than the goods-producing sector and continues to grow in relative importance.[9] The deflationary impact of foreign imports is much weaker in the service sector (though not absolutely lacking, as indicated by the fact that call centers and software contracts are increasingly outsourced to firms in India and elsewhere). Upward cost pressures in health care and education especially appear likely to continue contributing to rising inflationary pressures. The reappearance of government budget deficits under the influence of conservative politics and supply-side ideology is also likely to contribute to such pressures. Overall, the best outcome for the maintenance of the current SSA would be reflected in these opposing forces balancing one another, resulting in low inflation and low interest rates. Movement toward deflation or accelerating inflation cannot be ruled out, however, and either would weaken the current SSA.

Third, the ideology of free markets and deregulation continues to be powerful in the US, so major changes in regulation are unlikely to create direct problems for the current SSA. However, the lack of regulation and excessive deregulation can also generate serious systemic problems. One example is provided by the lack of regulation that prevailed during the postwar SSA under the capital–citizen accord. Environmental problems became so severe that they helped to generate a backlash in favor of extensive regulation. Another example can be found in the "deregulation" of the energy industry in California. Combined with the absence of regulatory oversight over energy trading, the result was price manipulation by utilities and energy traders, an enormous spike in energy prices that damaged both businesses and consumers, worsening fiscal problems for the state, and the bankruptcy or financial distress of major utilities.[10] The ideological appeal of deregulation persists, then, but not all its consequences are sanguine, and its net effect on the SSA depends on maintaining a proper balance between regulation and deregulation (the proper balance in turn is determined by the myriad exogenous forces that shape the outcome of deregulation).

Fourth, the "new" corporation in the United States—one focused primarily on shareholder interests—is certainly here to stay; one cannot imagine a return to companies that made long-term commitments to their employees, suppliers, communities, and other stakeholders. In fact, accounting reforms, the Sarbanes–Oxley Act of 2002, and measures to improve corporate governance and make boards of directors more accountable promise to promote the interest of shareholders even further by increasing corporate transparency and diminishing the power of senior managers to choose their own benefit over that of shareholders when the two collide. The shareholder-oriented corporation of the United States is much better suited to engage in international competition than the stakeholder-oriented corporation of continental Europe and Japan (because the US corporation can be much more ruthless in its pursuit of profitability, it can lower costs more drastically in the face of competitive pressures). The new American corporation, therefore, can be expected to continue its contribution to the new SSA.

Fifth, limited government is also likely to continue, but changes in the "external" environment appear quite likely to make it, over time, more of a detractor from than contributor to the maintenance of the new SSA. During the George W. Bush administration, conservative ideology reasserted itself, with the call for low taxes and limited government appealing to a large swath of the population. This conservative ideology, however, is running up against major changes in the external environment that appear likely to result in substantial economic damage:

1 In the wake of the terrorist attacks of September 11, 2001, major increases in expenditures on national defense and homeland security have become inevitable, pushing up government expenditures.
2 With the rising age of the population and the development of new, expensive medicines (reflecting in part the emergence of biotechnology), expenditures on social security and Medicare are likely to rise steeply over the next quarter century (from 2004).
3 Population growth significantly increases the need for new government services, as traffic and other costs of congestion grow disproportionately.
4 With changes in science and technology continuing to increase the importance of education, inadequate public expenditure on education is likely, over time, to have serious economic repercussions.

The belief in limited government, therefore, is likely to starve the discretionary budgetary items except for national defense and homeland security, while providing inadequate funding for social services and infrastructure. At the same time, the growing budget deficits likely to ensue if the Bush perspective holds sway are likely to drive up prices and interest rates over time. Under the changing external circumstances, then, the positive support provided to America's new social structure of accumulation by limited government may very well turn into its opposite, potentially undermining the new SSA severely.

Sixth, with regard to international agreements to facilitate international trade and investment, the outlook has become cloudy. On the one hand, the Bush administration did manage to win new "fast track" approval, meaning that trade legislation will not be subject to Congressional amendments—without this assurance, foreign countries are reluctant to negotiate freer trade measures with the US. On the other hand, political pressures have sustained protectionist measures in both the US and Europe, particularly in the agricultural sector. Such protectionism hurts especially the less-developed countries that are primarily raw material and agricultural producers. Unless it can be overcome, major new advances in international agreements will be difficult to achieve.

At the same time, the collapse of postwar SSAs in Japan and the heart of continental Europe (especially Germany), together with weakness in the Latin American economies, diminishes the potential upside of new, market-opening trade agreements. This is another example of a change in exogenous conditions undermining the American SSA. In both Germany and Japan, which at one time during the postwar period led their respective regions in economic dynamism, sclerotic institutions—most notably in their labor markets—have diminished their economic growth capacity. Institutional reform in those economies would probably prove to be a more significant factor than additional market opening in helping to maintain the current social structure of accumulation in the United States.

Finally, despite the severe setbacks experienced by the venture capital and investment banking industries in the US in the wake of the stock market bubble collapse, the financial infrastructure remains in place to support a renewed burst in entrepreneurial activity. At the end of the twentieth century stocks were rising in value at an unsustainable pace, excessive investment took place in telecommunications and Internet companies, and an increasing commoditization of technology products took place. In one respect, all of these phenomena represent an overexuberance of entrepreneurial activity rather than a fundamental problem with the underlying technological advances or their potential. Although many start-up businesses with unsustainable business models failed, Internet commerce is gaining traction, cell phone usage continues to spread throughout the world, and new products are continuing to appear. Once the inevitable industry shake-out has concluded, the advantages created by a financial system capable of supporting innovative companies are apt to become evident in the US once again.[11]

In considering the primary external forces that contributed to shaping America's new social structure of accumulation, I have focused on technological change and globalization (their impact will be assessed in much greater detail in Chapter 4). As I have just noted, the power of technological change is unlikely to diminish despite the setbacks experienced in the information technology and telecommunications industries. And in biotechnology we can actually expect an acceleration of innovation, given the advances made in our understanding of the human genome, the considerable research activity that remains underway, and the long lead time required for new products to gain approval.

The picture with regard to globalization is rather more mixed. Globalization has played a major role in creating and sustaining the new SSA in the US, just as it has in other countries (such as China) that have reformed their domestic institutions to take advantage of the opportunities it affords. However, in addition to the growth of protectionist forces—which reflects to a considerable extent the residual power of those industries that are not globally competitive—a global anti-globalization movement has gathered force. This movement reflects understandable concerns with the victims of globalization (ranging from child labor to workers unprotected from hazardous conditions), with the role globalization has played in weakening American labor, with the environmental havoc often wreaked by globalization, and with the cultural consequences of globalization—especially with the hegemonic spread of American culture.

In addition, the growth of international terrorism, which appears likely to be with us for a major part of the twenty-first century, has important consequences for globalization. As security concerns slow the transport of goods, worldwide supply chains will become less reliable and firms will have an incentive to concentrate a greater share of production locally. As far as the overall outcome is concerned, no one can predict it with any degree of certainty, but it should be recognized that with ongoing institutional reforms in China and some of the transitional economies in central Europe, with India's growing acceptance of institutional reforms reflecting the benefits it has already reaped from increased participation in the capitalist world economy, and with Russia committed to a growing economic integration with the West, there are countervailing forces that may enable globalization to continue to support America's new social structure of accumulation.

Once again, how long America's new SSA will persist is overdetermined by a multitude of factors and thus cannot be predicted with any degree of certainty. What we do know is that there are powerful forces tending to sustain any SSA once it is in place, and the forces tending to undermine America's new SSA confront forces that, at least in part, might well serve to sustain or even strengthen it.

Conclusion

As Chapters 2 and 3 have argued, capitalist economies are marked by extended periods of relatively strong growth alternating with extended periods of relative stagnation. The periods of strong growth are marked by a set of supportive institutions—a social structure of accumulation. Over time, internal contradictions emerge in all SSAs. These interact with changes in external conditions, ultimately undermining the periods of prosperity and ushering in periods of sluggish economic growth or stagnation. When recessions occur during these long-term downturns, they *may* turn into depressions or crises that threaten the very foundations of the capitalist system. This of course did not happen in America in the second half of the twentieth century (but it did happen in the first half). Recessions also take place during SSA periods, but they tend to be less frequent, milder, and shorter in duration when they do take place.

An understanding of SSAs helps us to go beyond the microeconomic calculations of profit and loss to understand the institutional conditions that support periods of extended prosperity and growth. They do more than this, however, by clarifying the manner in which capitalism has managed to survive over the centuries in the face of severe contradictions and crises. Essentially, capitalism manages to overcome its contradictions and survive by reinventing itself in each country where it prevails. In this sense, each stage of capitalism, each SSA, is unique, differing not only from the capitalisms that exist in other countries, but also from the capitalisms that have existed in previous stages within its own country.

Many factors play a part in the creation of new SSAs. During the periods of stagnation that precede them, social tensions and conflicts tend to rise. The resolution of these various social conflicts plays a major role in the establishment of new SSAs. In addition, the owners of capital seek to reestablish conditions that will once again make profitable investment possible on a wide scale. Further, external conditions interact with the social conflicts and the efforts of capitalists or firms to create a more favorable investment environment. Finally, the presence of favorable preexisting conditions and institutions also plays a role in determining whether a new SSA can be formed. If one is formed then it is the result of the interaction of all these factors, a result that is *overdetermined.*

In this chapter, I have focused on America's postwar SSA, on the forces that led to its dissolution, and on the reinvention of American capitalism at the end of the twentieth century as a new SSA was established. The American case studies are of interest in themselves, but the main reason for including them here is that they demonstrate general principles that are applicable to all capitalist countries; the creation of institutions that underpin the investment process determines the health (or lack thereof) of capitalist economies throughout the world. And each time a new SSA is formed in any country, that country's capitalism differs from its previous stage—it is reinvented.

One of the central factors that contributes to (or blocks) the formation of new SSAs in capitalist countries is the "exogenous" conditions that prevail. While as I have noted, nothing is truly exogenous (since all social processes and conditions emerge from their interaction with one another), treating certain conditions as exogenous is often a useful way of making analysis manageable. For that reason, I have chosen to treat globalization and technological change as "exogenous" when investigating their impact on the capitalist system in Chapter 4. These are the most important exogenous conditions, affecting SSA formation not only in the United States but throughout the capitalist world. Moreover, their influence extends beyond SSA formation to the long-term trajectory of the capitalist system in general.

4 Capitalism, globalization, and technological change

As I have suggested in previous chapters, capitalism overcomes its contradictions and moves on to new historical stages by repeatedly reinventing itself. It does not do so in a vacuum, however, but in a context defined by the "external" conditions that shape each stage. In the current era, one that promises to occupy much if not all of the twenty-first century, the principal external conditions are those defined by the prominent roles of globalization, technological change and their interaction. In the last analysis, of course, globalization and technological change are not truly "external." Both are influenced by numerous factors, not least of which is the demands of the capitalist system for ever-expanding profits and accumulation. Moreover, the principles of overdetermination suggest that all social processes are mutually determinative, with myriad interactions. Even so, treating globalization and technological change as exogenous factors provides a useful entry point for analysis.

Ever since the Industrial Revolution, technological change has been a core element in the development and spread of capitalism. Globalization as a core element in capitalism goes back even further; as Immanuel Wallerstein reminds us, it has been a part of the capitalist system since its inception in the sixteenth century.[1] At the end of the twentieth century and the beginning of the twenty-first, however, both globalization and technological change have assumed distinctive forms, influencing the ongoing development of capitalism in a unique and powerful fashion. Their impact, moreover, is magnified by the fact that as the capitalist system repeatedly renews and reinvents itself, new institutions have the opportunity to emerge—and existing ones reshaped—in response to the pressures created by globalization and technological change.

With regard to technological change, two sets of transformative technologies hold special significance. The first is the group of information and communications technologies (ICT) marked by the worldwide spread of computers, microprocessors, wireless devices, and the Internet, providing access to a vast array of databases, making it possible to communicate throughout most of the world instantaneously, to automate a wide range of production activities, and to transform the ways in which business is carried out. The second is the group that includes genetic engineering, nanotechnology and robotics (GNR). This group has not yet had the impact of the ICT revolution, but its role in transforming the world is likely to become increasingly apparent as the twenty-first century progresses.[2]

Globalization both spurs and responds to the ongoing changes in technology. With the improvements in communication and transportation, it is increasingly feasible to outsource production to the most advantageous sites in the world, however remote. Just like Britain in the nineteenth century, China has become the "workshop of the world" at the turn of the twenty-first. Moreover, since firms can communicate instantly with their far-flung suppliers or subsidiaries in different parts of the world, it becomes possible to integrate international supply chains. Even service activities like call centers can be globally outsourced, and the international division of labor can increase efficiency greatly, as the rapid growth of electronic contract manufacturing in East Asia reveals.

Globalization has multiple meanings, and different understandings emphasize different elements. In its most basic sense, globalization as an economic phenomenon refers to the growing internationalization of economic activity, from research and development to production and distribution. For many it has a range of negative connotations, including the spread of free trade/free market neoliberal (itself a pejorative term) ideology, the growing hegemony (imperialist or otherwise) of the United States, and the international march of corporate capitalism. While it is true that all of these elements tend to be true of globalization at least to some extent, I think it will be more useful to think of it first in its more basic sense, to explore its ramifications for the functioning of the capitalist system, and only then to approach its normative implications. Ultimately, I will argue, whether or not we happen to welcome it, globalization is here to stay, and an understanding of its distinctive role in the modern world, and of its interactions with other social and economic phenomena, is essential to reaching a reasoned evaluation of its consequences.

Globalization and technological change: the larger picture

There are several ways in which the interaction of globalization and technological change deeply influences the development of the capitalist system. In Chapter 1 a distinction was drawn among the three primary types of contemporary capitalism: state-led capitalism, the welfare-state capitalism of continental Europe, and the "harsh" capitalism of America and (to a lesser extent) the United Kingdom. Globalization and technological change have created conditions under which each of the other types is under growing pressure to emulate the American model, and the American model itself is under pressure—to which it is clearly responding—to become even harsher.[3]

Globalization means that competition is increasingly global. In any market, the advantages of being the low-cost producer(s) are legion, and with distinctions among the world's markets increasingly blurred by the forces of globalization, competition is growing more intense. This of course has many benefits for consumers as prices are forced down, and this should not be overlooked. At the same time, it means that firms and countries that have high labor costs because they pay their workers well and provide a wide range of benefits, as is commonly the case in continental Europe, have difficulty competing with products made in countries whose labor costs are extremely low. The problem is further exacerbated by the high tax rates common in countries that provide extensive state-supported benefits. High wages and high taxes make it difficult for companies to compete, creating strong incentives to automate production or to establish any new facilities where wages and taxes are lower.

The job-protection benefits that make it difficult to fire workers once hired create an additional hazard, since an employer who hires a worker in his/her twenties is possibly taking on a fixed cost for as long as forty years. Firms have difficulty envisioning their outlooks for even a few years, so the risk associated with adding full-time workers is considerable. Under these conditions, firms in high-cost countries like Germany and France have increasingly opted to carry out expansions abroad rather than at home, leading to sluggish economic growth and high levels of unemployment.[4] In addition to the mobility of capital, the increasing mobility of managerial employees and skilled professional workers intensifies problems in such countries.

A further problem is presented by the rapid aging of the population in continental Europe (and indeed in all of the industrialized countries). Since their pension and medical programs were established on a pay-as-you-go basis, with the current generation of workers paying for those already retired, the failure to expand employment also places in jeopardy the benefits going to those who have retired. Taken together, all of these effects have created great pressure on the social-welfare-oriented states to lower taxes and reduce worker benefits, benefits that either raise company costs or require higher taxes for public provision. The struggle to bring about economic reforms that will restore economic vigor (create a new SSA) in the face of intense and widespread public opposition has been at the forefront of European news since the 1990s.

The problem, moreover, affects the state-directed economies as well. In Japan, for example, high levels of public debt in relation to GDP combined with a rapidly aging population limit the role the public sector can play in assuring social welfare. Since the major public firms in industries like electronics and autos tend to be highly export-dependent, moreover, they can maintain their international competitiveness only through increased automation or outsourcing the production of a wide range of finished products and component parts to countries where labor costs are lower. Both choices diminish their ability to generate domestic jobs, thereby increasing the strain on public finances. Further, at the enterprise level, firms have been forced to become increasingly cautious about providing jobs with "lifetime" employment commitments, seniority-based raises, or other employee benefits—a reflection of the intense pressures created by global competition.

Technological change adds to the pressures on state-directed economies. In the first place, some elements of state direction are no longer feasible. State-owned corporations, for example, are unlikely to display the innovative character and flexibility that rapid technological change and intensified competition demand. In China, the leading sectors tend to be foreign-invested, private, or township and village enterprises, and a long-running process of state-owned firm privatization has accelerated in the first decade of the twenty-first century. Moreover, even in countries like Japan and Korea, where private ownership has been the norm, the role of the state in directing economic activity is being curtailed, reflecting the growing problems such direction has brought.

In Japan, the Ministry of International Trade and Industry (MITI; now renamed the Ministry of Economy, Trade and Industry or METI) once took a leading role in directing industrial organization, while banks and other financial-sector institutions followed the lead of the Ministry of Finance. Further, the Japanese government played a leading role in allowing major banks to count equity investments as a portion of their capital base in meeting international capital requirements, a measure which wound up intensifying the nation's financial crisis when the long bear market in stocks began at the end of 1989. In the future, it will no longer be possible for states to play a leading economic role in this way.

That is not to deny a major role for the state. The role of the state will change, however, to accommodate the forces unleashed by globalization and technological change. The state will need to facilitate international trade and investment, just as China has done, starting with the Special Economic Zones in 1980, entering the WTO in 2001, and paving the way to a massive infusion of foreign investment around the turn of the twenty-first century.[5] With regard to technological change, the state must play a major role in creating an institutional environment that fosters the introduction of new technology, research and development, and the prosperity of technology-oriented firms. Such an environment can include such elements as the development of educational institutions, research parks and venues for intellectual exchange, tax advantages for technology firms and their investors, requirements for technology transfer on the part of foreign investors, and the development of patent law. Under the new conditions of globalization and technological change, the role of the state will remain extremely important, but the relationship to the economy that characterized the old state-directed economies, one that often included direct ownership or micromanaging the private sector, will no longer be feasible.

East Asia is the region of the world where state-directed economies have become most prominent. As the relationship of the state to the economy changes under the pressure of globalization and technological change, it will also have to face some of the pressures encountered by the welfare states of continental Europe. In Europe, welfare was primarily provided by the family until the state assumed responsibility early in the twentieth century. In much of Asia today, the family still provides the safety net that the state provides in Europe, albeit in a less comprehensive, less certain fashion. Now rapid economic development and rural–urban migration, spurred by globalization and technological change, are fraying the family safety net. The developing and transitional countries of Asia will have to decide the extent to which the state will step in to provide a welfare safety net. In making this decision they will be confronted by the same pressures facing the modern-day European states; social welfare benefits will require higher levels of taxation than Asia has been accustomed to, and will be difficult to bring about as long as capital and highly skilled labor remain quite mobile. In this sense, the entire capitalist world is under pressure to emulate the American model of "harsh" capitalism.[6]

The impact of globalization interacting with the revolution in information and communications technology (ICT) impacts the capitalist world economy in three additional ways that are especially worthy of mention. First, as in the current American social structure of accumulation (SSA), the combination of the two plays a central role in strengthening capital over labor throughout the world. When capital is free to move wherever labor costs are lowest, and when the technical constraints that have inhibited such mobility in the past are eased, the bargaining power of labor becomes severely diminished. Increasingly, jobs being outsourced abroad include service-sector jobs, such as those at call centers, and jobs requiring technical skills, such as jobs in software development. Moreover, when the potential for automation makes goods production in factories requiring little or no labor increasingly feasible, the power of labor is weakened even further. As an increasing number of countries find themselves pressed to emulate the American model of capitalism, returns to capital relative to labor can be expected to rise on a worldwide basis, with a commensurate rise in inequality in the distribution of income and wealth.

Second, the interaction of globalization and technological change can be expected to accelerate the growth of world productivity and gross world product. The increased division of labor made possible by globalization, together with the productivity growth that the ICT revolution promises, could, as Gary Becker (2003) suggests, contribute to an economic growth boom lasting for decades. Labor productivity growth in the United States averaged 1.4 percent per year in the 1973–1995 period (Baumol and Blinder 2003: 115), increased to 2.5 percent from 1995 to 2000, and increased further (despite the 2001 recession) to more than 3.5 percent from 2000 to 2003 (Becker 2003, 2004). Becker notes that the previous major technological advance, the development of the electric motor and the internal-combustion engine at the end of the nineteenth century, took 40–60 years to become reflected fully in productivity improvement. Individuals, firms and nation-states all take time to adjust to technological revolutions. To process paper checks, for example, the cost to banks is considerable, whereas the (marginal) cost to process online payments is negligible. In the United States, millions of people are now paying online, and the number is increasing rapidly.

Changes in technology alone, of course, cannot account for productivity growth. The impact of new technologies depends on their interaction with the full range of social institutions and processes. Thus in continental Europe and Japan, inflexible labor markets, capital markets that make it difficult for new firms (capable of developing and introducing new technologies) to gain access to finance, high tax rates (in Europe), and so forth, create an institutional environment that discourages new investment and the new technologies it embodies. When SSAs appropriate to realizing the potentialities of the new technologies are established in Europe and Japan, however—and that is the probable outcome of the social struggles marking their current stagnation—we can expect productivity growth to increase sharply there as well.

The ongoing economic boom and rapid spread of new technologies in China, spurred in large part by the boom in exports and in incoming foreign direct investment—itself reflecting the strength of globalization—have begun in the twenty-first century to have a major impact on the smaller states of East and Southeast Asia, with the Chinese market now beginning to rival that of the US for many of them.[7] If the boom in India which began with its reform program in 1991 is sustained, the same type of spread effects are possible in South Asia, although they are not likely to become significant until perhaps the 2020s. The point remains that globalization and technological change bring with them the potential for a significant upward shift in the rate of world productivity and output growth.

Other factors enhance the likelihood of such an outcome. Globalization and technological change are associated with disinflationary economic forces.[8] In the industrialized countries, low or falling inflation makes it possible to pursue relatively easy monetary policies. The low interest rates this implies favor investment, as well as the purchase of houses and consumer durables. The ability to finance the new technologies cheaply promises to accelerate their introduction over time. Despite the US stock market collapse from 2000 to 2002 and the bankruptcy of many over-leveraged technology firms, the pattern of excessive enthusiasm and debt proving the undoing of many early firms when dramatic new technologies are introduced is not an unfamiliar one, and the long-term outlook for the introduction, spread, and impact of the new ICT technologies remains highly favorable. The lowering of prices is forced by international competition and made possible by cost reductions associated with technological progress, economies of scale, outsourcing to low-labor-cost countries, and the weakness of labor in the industrialized countries. The existence of low interest rates means that the introduction of the new technologies can be financed readily. Thus the forces that promise an extended period of accelerated economic growth on a worldwide basis are aligned.

The third major impact of globalization and technological change has to do with the vast increase in systemic risk. The financial crisis that began in Thailand in the summer of 1997 spread through much of Asia in that year, and throughout the world the following year, affecting Brazil and Russia with special severity. Despite the role of the IMF—which as Joseph Stiglitz (2002) has argued is not always benign—the development of international institutions to manage this risk remains limited. To choose perhaps the most obvious example, around the turn of the twenty-first century the central banks of Japan and China have been buying vast amounts of US currency—which is then used to purchase government securities—in an effort to prevent their currencies from appreciating in response to their trade surpluses. Normally, in the presence of such surpluses, significant currency appreciation would take place, undermining the favorable balance of trade. Since the economies of China and Japan are highly dependent on their export prowess, however, the two governments buy foreign currency from the exporters or intermediaries, and invest in US Treasury securities. This keeps their currencies lower in value than they otherwise would be (thereby supporting their export industries), and interest rates in the US lower as well.

The result of this has been the accumulation of substantial holdings of US government securities by the central banks of Japan and China.[9] This is taking place at a time when the US is running severe federal government budget deficits, projected to exceed $400 billion in fiscal 2004 (*Wall Street Journal*, 9/8/04: A2), lacks a credible plan to reduce the deficits in the future, and faces huge unfunded liabilities for social security and Medicare when the "baby-boom" generation retires in large numbers starting around 2010. What would happen if China and Japan decide that, given the poor outlook for the dollar, they are holding too large a portion of their reserves in US dollars, and proceed to diversify on a large scale into other currencies? A sharp slide in the value of the dollar would likely result, with interest rates spiking higher in the United States. This could well lead to a stock market crash and financial crisis in the US, and given the fact that the US dollar is a reserve currency for the rest of the world, and that important commodities like oil are priced in dollars, the crisis would quickly become a worldwide one. Since the governments of China and Japan are well aware of the consequences of dumping large amounts of US dollars on the market, they are likely to act cautiously in this regard. This reduces the likelihood that a crisis scenario will come to pass, but does not preclude it altogether. The growth of global economic and financial imbalances is simply one indicator of the considerable systemic risk associated with globalization and the ICT revolution that facilitates it.

Additional consequences of technological change

The preceding discussion of technological change has focused on the revolution in information and communications technology (ICT). Another group of technological changes is likely to emerge from the scientific revolutions currently taking place in genetic engineering, nanotechnology, and robotics. In these fields, many positive and profitable innovations are on the not-too-distant horizon. It is now possible, for example, to insert vitamin A in rice strains, so that in rice-consuming regions of Asia where widespread poverty is associated with millions of children suffering vision problems and early death from vitamin A deficiency, the disease could be prevented at nominal cost.[10] Advances in nanotechnology and robotics promise another set of scientific revolutions with wide-ranging consequences—from improving efficiency and human health to the development of new materials and such lifestyle-transforming phenomena as the development of household robots.

The new technologies also present a unique set of risks, which may broadly be divided into two categories. First, there is the risk associated with the afterthought status of externalities in the capitalist system. If something is profitable, there is strong pressure to introduce it commercially well before an understanding of the risks it poses, and well before laws are passed and procedures adopted to control those risks. Thus, for example, Aqua Bounty Technologies of Waltham, Massachusetts has developed a genetically engineered salmon that grows four or five times as fast as normal salmon, requiring less feed (Gillis 2004). Farm-raised salmon are now grown in ocean pens in a number of countries, and Aqua Bounty would like its salmon to be used along the East Coast of the US. The concern of many environmentalists is that some fish would escape and wipe out the stocks of wild Atlantic salmon by out-competing them for food and access to females. These concerns are magnified by the fact that even now the farm-raised salmon have been found to have far higher concentrations of mercury and other contaminants than their wild cousins.[11]

Cloning, including human cloning, is also on the genetic engineering agenda. Human cloning to create stem cells holds enormous promise for medical breakthroughs. At the same time, it is not entirely clear whether a fail-proof system could be developed that would prevent the use of the technology to clone existing people. The point is that rationally, the benefits and the costs of the new technologies should be considered fully before they are introduced. Under the capitalist system, however, many of the benefits will be private and many of the costs will be public, so that comprehensive, rational assessment is not possible before the technologies are introduced. This creates a potential for outcomes that range from the mildly inconveniencing to the catastrophic.

The other problem associated with the new technologies is the potential for them to be employed by individuals, small groups, or companies. In the twentieth century, weapons of mass destruction (WMD) tended to require the resources of a nation-state for their development and use. In the twenty-first century the new technologies will make possible the development of WMDs by individuals or small organizations, including terrorist organizations. Through genetic engineering, for example, new viral or bacterial pathogens might be developed that would wipe out entire populations. There are two ways in which the capitalist system increases the chances of such dysfunctional outcomes. First, the surplus that the system generates and the ongoing search for profits boost expenditures on research and development, with limited assurances that such research will remain within the public interest. Second, the uneven development that characterizes the capitalist system, and the grievances it engenders, have played a major role in the emergence of modern terrorism, a phenomenon that promises to persist for much of the twenty-first century. If the world's communities were organized along more humanitarian principles, with a sense of responsibility for those less fortunate replacing the sense of entitlement that often characterizes those successful in pursuing their own enrichment under capitalism, it is at least possible that the feelings of alienation, outrage, and helplessness that often give rise to terrorist actions would be meaningfully reduced.

Terrorism, of course, is not solely a response to rising inequality; it is overdetermined by a host of "external" factors, not least of which is the rise of religious fundamentalism in countries as diverse as Saudi Arabia and the United States. Nevertheless, the strength of the forces generating terrorism is such that in the middle of the first decade of the twenty-first century it appears as though the "war on terrorism" is likely to stretch on for the better part of the century. The reasons for this assessment are elaborated below, but one point must be mentioned in connection with the new types of technology that are beginning to emerge and which will create the possibility for small-scale attacks to create disproportionate damage. Increasingly, the capitalist world economy will require security measures in all manner of production, distribution, and daily-life activities. Although necessary, such measures will increase the requirements for unproductive labor, raise the costs of production and distribution, and reduce the levels of profit below what they otherwise would be. Required security measures, then, will in themselves reduce the rate of growth of investment and of world product (even while creating opportunities for profitable investment in the field of security itself). Although security concerns and the attendant need for unproductive defensive measures are likely to have a negative effect on the growth of world product, this effect is unlikely to outweigh the positive effects of globalization and technological change on world product in the decades to come. While any such assessment is inevitably somewhat subjective, the forces promoting an acceleration of the rate of growth of world product—and a corresponding intensification of the contradictions brought by the expansion of the capitalist system—are powerful.

Global prosperity and its contradictions

When dramatic new technological breakthroughs take place, as Becker has noted, it normally takes decades for their full impact to be felt in raising productivity and economic growth rates. Thus, for example, although computers were developed in the 1950s, and the personal computer in the 1970s (the IBM PC was introduced in 1981), it was not until the mid-1990s that a sustained increase in the rate of productivity growth became apparent in the United States.[12] The reasons for this are not difficult to imagine. Productive activity always takes place in a particular institutional context. When significant changes—like computerization—take place in one part of the production process, the complementary factors and institutions must change as well before the full potential of a given production change can be realized. Skills in computer use must improve, as must educational programs teaching such skills, and such changes may take a generation or more before their full impact can be realized. If information is to be filed and stored digitally, then the sources of such information must be using similar technologies for the greatest impact on productivity to be felt. Hospitals, for example, may maintain large computer systems, but until doctors begin to enter patient information on computers the potential benefits of computerized patient records cannot fully be realized.

More broadly, the ways in which work is organized must be changed in order to realize the full productivity potential of new technologies. Such changes will be required in managerial hierarchies as well as in the organization of directly productive activities. In the past, for example, one of the major functions of middle managers was to organize information in a manner that would be useful to senior managers charged with decision-making; the use of computers can simplify this task or, in some cases, eliminate the need for this activity at the middle-management level. Further, new technologies frequently require complementary innovations to realize their full potential. Thus, advances in microprocessors may require the development of new electronic devices or advances in application software to maximize their economic contributions.

From the standpoint of the consumer, changes in traditional ways of making purchases are necessary. Consumers must feel comfortable, for example, purchasing their tickets or doing their banking online, rather than going to a travel agency or bank to complete their transactions. In myriad ways, then, important new technologies typically require decades before their full potential can be realized.

These considerations suggest that the full potential of the revolution in information and communication technology remains to be realized, and that the acceleration in productivity and economic growth experienced over the past decade in the United States is just the beginning of a long-term phenomenon, one that is likely to spread more or less quickly to other developed and developing countries, with the speed of the spread likely to depend primarily on their success in developing the complementary institutions required to stimulate investment—that is, in sustaining or developing new social structures of accumulation. Globalization promises to speed the development and transfer of the new technologies to countries with appropriate SSAs.

International trade has been increasing more rapidly than global product, spreading the influence of new technologies throughout the world.[13] This increase actually understates the impact of globalization since a major share of multinational corporate sales is from their overseas facilities; when these take place within the countries in which they are located, they do not become part of the international trade data. China provides a good example of the realignment of institutions to reap the maximum benefit from the interaction of technological change and globalization.

Mao Zedong died in 1976 and, after a two-year transition period, Deng Xiaoping emerged as the modernizing leader of the new China at the Communist Party's Central Committee meeting in December 1978. China's commitment to modernization can be traced to that month, with institutional reform an ongoing process; as a result, China has had the world's most dynamic economy over the past quarter century, with an annual growth rate in GDP averaging approximately 9.4 percent (Zedillo 2004). Although it is not possible to provide a full discussion of China's institutional changes here, the institutional changes that facilitate the development of the new technologies and place China in a position to benefit from the growth of globalization should be mentioned. Institutional changes in the following areas constitute an important dimension of China's first SSA:

1 Market-oriented reforms replacing planning.
2 Opening to the global economy.
3 Education and labor market reform.

Although most countries are not faced with the extreme difficulty of having to make a transition from a planned economy to a market economy, the changes that China has instituted provide a good indication of ways in which countries can undertake institutional reforms to gain maximum benefit from globalization and the ICT revolution.

The market-oriented reforms replacing planning have occurred in agriculture, industry, housing and real estate, commerce, and—gradually—

finance (some of the equally important labor market reforms are noted separately on p. 83). The market system plays, of course, a critical role in efficient resource allocation. Equally important from the standpoint of globalization and technological change, it attracts both foreign investment and domestic private investment. This is essential for rapid economic growth since the role of the state in state-directed economies can no longer be as direct as it once was. Although state investment in social overhead capital (infrastructure) has played an important role in China, the boom that has taken place during the last quarter century has been driven by investment in the private sector, foreign-invested firms, and township and village enterprises (TVEs). The TVEs were initially organized within the communes at the brigade and village levels, and are now run as cooperatives owned by the entire community. Although they are collectively owned, the TVEs are typically professionally managed, are profit-oriented, and tend to reinvest most of their earnings, thereby creating highly valued employment opportunities; the rapid growth of the TVEs since 1978 would not have been possible without the widespread market reforms that China has adopted.

China's opening to the world economy has been dramatic, with foreign direct investment in China reaching US$57 billion in 2003 (*The Economist*, "A Survey of Business in China," 3/20/04: 9). Moreover, China has become an export powerhouse, with foreign exchange reserves of US$403.3 billion at the end of 2003, up 41 percent from 2002 and second in the world only to Japan (*Wall Street Journal*, 2/11/04: C4). China began in 1980 by establishing four special economic zones (SEZs) as independent cities with their own administrations (a fifth zone was added in 1988). The zones were successful in attracting a high level of foreign investment by streamlining bureaucratic procedures and by providing infrastructure support, tax advantages, and labor recruitment support, with the firms taking advantage of China's low labor costs to produce within them for export.

Soon after, China began establishing economic and technological development zones (ETDZs) within existing cities, zones that offered substantial advantages to foreign investors, although they were not as extensive as those offered by the SEZs. A broad coastal zone was also established with reduced but still significant benefits. The success along China's east coast has been followed more recently by the opening up of interior cities to foreign investment; since the interior is much less developed than the coastal regions, labor costs there tend to be much lower.

At the same time China has joined the World Trade Organization (WTO) to protect its trade rights, and is in the midst of gradually opening up its domestic markets to foreign firms. Initially foreign firms had limited access to the domestic market and were required to institute joint ventures with Chinese firms, restrictions that protected Chinese firms unprepared to compete with Western firms while they learned Western business practices, and which also facilitated the transfer of technology to China. As Chinese firms gain the strength to compete independently—and according to WTO rules—such restrictions are gradually being eliminated. At the same time, China has been a leader in promoting a broad East Asian free-trade zone, which starting with the ASEAN 10 is envisioned to include China, South Korea, and Japan as well (to become the ASEAN 10 + 3). By undertaking institutional reforms to participate fully in the global economy, China has created a development dynamic that is spurring economic growth in most of the East Asian region. In Thailand, for example, exports to China tripled between 1993 and 2001, and the number of Chinese tourist arrivals quadrupled (www.economist.com, from *The Economist*, 2/28/02 print edition). For Southeast Asia as a whole, however, trade with China did not begin to have a truly significant impact until the early years of the twenty-first century. China's trade with ASEAN countries increased by 45.3 percent in the first half of 2003, with exports from ASEAN countries up by 55.5 percent to US$20.47 billion and exports from China to ASEAN countries up 32.4 percent to US$13.77 billion (*People's Daily* English language website, 8/17/2003: http://english.people.com.cn). China's rapid economic growth promises to continue stimulating economic activity in the entire East Asian region.

China's educational system under Mao tended to focus on the socialist classics, and opportunities for technical and higher education were quite limited or altogether absent. During the reform period, a meritocratic examination system has been established for admission to the best schools; there has been a vast increase in the number of high school, college and graduate school graduates; training in science and technology has received great emphasis; and the school curricula have been revised accordingly. Instead of state labor bureaux placing new graduates in lifetime jobs, firms are free to recruit according to their needs. In addition, changes in government policy have made it possible for large numbers of students to be trained abroad. This whole set of changes has created a new generation comfortable with modern technology, and the number of internet users in China is expected to pass that in the US around 2006 (*Business Week*, 3/15/04: 54). The changes in education and the labor market have placed China in an advantageous position to benefit from the interaction of globalization and technological change.

Starting with a quite different set of initial conditions, India too set out on a path of economic liberalization in 1991, inspired to make changes in part by an economic crisis marked by a dramatic fall in foreign exchange reserves. Although there was extensive state ownership of major firms in various industries, India never had central planning of the Chinese type. Rather, an excess of regulations and bureaucracy had stifled the development of the private sector. While liberalization is a more uneven process than it is in China, both of the major parties are broadly supportive, and it appears that India is setting out on a course of domestic reform and engagement with the world economy that has the potential to lead to rapid economic growth as well.[14] If the experience of South Asia parallels that of East Asia, then with a lag of 15–20 years the spread effects that China has begun to bring to East Asia (with Chinese demand stimulating economies from Japan to Thailand) might well be paralleled in South Asia, with India serving as the major force.

There are reasons for believing that an extended period of global prosperity will emerge in the coming decades in other areas of the world as well. In the European Union, for example, globalization and technological change are creating strong pressures for economic reform. In principle, bringing twenty-five states into a common market should constitute a transformative institutional change with great economic potential. The EU has yet to realize this potential, however, thanks especially to high taxes and labor market rigidities, among other legacies of the welfare state. Faced with aging populations and the loss of jobs, moreover, sluggish economic growth has engendered severe fiscal problems in France and Germany, among other major states. As in the case of India, financial crises can be a powerful stimulant to economic reform, so there is every reason to believe that although it is likely to take time, the European Union will at some point make the reforms required to realize its economic potential.

As I have argued in Chapter 3, the United States has already created a new social structure of accumulation. With rapid Chinese growth set to continue in response to a continued commitment to reform, as Chinese growth spurs growth throughout East Asia (in 2003, Japan's exports to China, Taiwan and Hong Kong together passed those to the United States for the first time since 1873 [*Wall Street Journal*, 6/1/04: A17]), as the impact of India's modernization spreads in South Asia, and as the European Union states respond (however belatedly) to pressures for reform, an extended period of relatively strong growth in the capitalist world economy can be expected in the early decades of the twenty-first century. This growth, however, will be accompanied, inevitably, by the social and environmental contradictions associated with capitalist economic growth. These contradictions, in turn, are shaped by all the forces and social processes at work in the capitalist world economy, with globalization and technological change at the forefront in the current era.

Social and economic contradictions

From its inception, capitalism has been marked by uneven development within and among countries. This remains true during periods of rapid economic growth, although there are certain offsetting tendencies, including, most notably, the rapid increase in the size of the "middle" class in economically emerging countries like China and India. Since the institutions in most of the Middle East and Africa, and in much of South Asia, are not suited to attract investment, these regions are almost certain to continue to lag increasingly far behind those countries and regions experiencing strong economic growth. Globalization creates opportunities for less-developed countries to grow through exports to more developed ones, and on the supply side through transfers of technology and commercial knowledge. Countries without the requisite institutions, however, cannot be expected to take advantage of these opportunities, increasing the per capita income gaps between them on the one hand and the more developed and successfully developing countries on the other.

Within the successfully developing countries, disparities are also likely to intensify. China's investment boom, for example, has encompassed most of its broad coastal zone, while provinces in the interior (western region) are lagging considerably behind. In India, people with education living in certain urban areas have the opportunity to prosper, while extreme poverty remains deep-rooted among a large part of the 75 percent or so of the population living in rural areas. In both countries, the ownership of property, the possession of scarce skills, and the possession of political power provide opportunities for exceptionally high incomes.

Globalization and technological change, by creating an atmosphere conducive to accelerated economic growth, tend to intensify the process of differentiation, both within and among countries. In addition, since a range of special skills is required to make use of the new technologies, those lacking the required skills find their relative status diminished even more. In the United States, for example, unskilled workers after World War II could still aspire to "middle-class" lifestyles through well-paid factory jobs in selected industries. Such opportunities have been diminishing, and are likely to continue to diminish.

Accelerated economic growth and uneven development have two consequences of particular concern in the current stage of capitalist world development. First, if one thinks of terrorism in the current era as (in part) the revenge of the dispossessed, and recognizes that the consciousness of inequality is heightened by the spread of modern information and communications technology, then it appears that the forces stoking terrorism are likely to remain powerful (and indeed to grow) for much of the twenty-first century. This means that even in the absence of major wars, the peaceful conditions that inspire investor confidence will frequently be lacking. This is a contradiction confronting the capitalist world economy in the current era. Thus even an extended period of above-average growth in world product early in the century is likely eventually to confront severe headwinds.

Second, just as globalization and technological change have benefited capital immensely relative to labor in the United States, the same effect can be expected to hold sway worldwide. Since capital is mobile—and globalization and technological change have increased its mobility manifold—it always has the option to move to lower-labor-cost production sites if labor's demands for higher wages, better working conditions, or security become too strong. This option is not limited to the high-income countries. In China, for example, as wages rise in the coastal region, firms have the option to move production to inland sites or countries like Indonesia, where wages are considerably lower. As in the industrialized countries, moreover, automation always remains an option as well.[15]

As Gordon, Weisskopf, and Bowles (1996) argue, within a given capitalist country, capital can be too strong or too weak. If it is too strong, then the wages workers receive will be insufficient to enable them to buy the goods they produce. Aggregate demand will be insufficient to absorb the national product and capitalist firms will be unable to sell what they have produced; recession will ensue, bringing with it a fall in investment. If capital is too weak, then wages will be too high to permit high profits in production; this too will discourage investment. There are, however, six principal ways in which this core contradiction of capitalism can be held in check. Consideration of these helps in understanding how capitalism can thrive without labor benefiting proportionately.

The sustainability of capital's growing power

First, as in the postwar SSA in the US, a "capital–labor accord" can seek to strike a balance between the interests of capital and those of labor, permitting sufficient profits to attract investment and sufficient wages to maintain aggregate demand. This solution, however, becomes unlikely in the era of globalization, which is marked by an intensification of competition on a global scale; firms feel that maintaining low labor costs is a condition of survival.

Second, low labor costs at home may limit the home market, but as long as firms feel that they can increase their exports meaningfully and in a sustained fashion, limited domestic purchasing power need not discourage investment and production. The growth of overseas markets and investment opportunities appears to have played a role in the SSA that currently prevails in the United States. If capital worldwide, however, is stronger than labor worldwide, then purchasing power will be affected on a worldwide basis and exports will cease to provide a way out for capital. Given the strength of market fundamentalism in the US, conditions favorable to the growth in the relative power of capital have been established more quickly, but the global forces at work are beginning to move even Europe in the same direction. In the future, then, international trade and investment cannot be expected to resolve the contradiction posed by limited wage growth and weakening aggregate demand in the major capitalist countries.

Third, increasing access to finance can raise consumption above the levels supported by income alone. This can be especially helpful in increasing aggregate demand during a period of falling interest rates. Thus even during the 2001 recession in the United States and its aftermath, consumption and expenditures on housing were able to rise in the face of stagnant wages and falling employment. Financing consumption through rising debt, however, has obvious limits and makes the entire economic system more fragile in the event of a downturn or economic shock.

Fourth, potential slack in aggregate demand can be temporarily offset by increases in public expenditure or transfer payments. There are, however, two significant downside aspects to this strategy. First, sooner or later higher taxes will be required to finance increases in public spending. This lowers returns on investment and reduces purchasing power in the private sector; both factors discourage investment. Second, responding to political pressures, it is common for countries to avoid increasing taxes or even to lower them despite rising public expenditures. This strategy cannot be maintained indefinitely; ultimately, people will lose confidence in the public debt, interest rates will spiral upward, and a financial crisis is likely to emerge. Increases in public spending, then, while suited for countercyclical policies, cannot provide a long-term solution for deficiencies in aggregate demand.

Fifth, as people move from agriculture and the informal sector into the formal sector and begin wage labor, purchasing power can expand. This of course is an important factor in countries like China and in other developing countries as well. As these countries become increasingly developed, however, as in the case of the "Asian tigers," this source of additional aggregate demand will inevitably diminish. Even so, in Asia especially, the transition from agriculture and the informal sector to the formal sector can be expected to play a major role in sustaining aggregate demand during most of the twenty-first century.

Sixth, despite an imbalance in the relative strength of labor and capital (with capital holding the upper hand), aggregate demand can be sustained by high rates of investment. This requires an expansion of real investment opportunities as new markets open up, new technologies are deployed, and innovation proceeds apace. Together with the transition from agriculture and the informal sector, this appears to be the strongest source of support for strong global expansion in the early decades of the twenty-first century. Investment demand, however, is ultimately justified by increases in final consumption demand, so that if the superior power of capital relative to labor is sustained, limiting final consumption demand, at some point investment demand will be seriously affected.

The impact of globalization and technological change on the capitalist world economy, then, is multifaceted. It strengthens capital relative to labor and spurs innovation, raising profit rates and increasing the attractiveness of investment. At the same time, it spurs competition, which in itself can lower the returns on investment, but by requiring investment to remain competitive can spur innovation and sustain aggregate demand, both effects that promise to raise investment returns. Taken together, these factors promise to raise the rate of growth of world product in the early decades of the twenty-first century—especially as the forces of economic reform in Europe and Japan gain strength—with the negative impacts likely to grow increasingly significant as the century wears on. The aging of the populations in the industrialized countries, with the disproportionate increase in the number of the very old as medical technologies continue to progress, will create increasing fiscal problems for them, with higher taxes as the century progresses adding to the negative forces. The evolution of the capitalist system overall will be deeply affected by all of the "external" factors with which it interacts, but especially by the forces of globalization and technological change.

Environmental contradictions

The accelerated development of new technologies in the era of globalization and technological change promises a range of environmental benefits as, for example, fossil fuels are replaced by alternative energy sources. The social and political pressures generated by environmental preservation movements can be expected to intensify this effect. On balance, however, the accelerated growth in throughputs in the capitalist world economy can be expected to more than counterbalance the improvements, leading to accelerated deterioration in the environment. Chapter 7 explores the relationship between capitalism and the environment in some depth.

Environmentally friendly innovations may be coincidental, may be mandated by legislation, may involve a response to market pressures, or may involve a combination of all these factors. The development of cellular telephones and other wireless devices, for example, may replace the need for extensive fixed wireline investment, reducing the need for throughputs (although this effect will be partly offset by the need for cellular towers). Similarly, legislation can mandate the production of less-polluting vehicles, or encourage it indirectly by raising gasoline taxes. On balance, however, the rapid growth in gross world product, combined with some basic features of the capitalist system, suggests an overwhelming probability of accelerated environmental deterioration in the age of globalization and technological change. Numerous factors contribute to the likelihood of serious environmental deterioration.

First, the absolute size of gross world product will increase enormously. As India and China, each with populations in excess of one billion, reach "middle-income" status and ultimately begin to catch up with the wealthy countries in per capita product, the amount of pollution will increase enormously. Automobile manufacturers already consider China their "hottest" market, with sales growth expected to continue to be the strongest in the world.[16] China's superheated growth has increased the demand for energy dramatically, influencing world petroleum demand and prices (although coal remains China's primary energy source). As energy requirements increase the demand for fossil fuels worldwide, the problems of global warming can only intensify. And rising energy consumption is only one of the numerous ways that rising throughputs in developing countries—and the rest of the world—can be expected to increase pollution dramatically.

Second, the much greater size of the world economy in the decades to come increases the probability of accidental environmental hazards. I have already mentioned the tendency within the capitalist system to respond to profit opportunities first and to consider the environmental consequences later, if at all. The production of nondegradable plastics, for example, was under way for decades before an understanding of its negative environmental consequences became widely understood, and even today there are few checks on its production. As the world economy grows much larger, the tendency to introduce new elements into the environment without a clear understanding of their impact, together with the rising cumulative impact of known pollutants, can be expected to intensify environmental deterioration significantly.

Third, political pressures against environmental protection and against taxation (which could discourage polluting activities or provide public funds for remediation purposes) can be expected to persist. As will be discussed in Chapter 7, the interests in abusing the environment tend to be much more focused than the interests in preserving it. Timber interests and communities dependent on logging jobs have a much more focused interest in cutting down trees than the remainder of the population has in preserving them, and automobile companies and their workers have a much more focused interest in promoting the sales of highly polluting SUVs than the remainder of the population in limiting them. This dynamic is always present under capitalism, but as globalization and technological change drive the expansion of the world economy, the polluting consequences can be expected to increase disproportionately.

Fourth, the uneven development that characterizes capitalism at all times is likely to interact with rising population densities to increase stress on the environment. As world demand for forest products rises, for example, deforestation pressures will continue to rise in Indonesia and other Third World countries. Specific capitalist interests benefit from the sale of timber or other forest products, of course, but for the hundreds of millions of people marginalized within the capitalist system, logging jobs may be the only ones available, or the clearing of forests for subsistence agriculture may be the only means to survival. Globalization intensifies such forces by increasing the size of the global market for timber and other forest products.

Fifth, the problem of the global commons (discussed in Chapter 7) is intensified greatly by the forces of globalization and technological change. The consequences of pollution are increasingly becoming international or global in scope. Environmentally damaging forestry in Indonesia, for example, contributed to raging fires there leading to choking smog in

Singapore and Malaysia, and the increased use of coal in China has contributed to acid rain in Japan and South Korea (*Los Angeles Times*, 9/25/97: A1). More broadly, however, as globalization and technological change drive the growth in world product, the overall stress on the global environment rises disproportionately. If we consider truly global problems like global warming, holes in the ozone layer, or the fate of the oceans, the problems become much more difficult to deal with than pollutants with identifiable sources crossing national boundaries.

Global warming results from the cumulative effect of fossil fuel use by the entire world, which results in rising concentrations of carbon dioxide in the atmosphere. As globalization and technological change contribute to the accelerated growth of world product, the demand for energy rises, intensifying the problem of global warming. No single country—and no small group of countries—has the power to stop it. If a single country curtails its own use of fossil fuels, thereby sacrificing its living standards to some degree, the impact on the global environment will be negligible. As far as the oceans are concerned, each country tends to use them as an inexhaustible dumping ground for its wastes, and once again any single country resolved to act more responsibly can have only a negligible impact. These are classic global commons problems.

Collective action through international treaties is essential if the environment is to be protected. Since such treaties involve reducing growth rates, and therefore profit opportunities, they tend to spawn violent opposition in capitalist countries. The opposition, moreover, does not come only from capitalists. Since capitalism spurs and glorifies the pursuit of wealth, and at the same time generates personal insecurity as people must fear for their employment and livelihood, any action that discourages growth tends to generate broad opposition. The immediate desire for profit or need for income tends to outweigh the longer-term consequences of a destroyed habitat in social decision-making.

Globalization and technological change, then, interacting with population growth and all of the other "external" forces shaping capitalist development in the current era, promise to intensify environmental destruction over the course of the twenty-first century. A more comprehensive assessment of the relationship between capitalism and the environment appears in Chapter 7.

Conclusion

Chapters 2 and 3 explored the manner in which the capitalist system overcomes its contradictions by repeatedly reinventing itself and establishing new social structures of accumulation. In doing so, it generates extended periods of relative prosperity (when a new SSA is established) alternating with extended periods of relative stagnation (when the SSA succumbs to its contradictions). This takes place differently within each country, according to its own institutions, conflicts, and contradictions. As capitalism moves from one stage to the next within each country, however, the "external" factors with which it interacts also play a vital role. At the end of the twentieth century, and most likely for the better part of the twenty-first, the forces of globalization and technological change are the "external" factors most likely to influence the evolution of the capitalist system.

As I have argued in Chapter 1, the advent of capitalism in the sixteenth century brought with it a significant rise in living standards in (the industrialized) part of the world, especially since the Industrial Revolution. This remains true even though the early stages of "primitive" capitalist accumulation are often harsh in the extreme. In the second half of the twentieth century and over the course of the twenty-first century, there are strong indications that the improvements in living standards that capitalism has brought are spreading to some of the less-developed regions of the world, with East Asia leading the way. Globalization and technological change, and their interaction, have played a central part in this process.

In this chapter, my focus has been on exploring the manner in which the forces of globalization and technological change shape the continuing evolution of the capitalist system. They do so in numerous ways, some of which aid the human condition and others of which do not. The prospects for continued improvements have been demonstrated most clearly by China's ability to follow the pathbreaking success of the Asian "tigers," taking full advantage of the forces of globalization and technological change, and the positive economic impact this is having throughout East Asia. In time, India may have a similar impact on South Asia, and while other regions of the world may well continue to lag, there is reason to think that over the course of a century or two all of the Third World has the potential to participate in the expansion of the global economy.

As I indicated in Chapter 1, however, the impact of the capitalist system on the human condition is not altogether positive. In this chapter I have laid special emphasis on the problematic and dysfunctional aspects of capitalist expansion. Globalization and technological change, and their interaction, have served throughout the world to strengthen the power of capital relative to that of labor, and to promote the "harsh" form of capitalism rather than the more humane forms of capitalism found in the more mature economies of continental Europe and (to a lesser extent) in the state-led economies of East Asia. In addition, even when the movement of large masses of people into the "middle" classes in China and India is taken into account, the forces of globalization and technological change appear likely to continue to promote greater inequality, both within and among different countries.

The same forces increase systemic risk, especially in international currency transactions, as an increasingly integrated global economy transmits shocks throughout the capitalist world economy with great rapidity, and as international institutional reform lags behind the requirements of global economic integration. The greatest danger posed by growing globalization and technological change, however, is likely to be that posed by environmental degradation. Chapter 7 is devoted in its entirety to an analysis of the dysfunctional relationship between capitalism and the environment, but the role of globalization and technological change are so important in this regard that some assessment, however brief, is called for in this chapter.

There are various ways in which the capitalist system is, in general, hostile to the environment. Since economic activity passes regularly through the prism of markets, the externalities generated by those engaged in market transactions are characteristically ignored. Most of these externalities—which affect those other than the market transactors—are environmentally damaging, some of them extremely so. Moreover, their cumulative effect can increase environmental damage disproportionately. Thus, for example, the atmosphere can absorb a certain amount of carbon dioxide and other greenhouse gases without the problem of global warming reaching crisis conditions. As globalization and technological change accelerate the growth of world product, however, the accompanying destruction of the environment will increase disproportionately.

It appears almost inevitable that this will be the fate of the atmosphere—and more broadly of the environment in its entirety—over the course of the twenty-first century. Moreover, the capitalist system is structured in a way that makes economic growth its *raison d'être*. Competition generates pressures to introduce an endless stream of new products, and people welcome growth as the source of their jobs and benefits. As globalization and technological change accelerate economic growth and promote its spread worldwide, the destruction of the environment can only accelerate as well.

While I place special emphasis on capitalism's environmental contradictions in this book, however, the capitalist system is multifaceted, and its contradictions have been seriously explored by others in a variety of rich traditions. Before turning to capitalism and the environment I will use Chapters 5 and 6 respectively, to investigate the relations between capitalism and the surplus, and between capitalism and class. The extensive literature in both traditions is worthy of serious consideration, and explorations of that literature, even when critical, are capable of providing insights into the nature and dynamics of the capitalist system that deepen our understanding of it.

5 Capitalism and the economic surplus

Chapters 2 and 3 focused on the manner in which capitalism repeatedly reinvents itself, moving to new stages of qualitatively different forms of social organization as it overcomes its internal contradictions and adjusts to changing external circumstances. Chapter 4 extended the analysis to an exploration of the principal external conditions shaping the evolution of the capitalist system, with a focus on globalization and technological change. This chapter seeks to provide an alternative theoretical perspective for approaching capitalism—one based on an analysis of the economic surplus—but one that is not at all in conflict with the social structure of accumulation approach.

As I noted in quoting Dudley Dillard in Chapter 1, capitalism differs from prior social formations in that the economic surplus is channeled into capital formation rather than into the building of monuments and other nonproductive uses. This of course is the very process of accumulation that stands at the heart of capitalism, and it is the reason for which the explosion in output per capita and living standards has taken place over the last four and a half centuries in the industrialized countries.[1] Considering the accumulation process from the standpoint of the generation and use of the surplus provides additional insight into the nature of the capitalist system, including its internal dynamics and contradictions. The significance of the surplus and of who appropriates it can be grasped most fully in conjunction with class analysis, which will be the subject of Chapter 6.

The surplus can be defined in different ways, and in the pages that follow I will examine some of the ways in which the concept has been used in the radical political economy literature. Here I would like to explain why I have found it most useful simply to think of the surplus as that portion of national income that is not required for the essential consumption, both private and public, of the entire population. If we consider society's essential consumption requirements as having a priority claim on social output, then the surplus can be regarded as society's discretionary income, with each society defining and differentiating itself from other societies by the manner in which it "chooses" to dispose of the surplus.

Under certain circumstances, when there is a dominant class in society, then we can think of the dominant class as being composed of that group of people who control the surplus and determine its use. When approached from this perspective, the analyses of class structure and surplus use become intertwined. In Chapter 5, however, I would prefer to focus on the concept of the surplus independently for the most part, reserving the analysis of the interplay between class structure and surplus use for Chapter 6. The analysis presented there should help to clarify the reasons for which capitalist development has not yet begun to any substantial degree in many of the less-developed countries in the world today.

In this chapter, the analysis of the surplus will focus on its role in the dynamic evolution of the capitalist system, and its potential for generating core contradictions in that system. In the middle of the nineteenth century, Marx's analysis of capitalism focused on a competitive world of small producers with little or no power to set their own prices (they had to accept market prices as given and devise their production and distribution strategies accordingly). In the middle of the twentieth century, Paul Sweezy and Paul Baran sought to update the Marxian analysis of capitalism to a world in which giant corporations with substantial pricing power had become dominant.[2] While their focus was on the American economy, they argued that modern capitalism in general should be thought of as "monopoly capitalism"—although what they really had in mind was "oligopoly capitalism." Monopoly refers literally to cases of a single seller, while oligopoly refers to industries dominated by a few sellers; in both cases, however, the seller or sellers have substantial power to set their own prices.

According to the analysis of Baran and Sweezy (1966), the central contradictions on which Marx focused were no longer applicable in the era of giant corporations. Rather, Baran and Sweezy saw the central contradiction of contemporary capitalism as the tendency of the surplus to rise (1966: Chapter 3). The result of this was an underlying tendency for capitalist societies to stagnate economically, a tendency that could only be postponed and not overcome through vastly expanded military expenditure, a Herculean sales effort (including advertising and marketing) and enormous waste. A substantial literature has emerged endorsing this approach and developing it, and as one of the few substantive efforts to update the Marxian critique of capitalism it deserves to be taken seriously.[3] For the reasons I will outline below, however, the argument that there is a tendency for the surplus to expand under contemporary capitalism is mistaken; if anything, there may well be a tendency for it to shrink—posing, if this should be the case, a distinct set of problems for the capitalist system.[4]

In this chapter, then, I would like first to explore different conceptions of the surplus, arriving in this way at a definition that I have found to be the most useful in thinking about the capitalist system. That section will be followed by an analysis of the "monopoly capitalism" thesis of an expanding surplus, a thesis that focuses on the purported contradiction between capitalism's capacity to lower costs of production and increase supply, on the one hand, and the social relations under capitalism that prevent the expanded output from being used to meet individual and social needs on the other. A final section will consider alternative ways in which the concept of the surplus can be employed to enhance our understanding of the capitalist system. Of special interest here is an exploration of the relation between the surplus and environmental sustainability. Although the analysis of capitalism and the environment will be treated more fully in Chapter 7, the existence of a surplus makes feasible, in principle at least, a transition to a sustainable economy that would otherwise be much more difficult to achieve.

Conceptions of the surplus

The modern conception of the surplus emerges from Paul Baran's book, *The Political Economy of Growth* (1957). Baran's work, however, is related to the earlier development of the concept of surplus value in Karl Marx's *Capital* (1961–62). Marx assumed that workers would receive a subsistence wage under capitalism, and in earlier modes of production (such as slavery or feudalism) received its equivalent. It was, after all, in the interest of the dominant half of each class duality (capitalist and worker, slave-owner and slave, lord and serf) to provide enough sustenance to enable the productive worker to continue to produce, and to raise the next generation of productive workers as well.

The output generated above this subsistence requirement was the surplus value. It took different forms under different modes of production: profits under capitalism, the output produced by serfs on the lord's land under feudalism, and so forth. The surplus value could be increased in two ways under capitalism. First, as under other modes of production, *absolute surplus value* could be raised by extending the working day or increasing the required intensity of work. There are physical limitations to this, however, and beyond a certain point demanding additional work becomes counterproductive as the health of workers suffers and their productivity diminishes.

Second, *relative surplus value* can be increased when additional capital and/or technological improvements enhance the productivity of labor, reducing the number of hours it takes each worker to produce his or her subsistence requirements (or their equivalent). Under capitalism—as capital accumulation proceeds over time—this becomes much more important than it was under previous modes of production. For Marx, surplus value was not equivalent to profit, but profit had to come from surplus value. This in turn provided the basis for one of the core contradictions that Marx perceived in capitalism.

Since Marx believed that competitive forces would force the price of capital goods down to their cost of production, he saw living labor as the only source of surplus value. As the accumulation process proceeded over time, the amount of capital used in the production process relative to the amount of labor would inevitably rise, leading to a fall in surplus value and ultimately to a fall in the rate of profit (Marx 1961–62: part III; Weisskopf 1996: 369). Marx felt that the "law of the falling rate of profit" was one of the core contradictions in the capitalist system. If profits rates fell too far, capitalists would cease investing, the accumulation process would grind to a halt, and massive unemployment and social unrest would lead to the overthrow of the capitalist system. Although he was hopeful of this outcome, he was not of course making specific predictions; rather, he was attempting to analyze the internal logic of the capitalist system—the way in which it would function in the absence of conscious interventions.

The law of the falling rate of profit, based as it is on Marx's labor theory of value, is, I believe, incorrect and not very helpful to our understanding of the capitalist system. The labor theory of value is deficient in ascribing no contribution to the value of production by any input other than directly productive labor (thereby excluding entrepreneurial innovation, managerial and engineering skills, capital, and so forth). It is also deficient in allowing no role in value creation to demand and usefulness. Ultimately, the profit rate *may* tend to fall over time due to the law of diminishing returns, but that assumes a lack of innovation and new products that is entirely uncharacteristic of the capitalist system. Profits may fall over time, therefore, or they may not, but as far as the internal logic of capitalism is concerned there is no necessary tendency in either direction.

Marx's use of the concept of surplus value to explore the internal contradictions of the capitalist system is of interest, however, because it served as one of the starting points for the quite different analysis of Paul Baran. Baran presented multiple definitions of the surplus: four in *The Political Economy of Growth* (1957), a fifth in his foreword to the book's 1962 printing, and a sixth in *Monopoly Capital* (1966), the book he co-authored with Paul Sweezy. Without going into all of his definitions in detail, I would like to explore the implications of the most interesting of his first definitions—one which in modified form provides the most useful approach to the concept of the surplus. Later, in order to analyze the *Monopoly Capital* interpretation of contemporary capitalism, I will turn as well to the conception of the surplus that Baran and Sweezy developed jointly.

The *potential surplus* is defined by Baran (1957: 23) as "the difference between the output that *could* be produced in a given natural and technological environment with the help of employable productive resources and what might be regarded as essential consumption." Whereas Marx develops his conception of surplus value from the production relations between the worker and capitalist (or, more generally, between the direct producer and the owner of the means of production), Baran starts from a national income accounting framework that focuses on national output and its constituent parts. There is a twist to his approach, however, since most of the elements he uses cannot be found in *conventional* national income accounting.

The concept of the surplus itself is not to be found there. The potential national output or income (they would amount to the same thing) is greater than full-employment national income, since it includes the output lost due to the "misemployment of productive resources" (1957: 23). This includes, in Baran's view, output lost to unproductive workers, output that would not be produced in a rationally ordered (noncapitalist) society, output lost due to the underutilization of productive capacity that is present under capitalism even during periods of so-called full employment, and so forth. My own view is that these concepts are of interest, but they are so tenuous and ill-defined as to allow no means of practical assessment or quantification. In my own presentation of the surplus, I will suggest that "potential national income" should be replaced by "national income," a category that can readily be found in conventional national income accounts.

The concept of *essential consumption*, by contrast, can be quite useful, and marks an important contribution to the surplus literature. Essential consumption is not a physiological minimum, but the equivalent of a poverty line based on community standards of what constitutes the minimum requirements for living decently. It includes government consumption as well as private consumption, so that the costs of maintaining, say, basic bus service, medical clinics, and a sixth-grade (or high school in the case of the United States) education might be included in essential consumption. As far as private consumption is concerned, the cost of owning and maintaining an automobile would be part of essential consumption in most of the United States (since access to shops, jobs, and medical care is dependent on it), but not (yet) in China.

Returning then to my own preferred definition of the surplus, it can be thought of simply as the difference between national income and essential consumption. The surplus can be used in many different ways, including investment, luxury consumption, military expenditure, higher education, the building of monuments, research and development, and so forth. Since the dominant classes or groups in society can be thought of as the ones who control the use of the surplus, they define themselves and their societies by the decisions they make, whether explicitly or implicitly. Moreover, whenever a society is faced by severe challenges, the existence of a surplus provides a means to confront them. This will prove to be of importance when we consider some of the contradictions of contemporary capitalism, both in this chapter and more fully in Chapter 7 on the environment. First, however, since Baran and Sweezy place their conception of the surplus front and center stage in analyzing the core contradiction of contemporary capitalism, an examination of their argument appears in order.

Paul Baran, Paul Sweezy, and the "monopoly capital" thesis

In *Monopoly Capital*, Paul Baran and Paul Sweezy define the economic surplus simply as "the difference between what a society produces and the costs of producing it" (1966: 9). In using this concept to explore the core contradictions of contemporary capitalism they organize their argument around the nature and behavior of the representative firm, which they see as large in size and as a member of an oligopoly, capable of influencing the prices at which it sells its output. The behavior of this firm differs from that of the representative firm in Marx's era, since the latter confronted numerous small competitors, was small itself, and had to accept prices established by market forces. The firm of Baran and Sweezy, by contrast, could maintain prices above those that would be determined by competitive equilibria, while bringing its enormous resources to bear on improving production processes and lowering production costs. The result would be a widening gap between the value of output and the cost of production; on a national level, this would mean a rising (economic) surplus.

Since the number and purchasing power of the necessary production workers would not be rising as fast as total output, the macroeconomic implications of this situation are an inability of the firms to sell their entire output, discouraging further production and investment. Without a variety of interventions, the natural outcome would be a tendency toward stagnation in the economy, and capitalism would lose its ability to generate economic growth and rising living standards. At the firm level, the successful enterprise would have high profits in production, but would be unable to sell all its output or expand its production. These outcomes would present a quite serious challenge to the continuity of the capitalist system.

The contradiction thus posed is addressed, according to Baran and Sweezy, by the emergence of a multitude of ways to absorb the surplus. They focus especially on the sales and marketing effort at the enterprise level, and military expenditure at the national level. They also take note of exceptional levels of wastefulness, as when firms hire teams of lawyers and investment bankers to take over other firms, who respond in kind by hiring defensive teams of their own, thereby compounding the waste. Contemporary capitalism emerges, as a result, as a wildly irrational society, one that has the productive capacity to meet the full range of individual and social needs, but which instead uses its capacity in ways that produce waste, militarism, and crassly commercial culture.

There are two principal antecedents to the monopoly capital thesis. On the one hand, it was shaped by the social criticism of the 1950s, by the view of the world reflected in such works as John Kenneth Galbraith's *The Affluent Society* (first published in 1958) and Paul Goodman's *Growing Up Absurd* (1956). On the other hand, it represents a serious attempt to modify the Marxian analytical framework to take into account the emergence of giant corporations with considerable pricing power, and to reconsider the fundamental contradictions of capitalism accordingly. While many aspects of its social criticism continue to be of interest, the thesis of an expanding surplus was unconvincing when the book appeared in 1966 and appears even less valid today.

In their book, Baran and Sweezy refer to the findings of Joseph Phillips, which are presented in its statistical appendix. Phillips attempted to estimate the surplus for the United States, and found it rose from 46.9 percent of gross national product (GNP) in 1929 to 56.1 percent in 1963. Baran and Sweezy cite this finding (p. 11) as evidence supporting their thesis. It is of interest to note, however, that Phillips divided the surplus into six categories, according to the theoretical framework laid out by Baran and Sweezy, and that only one category, government spending, accounts for over 100 percent of the reported increase in the surplus as a percentage of GNP (p. 389). Alternatively stated, the other five surplus categories, taken collectively as a percentage of GNP, declined between 1929 and 1963.

The *Monopoly Capital* thesis, moreover, has theoretical deficiencies that are far more significant than those revealed in the statistical findings. As I have indicated earlier, Baran and Sweezy define the surplus as the difference between national product and the socially necessary costs of production. Their statistical appendix reflects the principal categories into which the surplus is divided in the text, and a consideration of these categories reveals their problematic nature. The categories include (1) total property income; (2) waste in distribution; (3) nontrade corporate advertising; (4) employee compensation in finance, trade, and real estate; (5) employee compensation in legal services; and (6) government expenditure.

The first category, total property income, reflects the roots of Baran and Sweezy in Marxian theory; this is the modern variant of capitalists' (profit) income. *As a first approximation* it is indeed appropriate to treat such unearned income—consisting of profit, rent, and interest—as a socially unnecessary cost of production. There are, however, several points that should be considered in this regard. First, insofar as profit represents a return to innovation and entrepreneurship, it may be a necessary cost of production. Second, as class lines become somewhat blurred in contemporary capitalist society, a number of problems arise from treating all of property income as part of the surplus.

Pension funds and retirement plans, for example, own a sizable portion of corporate stock in the United States (Lippit 1992: 77). Most of this is used to help finance the retirement of workers, contributing to their essential consumption. The California Public Employees' Retirement System alone has some $134 billion (*Los Angeles Times*, 3/18/03: C7) under management. Income accruing to funds like these simply cannot be regarded as "surplus" in the sense of constituting a portion of society's discretionary income. The living costs of childhood and old age, as well as those of currently active members of the labor force, are properly part of socially necessary costs. In contemporary capitalist society, a portion of these costs appears under the guise of "property income," but must nevertheless be excluded from the surplus.

"Waste in distribution" is the second surplus category. Presumably distribution costs reflect the retail sales price less the cost of goods produced at factories. This would include transportation costs, the commissions and salaries of salespeople, marketing and advertising expenditures, and so forth. Baran and Sweezy recognize that some of these costs are necessary, as does Phillips. In the case of transportation costs they are, for the most part, clearly necessary. In the case of salespeople, the calculation becomes, perforce, more tentative. If people were forced to wait an hour on supermarket checkout lines it is not clear whether they would regard the services of checkout workers as superfluous. Even advertising and marketing expenditures raise more complex issues than might be apparent at first glance.

Presumably, these expenditures are able to raise the scale of production and lower the costs of production. At the beginning of the twentieth century, the United States had over one hundred automobile producers; today the figure is more like two and a half (the figure excludes foreign-based producers except for the half, which represents DaimlerChrysler). Cars that are made in small volume are extremely expensive to produce and are generally associated with super-luxury models. If the US still had over one hundred producers, the cost of automobiles would inevitably be far higher. The marketing expenditures of automobile companies have contributed to brand awareness and larger sales volumes, thereby leading to industry consolidation and lower unit costs of production. Treating these costs as purely wasteful, therefore, as an unadorned part of the surplus, is problematic.

The problem is further compounded by the role of advertising, the third of the surplus categories. Without advertising, newspapers, magazines, and television, among other media, would undoubtedly be more expensive. In effect, advertising expenditures are subsidizing these media, so that treating advertising expenditures as purely part of the surplus fails to take into account the contribution they make to the output of goods and services that are not included in the surplus. We can sympathize with the dislike of commercial culture, but we cannot fail to acknowledge that a portion of this expenditure makes a positive contribution to essential consumption.

The fourth and fifth categories similarly represent some rather cavalier assumptions about what is socially necessary. These categories sweep into the surplus value added via employee compensation in finance, insurance, real estate, and legal services. Again we find the prejudice that tends to exclude service activities from the sphere of the productive. Some people do choose to sell their homes by themselves, others pay the typical 6 percent commission to real estate agents. Presumably they do so because they find the service provided to be of value. Similarly, people do benefit from being able to use the services of insurance agents, make deposits at banks, and so forth. To suggest that people in these industries provide socially unnecessary services appears quite arbitrary.

Monopoly Capital's sixth and final surplus category, government expenditure, is the most problematic of all. Treating all of government expenditure as part of the surplus is simply unacceptable. *Most* of government expenditure contributes to essential consumption, and a large part of it represents, either directly or indirectly, essential costs of production. Part of essential consumption represents collective rather than individual goods and services: police and fire protection, roads and bus service, public schools, and so forth. In addition, without these services, the essential costs of private producers would inevitably be considerably higher. Finding ways to get workers to and from work in the absence of paved roads and public transport, providing workers with the literacy and minimum educational requirements needed for their jobs, providing the firm's own security force in the absence of police, and so on, would raise costs directly. And without a system of laws and courts to enforce contracts and create a stable institutional framework, a great deal of business activity could not be carried out at all.

Above and beyond the problematic nature of the different surplus categories indicated by Baran and Sweezy, another central issue has arisen as a result of the reinvention of American capitalism at the end of the twentieth century. During the middle of the century, a theoretical framework that focused on the oligopolistic market structure of the industrialized countries had considerable force. In the contemporary era, however, the interaction of technological change and globalization has dramatically diminished the purported pricing power of the typical corporation.

Under conditions in which both production and supply chains are increasingly global, the production of physical goods has increasingly been automated or shifted to countries with low labor costs. Both phenomena—but the latter especially—create strong downward price pressures, which the growth of international competition has intensified. These pressures are unlikely to diminish in the foreseeable future. China, increasingly the workshop of the world, is rapidly increasing the sophistication of its production capabilities, and its massive underemployment assures continued low labor costs. Increasingly, services can also be produced abroad, as exemplified by the rise of the Indian software industry. Domestically, the rise of giant discount chains (such as Wal-Mart) threatens other forms of retailing, from department stores to supermarket chains. Their buying clout and worldwide sources enable such chains to force down wholesale prices to minimum levels. If (with obvious exceptions), corporations have pricing power that is non-existent or quite limited, then the entire monopoly capital thesis of a rising surplus cannot be regarded as viable.

An alternative perspective on the surplus

I have suggested above that the surplus can most usefully be regarded as the difference between national income and essential consumption. National income or product can be thought of in either gross or net terms, as GDP or NDP. Essential consumption is both private and public, so that it would include essential government consumption. After briefly restating some of the principal forms the surplus can assume, I would like to proceed to an examination of the ways in which the analysis of the surplus can yield important insights into the nature, functioning, and core contradictions of the capitalist system.

If we start with the assumption that a nation's entire citizenry has a basic claim on the goods and services needed to provide essential consumption, then the surplus is, in essence, society's "discretionary" income. It can assume a variety of forms, including investment, luxury consumption, the provision of education above and beyond what is included in essential consumption, the building of monuments, military expenditure, research and development, the maintenance of religious institutions, the entertainment industry (including professional sports), and so forth. Some of these activities contribute to further growth and development, some do not, and some make a partial contribution, as when they enhance the stability of the social order.

Compared with previous social formations, such as feudalism or ancient slaveowning societies, under capitalism a substantially larger share of the surplus goes into capital formation and other activities that promote further growth, activities such as research and development or higher education. Since accumulation is at the core of the capitalist system, one way of thinking about capitalism is as a system that is focused on channeling the surplus into expanded productive capacity, and into the ancillary activities (like research and development) that facilitate this. Since other social formations—like feudalism—have not had the same imperative driving their dominant classes, capitalism distinguishes itself in this respect.

Chapters 2 and 3 approached the central role of accumulation under capitalism through an exploration of the institutional structures needed to support the accumulation process. Considering accumulation from the standpoint of the surplus raises a different set of issues. National income can be thought of as either the sum of incomes received in society or the total expenditures made on final goods and services; the two must always be equal by definition (assuming that inventory changes and net exports are taken into account). If we consider national income from the expenditures side, it can be divided into four categories: consumption, investment, government expenditure, and net exports (exports minus imports). Since government expenditures can also be divided between consumption and investment, and since net exports are usually relatively small and in any event can initially be treated separately (in a "closed economy" model), we can simplify the basic national income accounting by presenting national income as equal to consumption plus investment (Y = C + I).

Investments are undertaken in the expectation of generating future revenues and profits. Since the future is inherently unknowable, capitalists or firms must have a certain degree of confidence or optimism about probable future economic outcomes. Future sales will depend on the future demand for consumption and/or investment goods and services, but at some point there must be a rising consumption demand to justify further investment demand. Consumption demand depends most importantly on the levels of income earned, but since the higher personal incomes depend primarily on wage and salary growth, they are typically reflected in corporate ledgers as higher expenses—and lower profits. With lower profits in production, there is a lower inducement to invest. In other words, investment must ultimately be justified by high levels of consumption, but high levels of consumption ultimately imply high wage and salary costs—and lower profits, which discourage investment. This is one of the core contradictions with which capitalism is always confronted.

If the accumulation process is to proceed smoothly, then the surplus must be large enough to accommodate rising investment. If the surplus is too small, then the economy will tend to stagnate; the negative demand effects of limited investment will be compounded by the limited ability to incorporate the new technologies that are often embedded in new investment. On the other hand, if the surplus is too large relative to investment opportunities, then sales will fall short of the output produced. In that case, unsold goods will pile up, prices will be cut to eliminate unwanted inventories, and investment will be discouraged. As a result, the economy will not produce at its full-employment capacity.

The monopoly capital thesis assumes that this latter situation is endemic in contemporary capitalism. It suggests that *without intervention*, capitalism would tend toward stagnation. It argues as well, however, that intervention is the norm, with aggregate demand sustained by the sales effort, military expenditure, and multiple forms of waste. Without denying the presence of these phenomena, I have already tried to explain the reasons for which the theory of a rising surplus is inadequate as a basis for understanding the central dynamics of contemporary capitalism. Here I would like to go a step further by suggesting that there may well be a tendency for the surplus to diminish over time, posing a quite different set of problems for the capitalist system.

A diminishing surplus?

If we think of the surplus as society's discretionary income, then we can think of it as representing a set of resources that enables society to confront serious challenges or problems. If the surplus diminishes over time, then society's ability to respond to such situations will be increasingly circumscribed. In this section, I would like to explore first what the implications of a diminishing surplus might be, and second, the forces at play that may well bring about a diminishing surplus.

First, consider the situation of a peaceful society that suddenly finds itself confronted with the likelihood of a military attack. If it has a surplus, then it can mobilize resources to respond. Suppose it experiences a natural catastrophe, such as a massive earthquake. If it has a surplus it can mobilize resources to rebuild. Now if it does not have a surplus, that does not mean it will be completely incapable of response. Rather, it will mean that at least some portion of the population must have its consumption pushed below the socially agreed-upon minimum. Whoever is victimized by this process will have a grievance. The result will be social conflict, and if the prospective victims have any political strength, then all or part of the resources sought will prove unavailable. Further, the very existence of social conflict will absorb resources and make response to the "external" threat, whether natural or manmade, more difficult.

These examples are meant to clarify the theoretical point. Of much greater actual significance is the real threat posed by environmental deterioration. While this will be explored more fully in Chapter 7, which will attempt to spell out the nature of the threat, its connection to a diminishing surplus requires some discussion here.

Under capitalism, economic growth is part of the logic and justification of the system. Since accumulation is at the core of capitalism, both the growing capital stock and the new technologies it incorporates are likely to lead to significant economic growth over time. The historical evidence strongly supports this; to cite just two examples, per capita output in the United States grew by some seventeen times between 1820 and 1989, while that in Japan grew even more (by twenty-four times) between 1870 and 1989 (Maddison 1991: 7). While a certain amount of growth undoubtedly improves the human condition, there is no simple correlation between levels of per capita output and social well-being once incomes have reached a point at which basic levels of comfort have been attained. There are good reasons to think, for example, that the levels of happiness in the US today (in 2004) are less than they were half a century ago, despite vastly higher income levels.[5]

In addition to being a natural consequence of the capitalist social formation, economic growth plays a key role in its stabilization. Since capitalism generates its own distinctive forms of inequality, alienation, insecurity, and frustration, the stability of the system relies in part on its material promise. People who are deeply unhappy with the state of their lives may nevertheless support the system if it appears to offer the prospect of material improvement or even moving up into the property-owning class (whether or not they are actually successful is not the issue). In the absence of meaningful economic growth, the social conflicts inherent in capitalism may therefore assume a much more virulent form.

If the surplus is diminishing over time, then the level of investment is likely to fall, intensifying social conflicts. In addition, the ability of capitalist societies to address serious problems will weaken. Finally, the ability of the world economy to adjust to a "steady state" will be undermined severely. This issue is intimately connected to the environmental problem, which we might think of as follows. If we start with a room of specified size and there is a steady stream of people entering it, it will soon fill up. Although additional people may be pressed into the room, it will reach a point at which it cannot hold even one more person. In like fashion, if we regard the earth as having a fixed set of resources (except for energy derived from the sun, gravitational pulls, and other external sources) and a fixed capacity to absorb wastes, then it cannot accommodate an indefinitely expanding set of throughputs—production, consumption, and waste disposal. Yet capitalism demands precisely that.

We cannot think of capitalism apart from indefinite expansion based on an ongoing process of accumulation. Consider the issue from the standpoint of the firm. Profit growth can be pursued through increased sales revenue or decreased costs. In the most extreme case, however, costs cannot go below zero. On the other hand, there is no apparent limit to revenue growth. Ultimately, therefore, firms seeking to maximize their profits must rely primarily on revenue growth. The result is an indefinitely expanding set of throughputs in the capitalist world economy, taking place in a constrained environment. The end result of this process will be the earth's diminished capacity to sustain human life—and may well be the complete loss of such capacity. This is the ultimate contradiction which capitalism faces.

There are already many warning signs of this most unfortunate of outcomes. If we think of global warming, climate change, species loss, desertification, water shortages, pollution of water, earth and air, deforestation, and loss of the upper ozone layer, then the list of serious threats is already quite substantial. It is striking to think that this has been managed in just four and a half centuries of capitalism, whereas dinosaurs, with brains rather smaller than those of human beings, managed to survive for some 165 million years.

If human beings are to survive capitalism, then measures must be taken to prepare for post-capitalist society. We can envision such a society as involving a modified steady state, eliminating the steady growth of throughputs that the earth, with its limited capacity, cannot absorb indefinitely. The term "modified" is inserted to suggest that a completely frozen economic environment is neither possible nor desirable. There is no reason why innovations that open new frontiers, improve health, or reduce resource use—to cite some possibilities—should be barred. The important objective is to avoid the mandatory increase in throughputs that capitalism demands in the unending search for ever-higher profits. When firms create demand where none existed previously, and when the capitalist system creates the illusion that there is a one-to-one correlation between happiness and greater material prosperity, the rising throughputs and environmental destruction that result represent nothing more than the dysfunctional quality of the capitalist system.

Since open-ended growth in a constrained environment is ultimately unattainable, and since the pursuit of such growth in the extreme case is likely to lead to the end of human life on earth, it behooves us to begin preparations for a modified stationary state. Such a state could never be implemented immediately, because the legacy of capitalism is an enormous range of unsolved social problems. To prepare for such a state will take a sustained social effort extending over many generations, and the resources to deal with these problems must come out of the economic surplus. For this reason, the possibility that the surplus will tend to diminish over time must be considered seriously.

Since the surplus is the difference between national income and essential consumption, any tendency for the surplus to diminish over time must be reflected in rising essential consumption. There are a number of forces that can contribute to this. First, since essential consumption is socially determined, there is a natural tendency for it to rise as new goods and services become part of daily life. Initially the telephone was a luxury, but now to be cut off from telephone service is to be isolated from basic communication with other human beings. Similar transitions are now taking place with regard to cellular phones and Internet access. Automobiles were once a luxury and now a necessity in most of the United States. As an increasing range of goods and services becomes part of everyday life, essential consumption rises accordingly. To the extent that rising national income is matched by rising essential consumption, tendencies for the surplus to rise with national income will be offset.

An aging population—characteristic of most of the West and Japan, and soon to be reflected in the successfully developing Third World countries, where population increase rates are falling—also tends to eat into the surplus. It does so in several ways. First, it increases the dependency ratio in society, so that each productive worker is in effect responsible for supporting an increased number of people. In addition, there are certain costs that increase disproportionately with aging—most notably medical costs. Given the ongoing breakthroughs in biotechnology and other fields of medicine, it seems likely that life expectancy in the industrialized countries will increase significantly, and the disproportionate increase in the very old will be especially costly. The changing age composition of the population, therefore, will tend to eat into the economic surplus.

Finally, there are increasing costs associated with population concentration and congestion. Removing waste from congested urban areas becomes disproportionately expensive as population grows and the distance the waste must be shipped increases. The cost of solutions for traffic congestion rises disproportionately as the congestion becomes more and more severe. In general, factors such as these are reflected in the fact that the cost of living in large cities with dense populations tends to be significantly higher than it is in rural areas or small towns. This is simply a reflection of the fact that the cost of essential consumption is greater. As the world becomes increasingly urbanized, therefore, the diseconomies associated with growing population densities tend to lead to a falling surplus.[6]

The argument I have presented here addresses one of the core, long-term contradictions of the capitalist system. Indefinite expansion of throughputs in an environment that cannot sustain indefinite expansion is not feasible. For that reason, capitalism is ultimately unsustainable and, if human life is to continue, will ultimately have to be replaced by a social formation that is consistent with a modified stationary state. If one were to propose that such a state be instituted immediately, however, it is not only the capitalists who would object. The sizable share of the world's population living in poverty would surely not agree to a freezing of the status quo, and even the increasing middle class population in the developing countries would, for the most part, be unwilling to abandon its material aspirations. The same is likely to be true of the majority of the population in the industrialized countries. Economic growth will have to continue for some time, then, and the capitalist system is likely to be the driving force behind that growth. To maintain the possibility of preserving human life on earth, however, growth will have to be curtailed at some point.

To make that possible, the sense of economic deprivation and injustice experienced by a large portion of the world's population will have to be addressed. This can be done most readily if a sizable share of the economic surplus generated under capitalism is dedicated to addressing the problems of poverty, inequality, and the economic development of Third World countries. If the surplus is diminishing over time, the need for early action becomes all the more imperative.

It might also be noted in this regard that a second core contradiction of capitalism derives from the sense of exclusion, deprivation, and social injustice experienced by a large portion of the world's population. In an era of weapons of mass destruction, the sense of alienation that capitalism helps to generate on both a global and national scale through its pattern of unequal and exploitative development creates an intensified threat to modern civilization. For this reason as well, using the surplus to bring about development in the Third World and eliminate deprivation in the industrialized world, bringing about greater economic and social equality throughout the world, is more than an altruistic objective. It is likely to be one of the conditions for sustaining human life on earth over the long term. If the surplus is indeed diminishing over time, then the window of opportunity for meeting this condition will not be open indefinitely.

6 Capitalism and class

Ever since the classical era in economics, the century ranging from Adam Smith to Karl Marx, political economy has accorded a central place to the analysis of class and class struggle. David Ricardo, writing early in the nineteenth century, identified three principal classes: landlords, capitalists, and workers. Since he assumed—like many of his contemporaries—that workers would be limited to a subsistence wage over the long term under any circumstances (any significant rise in wages would increase the working population and the ensuing competition would bring wages back down to the subsistence level), Ricardo believed that the competition over the economic surplus would be carried out between the landowners and the capitalists. Since the landowners used their income (from rent) for luxury consumption whereas the capitalists used their profits for reinvestment, economic growth and the progress of society depended, in Ricardo's view, on the capitalists prevailing. Ricardo's analysis suggested that over the long term the share of rent in national income would tend to increase with the growth of population, but that public policy (such as the 1846 repeal of the Corn Laws) could postpone the ultimate decline in profits and the corresponding end of economic growth.

Writing in the middle of the nineteenth century, Karl Marx shifted the focus on the primary contending classes to the proletariat (the workers) and the bourgeoisie (the capitalists). Ever since then, the rich outpouring of Marxian literature has given a central role to the analysis of classes and class struggle in capitalist society. Since Marx used the term "class" in different ways in his own writings, since class analysis has often been central to radical political programs throughout the world, and since many problems are inherent in class analysis in any event, it is quite natural that this literature has incorporated intense debates. My purpose in this chapter is to clarify some of the issues that have been raised in the debates over class with a view to illuminating a number of the core features of capitalism and of the factors driving change within it.

The next section addresses some of the key problem areas associated with class analysis. This section is a necessary precursor to the discussion later in the chapter that suggests ways in which class analysis can nevertheless be a useful if limited means of gaining insight into capitalist society. After the discussion of problem areas, I will turn selectively to some of the major writings on class, followed by a section assessing the strengths and weaknesses of the different approaches in facilitating an understanding of the capitalist system. The focus here will be on selected writings of Eric Olin Wright, Immanuel Wallerstein, and Stephen Resnick and Richard Wolff. Following this review and critique, I will turn to a section assessing ways in which the concept of class can properly be applied to an interpretation of capitalist society, focusing on the interrelation between class and surplus use.

Capitalism and class: problem areas

In the last chapter of volume III of Marx's *Capital*, a chapter broken off after one and a half pages, Marx refers to the wage-laborers, capitalists, and landowners as the "three big classes of modern society based on the capitalist mode of production" (1961–62: 862). In the same fragmentary chapter, however, Marx notes that "physicians and officials . . . would also constitute two classes, for they belong to two distinct social groups" (ibid.: 863). In this passage, Marx appears to have been preparing to address the problem of the "intermediate" classes, those who do not fit neatly within the category of the "three big classes." The problem of the intermediate classes has become much more significant in contemporary capitalism, simply because the portion of the population that fits within this category has swelled enormously, with teachers, engineers, accountants, other professionals, and government employees, among others, constituting a large and growing portion of the population in the industrialized capitalist countries.

There is definitely a power to the imagery Marx presents in *The Communist Manifesto*, and elsewhere, of two principal contending classes characterizing each major social formation. Thus in ancient slave-owning societies there were the slave-owners and slaves, under feudalism there were lords and serfs, and under capitalism there are capitalists and workers, with the former class in each duality living off the surplus above and beyond its own subsistence requirements produced by the latter class, constituting in each instance the direct producers. The picture presented by Marx of contending classes struggling over the surplus—and in the process driving historical change—does not, however, appear to be consistent with the hundreds of millions of people in contemporary capitalist society who do not fit neatly into the "big" class categories to which he referred.

A second problem in applying class analysis to contemporary capitalist society lies in the existence of single individuals incorporating multiple class identities. Is an owner of a small firm who works alongside his/her employees a capitalist or a worker, or both? Is a wage-earning foreman, whose job it is to oversee workers' efforts in the interest of his/her employer, to be regarded simply as a representative of the interests of capital, or does the earning of wages and the exclusion from participation in the firm's profits suggest a different class categorization? How does one ascertain the class status of a skilled worker or professional who has sizable shareholdings in a number of companies? Problems such as these arise from the fact that individuals may participate in multiple roles in their economic activities, and a focus on the major class dualities may be unable to take account of this fact adequately.

A third problem in class analysis is associated with the role of women, children, and the family in general. Do women automatically have the class status of their husbands? What if a husband is a capitalist and his wife a worker or a housewife; or what if the wife is a capitalist and the husband a househusband? Is Mao Zedong, who was born into a rich peasant household, simply to be classified as a rich peasant? The issue raised here is actually broader than one of gender. People fulfill multiple roles in life. To categorize them solely on the basis of their class roles is problematic. To do so based on the class roles of their relatives is even more so.

A fourth problem with using class analysis to analyze capitalist society derives from the weak emotional identification or even the absence of any identification with a particular class that even those who apparently belong to one often display. As a driving force motivating individual behavior, religious, ethnic, tribal, and other forms of identity are typically far more powerful than class. Some have argued that "class consciousness" is a necessary part of a group becoming a class, with the consciousness of common class interest a necessary component of class struggle. Be that as it may, it is possible that people fail to develop a strong sense of class because class is a relatively weak component of all the processes and relationships that shape individual identity.

A fifth problem with applying the concept of class to capitalist society is tied to this question of class consciousness, together with the related issue of class struggle. As Barry Hindess (1987: 120) has pointed out, when politics is analyzed in terms of class struggle, implicit in the analysis is the notion of classes as "actors," consciously choosing a course of action, as well as the idea that class interests are objectively given by the structure of society. Hindess argues that neither notion is acceptable. As Hindess points out:

> An actor is a locus of decision and action, where the action is in some sense a consequence of the actor's decisions . . . Reference to an actor . . . always presupposes some definite means of reaching and formulating decisions, definite means of acting on them, and some connections between the two.
>
> (Hindess 1987: 110)

Thus Hindess argues that in addition to individuals there can be social actors such as capitalist enterprises, state agencies, or political parties. Classes, however, like societies, "have no identifiable means of formulating decisions, let alone of acting on them" (ibid.). Hindess concludes, accordingly, that the entire notion of class actors driving social change under capitalism (or any other social formation) is unacceptable.

A sixth problem with the use of class analysis is associated with one branch of Marxian thought. According to this interpretation of Marx, which follows especially the Preface to his *A Contribution to the Critique of Political Economy* (Marx and Engels 1958, vol. I: 362–363), the social structure of institutions and ideas is erected on the economic base of society.[1] In that base are class relations of production that correspond to a particular level of development of the forces of production. The class relations initially facilitate the continued development of these forces (that is, they contribute to ongoing economic growth), but at some point the class relations begin to hinder their further development. This ushers in a period of social crisis marked by intensified class conflict and, ultimately, the overthrow of the existing system and its replacement by a new mode of production with new class relationships capable of supporting renewed development of the forces of production.

This theoretical vision of the forces promoting historical change—and especially systemic change—has captured the imagination of millions. There are a number of problems with it, however, with that of essentialism the most prominent. Since historical change always comes about in complex ways as a result of multiple causes, one cannot legitimately claim that there is an economic "base" ultimately responsible for the changes in the economic "superstructure," or that conflict within the base—within the class relations of production—transforms the base and therefore the superstructure. While it is certainly true that conflicts within the economic sphere will have effects throughout society, it is also true that changes in the rest of society will have effects on the economic sphere, including class relations. If essentialism is rejected as the basis for social analysis—as indeed it must be—then the branch of Marxian thought that treats classes and class struggle as *the* basis of society and social change must be viewed with considerable skepticism.

A seventh problem with the use of class analysis is tied to the secondary point raised by Hindess in the discussion above. Since "class interests" are not objectively given, various problems are raised for class analysis. It has often been noted that among capitalists, interests may be fiercely opposed (sometimes efforts are made to circumvent this problem through the recognition of class "fractions"). Thus, for example, exporters may wish to promote free trade while those fearful of import competition seek to block it. Or large firms may have different interests from small firms, financial firms from producing firms, and so forth. Among workers, those who allow their health to deteriorate by smoking, weight gain, and so forth, usually add to the health costs of other workers by increasing health coverage copayments. Airline pilots who seek to maximize their own pay and minimize their own working hours have contributed to the financial distress of major American airlines, driving several into or near bankruptcy. This in turn has resulted in lay-offs for flight attendants, workers at Boeing (who produce many of the planes), and others. There are many problems, therefore, with the simplistic assumption that class analysis provides the single key to understanding economic conflict.

Another problem with the class analysis of social conflict arises from essentialism of a different sort. By focusing on classes to the exclusion of consumers, suppliers, communities, and so forth, class analysis often oversimplifies the vast array of social interests affected by economic activity. At times capital and labor have a common interest, as for example in those cases of oligopoly and monopoly where firms charge higher-than-competitive prices, and pay their workers high wages with a portion of the extra revenue obtained.[2] Or business firms may stay in business by economizing on the use of pollution controls, preserving jobs and serving their own profit objectives at the expense of the local community, which suffers from the pollution. Class analysis of course does not necessarily reduce all social conflict to class conflict, but the literature on class conflict often moves in this direction by exaggerating the importance of class conflict relative to other social conflicts.

Finally, different writers on class have defined class in different ways. If there is a lack of agreement on what constitutes a class, that will inevitably diminish the ability of class analysis to illuminate social reality. A great deal of class analysis has assumed that class can be defined in terms of ownership, power, and consciousness, or some combination of these factors.[3] The lack of agreement on what constitutes a class can lead to sharply differing conclusions. For example, with the elimination of private ownership of the means of production in the former Soviet Union, some have argued that a classless society was created. Others, who argue that there remained a ruling class, focused on power as the defining element in class relationships. As we will see in the discussion of some leading class theorists (pp. 112–117), Resnick and Wolff have come up with an elegant way of addressing this problem. In general, the theorists discussed in the following sections have addressed a number of the problems with class theory presented here, and an analysis of their positions will pave the way to a discussion of the reasons for which class analysis, despite the problems noted here, can still provide useful insights into the nature and working of the capitalist system.

Eric Olin Wright on class

An interesting project underlies Eric Olin Wright's analysis of class structure. In his writings (1989 and 1997, for example) he attempts to make

Marxian class theory operational at a microeconomic level. Much of his work addresses the problem of how to conceptualize the position of the so-called "middle classes," including professionals, state employees, and so forth. Wright explains his objectives as follows:

> The central thrust of my work on class structure has been to try to produce, within a broadly Marxist theoretical framework, a class structure concept capable of being used in analyses of micro-level processes at a relatively low level of abstraction. It has been driven by two overarching questions: first, how can we best explain the empirical variations in patterns of class formation across advanced capitalist societies? and second, under what conditions are class formations likely to embody projects of radical social change? My assumption is that any viable democratic socialist politics in advanced capitalist societies must contend with the formation of durable political coalitions between segments of the "middle class" and the working class. Overly abstract and macro-level concepts of class structure do not seem to provide the categories necessary for exploring such coalitions.
>
> (Wright 1997: 43)

In order to pursue his project, Wright recognizes that the concept of class must be made more nuanced, more complex, in order to address a variety of difficulties posed by the simple class dualities, including especially capitalist–worker, that much of the Marxian literature has emphasized. He introduces the needed complexity in several ways, recognizing that his analysis is a work in progress, and that different conceptualizations seem more suited to addressing different problems.

First of all, Wright recognizes "that individual jobs can, in different ways, have multiple, and sometimes even *contradictory*, class characters" (1997: 45). Thus, for example, Wright notes that managers "could be understood as simultaneously in the working class and the capitalist class: they were in the working class insofar as they had to sell their labor power in order to obtain their livelihood; they were in the capitalist class insofar as they dominated workers within production" (ibid.: 52–53). Wright recognizes further that the class position of many individuals is *mediated*. That is, they derive their class status, at least in part, from others, or, their class status is determined by the role they play within capitalist society. Thus, for example, children, retired people, and others not in the labor force may derive their class status in part from that of family members, whereas employees of the state may be thought of as related to the capitalist enterprise working class through participation in the same labor markets; or elite state employees who follow career trajectories that carry them back and forth between the public and private sectors and have the ability to capitalize surplus income can be thought of as holding class positions comparable to that of senior managers of capitalist enterprises, although their positions are mediated rather than direct (ibid.: 68).

Further complications can arise from differential life experiences. There may be two workers, one of whom remains a worker while the other becomes a senior manager. The senior manager in turn may have an income well above the maintenance level defined by subsistence, and put his/her savings to work accumulating capital (alternatively, the same individual may receive stock options or restricted stock). Such temporal factors are complicated even further when we recognize the fact that there may be no means of distinguishing between the two workers initially, or in a different way when we recognize the fact that certain career trajectories may routinely involve experience at a variety of working-class jobs prior to elevation into the ranks of management.

As a result of his rethinking the issues of class structure, and of the "middle" classes especially, Wright recognizes the possibility of *contradictory locations*, with particular jobs incorporating elements of working class, capitalist class, or petty bourgeois class status (with the latter reflecting the situation of independent proprietors). The latter group would include—among others—professionals such as doctors who may be wage earners but who would have, at least in principle, the option of going into business for themselves. Following the work of John Roemer, Wright also recognizes the possibility of individuals earning monopoly rents through their scarce skills or organizational positions, and who therefore have the possibility of accumulating sufficient capital to enter the capitalist class. In effect, these rents form the basis for what Wright calls *secondary exploitations*, differing from but related to those based on capital ownership.

In addition to these class-differentiating factors, Wright also recognizes the *mediated locations* and *temporal trajectories* discussed above. In conclusion, Wright suggests that "[i]nstead of a simple historical vision of the epochal confrontation of two class actors, we have a picture of multiple possible coalitions of greater or lesser likelihood, stability and power, contending over a variety of possible futures" (1997: 71).

The efforts of Wright to grapple with the problems raised for class theory by the existence of a large and growing "middle class" in the capitalist countries helps to highlight many of the problems inherent in the oversimplified dualistic class model employed in some of Marx's writings and repeated in much of the Marxian literature. At the same time, some of the problems with class theory I have discussed previously remain. The complexity introduced by Wright has the advantage of making analyses potentially more realistic and applicable to the interpretation of actual class structures. At the same time, Wright's main objective of making possible class coalitions leading toward progressive social change may be undermined by the open-ended possibilities for fragmenting economic groups into different class subcategories, and the weaknesses of class identity as a motivating force for individual action are highlighted by his approach. I will return to a more comprehensive critique of all the class theorists discussed after presenting some of the important contributions of Wallerstein and of Resnick and Wolff.

Immanuel Wallerstein on class

Immanuel Wallerstein places the analysis of capitalist classes within the framework of his overall analysis of capitalism as a world system. Since Wallerstein characterizes that system as the production of commodities for sale on the world market, he sees the capitalist and working classes as global in scope. His analysis does not start with the division between the bourgeoisie as the owners of capital on the one hand and "free" workers selling their labor power on the other. Rather, he focuses on the process of the direct producers receiving the value of their labor power and an exploiting class of capitalists receiving the surplus value they produce. According to Wallerstein, a variety of different mechanisms of labor control is possible and used in capitalism, ranging from slavery and indentured servants to "free" labor. The methods of labor control vary, but all are encompassed within the capitalist system as long as production for sale is emphasized.

According to Wallerstein's analysis, wage labor has long been used, but direct-producing families have traditionally received their income from a variety of sources, ranging from subsistence farming and handicraft production for direct sale to wage labor. Over time, the process of *proletarianization* is one in which wage labor becomes increasingly important as a share of the total subsistence income. Wallerstein observes that the payment of wages may be among the most costly methods of paying workers their subsistence allotment, but it reduces the costs of supervisory labor. From the standpoint of the sustainability of the capitalist system, the ongoing contradiction between capitalists seeking to minimize their costs and the need for growing purchasing power to enable them to sell their products is eased by the growth of wage income.

In Wallerstein's view, the bourgeoisie are "those who receive a part of the surplus value they do not themselves create and use some of it to accumulate capital" (Wallerstein and Balibar 1991: 117). By contrast, "the proletariat are those who yield part of the surplus they produce to others. In this sense there exists in the capitalist mode of production only bourgeois and proletarians. The polarity is structural" (ibid.: 120). Since, in Wallerstein's view, exchange can be a means of appropriating surplus, proletarians can include (in addition to wage workers) petty producers, middle peasants, tenant farmers, sharecroppers, peons, and slaves (ibid.). Thus Wallerstein's conception of class is divorced from the mode of production and focuses exclusively on two groups in society: those who produce surplus value and those who appropriate it.

Given this conceptual base, Wallerstein can argue that "at a certain level of expansion of income and 'rights', the 'proletarian' becomes in reality a 'bourgeois', *living off the surplus value of others* . . . The twentieth century bureaucrat/professional is a clear instance of this qualitative shift" (Wallerstein and Balibar 1991: 122). By (1) dividing the entire world into two classes, the producers and appropriators of surplus value; (2) including the process of "unequal" exchange among the mechanisms for appropriating the surplus produced by others; and (3) by including within his conception of capitalism a wide variety of methods of labor control, Wallerstein has no problem dealing with the so-called middle classes. They are, for him, simply part of the bourgeoisie, and their relatively large numbers in the industrialized countries are offset by the larger number still of proletarians in the world's peripheral states: all are incorporated within a single social system—the capitalist world economy.

Resnick and Wolff on class

Stephen Resnick and Richard Wolff have developed the most sophisticated and nuanced conception of class among modern theorists writing in the Marxian tradition (1987, 1996, 2002). They are highly critical of the manner in which various theorists have used the concept of class without clarifying the core assumptions underlying their usage. According to Resnick and Wolff, class theorists have tended to emphasize concepts of class that are based on ownership, power, consciousness, or a composite of two or three of these elements. They find all of these approaches to be unsatisfactory, as well as the source of a great deal of confusion. Thus, for example, when the Soviet Union eliminated the ownership of private property in the means of production, class theorists who focused on ownership argued that a fundamental social shift had taken place and class society eliminated. On the other hand, those who focused on power, argued that a state elite had simply replaced private capitalists as the source of exploitation of the direct producers.

Based on their reading of the mature Marx, especially on volumes II and III of *Capital*, Resnick and Wolff argue that class can be most usefully conceptualized as the production and distribution of surplus labor (or, what is the same thing, surplus value). They argue accordingly that under capitalism there is a *fundamental* class process, in which surplus value is produced. This is a value of output that exceeds the (socially determined) subsistence requirements of the direct producers. In the fundamental class process there are the (direct) producers and appropriators of surplus value. This process does not take place in isolation, however; there are many necessary conditions required to allow it to take place.

Thus, for example, in a capitalist enterprise producing, say, consumer goods, there will be people responsible for purchasing, marketing, security, accounting, hiring, and so forth. Without such people the enterprise could not operate. Further, it makes no difference whether the enterprise outsources many of these functions or carries them out internally. It can hire an outside firm to provide security or it can hire its own security guards; similarly, it can hire an outside employment firm or use its own personnel department to recruit directly. In either case, it must transfer a portion of the initially appropriated surplus value to the individuals providing such services; Resnick and Wolff refer to this as a *subsumed* class process. Despite the terminology, the fundamental and subsumed class processes are equally necessary; neither can take place without the other.

In addition to the fundamental and subsumed class processes, Resnick and Wolff recognize a set of nonclass processes that are needed to enable the fundamental class process to proceed: these include political, economic, natural, and cultural processes. A political process might involve the maintenance of a legal and court system, or an economic process the maintenance of a central bank responsible for setting interest rates. To the extent that individuals are needed to run such institutions, a portion of the surplus labor will have to be transferred to them as well. This might be done through fees or taxes required of the capitalist as recipient of the surplus labor in the fundamental class process. In this way, the fundamental class processes, the subsumed class processes, and the nonclass processes interact to constitute social reality.

The elegant class analysis presented by Resnick and Wolff enables us to overcome many of the problems I have noted above. Since their focus is on class as a process rather than on particular groups of people, it poses no problem to deal with the fact that people may—and typically do—participate in numerous class processes. The problem of how to categorize the middle or professional classes disappears if we think of class as an adjective rather than as a noun specifying particular groups. Thus the capitalist who receives the surplus value created by the direct producers and distributes it to various providers of the conditions necessary for such production is participating in both the fundamental and subsumed class processes, while a human relations specialist employed by the firm is participating in the subsumed class process as a recipient of a portion of the surplus value.

Problems with existing class theory

Problems remain with each of the class theories discussed above, both in terms of their internal logic and in terms of the problems one would encounter in any effort to apply them to the reality of contemporary capitalist society. Eric Olin Wright properly recognizes the inadequacy of any simple duality to portray this reality, and his attempt to theorize the place of the "middle" and professional classes is certainly a welcome one. Unfortunately, as Wright himself recognizes, one approach makes it possible to address certain problems, while other approaches facilitate dealing with others. He is therefore unable to present a consistent, unified theory (and Wright himself is well aware of this; 1997: 42).

As I have mentioned, one of the approaches Wright uses is to recognize the possibility of contradictory locations, as for example when a manager sells his labor power to his employer but at the same time exercises power over the workers beneath him. Wright himself recognizes several problems with this approach (1997: 54). First, he treats exploitation as the central element in defining the material interests that determine class location, but the exercise of power rather than exploitation *per se* becomes central in defining those in contradictory class locations. Second, again following Wright's self-critique, employment by the state is not directly addressed. Finally, although Wright makes reference to "semi-autonomous employees," he acknowledges the difficulties in operationalizing this concept.

To address the shortcomings associated with his concept of contradictory locations, Wright introduces the concept of multiple exploitations. Following the work of John Roemer, he distinguishes four types of assets, each with its own unique form of exploitation; unequal ownership of or control over the different assets enables the exploiting class to appropriate part of the socially produced surplus (1997: 55). The four types of assets and the corresponding forms of exploitation are labor power assets (feudal exploitation), capital assets (capitalist exploitation), organization assets (statist exploitation), and skill or credential assets (socialist exploitation). Wright observes that there are several advantages to this approach compared to the contradictory locations approach, such as an ability to understand the role of professionals as appropriating part of the surplus thanks to their monopoly over certain skills rather than to the self-directed nature of their work within enterprises.

At the same time, Wright recognizes serious problems with the multiple exploitations approach. He notes, for example, that in principle managers who are exploited by capital, but benefit as "organizational exploiters," should have an objective interest in eliminating capitalism and promoting "the creation of a society within which organizational exploitation is the primary basis of class relations" (1997: 57). Since managers, and especially senior managers, tend to be strong supporters of the capitalist system, such a conclusion appears to fly in the face of common observation and common sense.

In the final analysis, Wright correctly discerns the need to analyze contemporary capitalist society using a model of class relations that goes well beyond the simplistic duality of the two-opposing-class model to incorporate the so-called intermediate classes. In attempting to do so, however, he is unable to come up with a consistent theoretical framework. One possible problem with his approach may stem from the fact that he starts out with the desire to use class analysis to identify possible class coalitions that will support progressive social change. Since classes, as Hindess notes, cannot be "social actors," however, it is entirely possible that Wright's quest is quixotic, that the sources of ultimate change in the capitalist system will lie somewhere outside the sphere of class action or class coalition.

The starting point of Wallerstein's analysis is quite different from that of Eric Olin Wright, as well as from that of Resnick and Wolff. Wallerstein starts with the capitalist world economy (CWE) as his sphere of analysis, rather than with the capital–labor relation in the individual enterprise. There are both strengths and weaknesses inherent in this different approach. As the global integration of economic activity becomes an increasing reality, conceptualizing economic activity and corresponding class structures in terms of the world economy has obvious appeal. At the same time, the simple lumping of the entire world into two groups, the exploiters and the exploited; the lumping together of all those producing surplus value, whether they are workers, serfs, or slaves; and the lumping together as bourgeois all those who receive any part of the surplus value ostensibly created by the direct producers, inevitably creates numerous problems and conceptual confusions.

In the first instance, when classes are identified as particular groups, the concept of class has usually been tied to particular modes of production (MsOP), such as the capitalist MOP (capitalist–worker), the feudal MOP (lord–serf), the landlord–tenant MOP, and so forth. Wallerstein's treatment completely ignores these relations of production and focuses rather on the extraction or receipt of surplus labor. Further, since this process in Wallerstein's world can take place via exchange, the peasant in Latin America who produces coffee and sells it for less than its "value" is a member of the proletariat, while a doctor who drinks the coffee in the US paying less than its value is a member of the bourgeoisie. If the focus is purely on the beneficiaries and victims of the CWE this approach may have some merit, but by moving the locus of class away from MsOP it does little to illuminate the dynamic forces driving contemporary capitalism. In a sense, class here is based really on levels of consumption. Moreover, even the assumption of exploitation implicit in this example requires qualification—although this is generally true within the Marxian framework—since it is entirely possible that without producing coffee, the peasant would be materially worse off (indeed, this is likely the case if his labor is not coerced).

In the class analysis of Resnick and Wolff, the problems are of an entirely different kind. Despite the logical consistency and theoretical sophistication of their approach to class analysis, a number of problems become apparent in attempting to apply it to interpreting the reality of contemporary capitalism. Here I would like to focus on three in particular. First, by turning class into an adjective rather than a noun identifying distinct groups of people in potential conflict, the power of class analysis to illuminate such conflicts is dissipated. Agreed that given the complexity of contemporary industrialized capitalist society, the nature of class conflict is much murkier than it was in earlier centuries. Nevertheless, it can reasonably be argued that the analysis of class conflict provides core insights into human history and social change, and that focusing on class as process rather than as distinct groups of people defined by their relation to a particular mode of production weakens the possibility of attaining such insights.

The Chinese revolution, for example, can be thought of largely in terms of the Communist Party representing the interests of the landless, poor, and middle peasants, together with the much smaller class of industrial workers, confronting the Nationalist Party (Guomindang) as the representative of the interests of the capitalists, (larger) landowners, rich peasants, and senior government officials. Much of the conflict in Central America in the second half of the twentieth century can be understood in terms of the class conflict between the large landowners and the peasantry. To think of class in terms of processes rather than in terms of specific groups undermines our ability to evaluate the role of class conflict in historical change.

A second problem with the framework for analysis provided by Resnick and Wolff derives from their focus on surplus labor or surplus value, itself a core part of Marxian value theory. Marx's analysis emerged from a society shaped by the industrial revolution. The nineteenth-century capitalist could indeed be represented as the captain of industry confronting a mass of relatively undifferentiated laborers. The idea that the laborers produced value in excess of what they were paid was clearly suited to the age. Its logic is reinforced by the observation of Stephen Marglin in "What Do Bosses Do?" (1996) that it was not new forms of power or technology that drove the formation of the giant early "manufactories" but the ability to control labor and intensify it.

The image of surplus labor/value on which Marx focused, however, is much more problematic in contemporary capitalist society, where value added in the service sector has become much greater than that in the physical goods sector. Even in the physical goods sector, the nature of production has changed dramatically. Take for example the pharmaceutical industry. A few workers may be producing pills using highly automated processes. Are we to say that they are being exploited because they are not being paid the full value of their production, or that the surplus value of the pharmaceutical enterprise is being generated by their activity?

Alternatively, one could reasonably argue that the vast research activity of the modern pharmaceutical firm is the primary source of the value it creates, interacting with the demand for its products created by those hoping to be cured of disease. In general, a large portion of factory production is amenable to automation; with the spread of robots in production, completely automated factories may well be feasible in the not-too-distant future. Where factory jobs are not amenable to automation they are increasingly shifted to low-wage countries like China. In the goods sector of the economy, then, the usefulness of a surplus labor model in analyzing the economic process is quite limited, while in the service sector, ranging from transportation to education and medical care, it is even more problematic. Within the framework provided by Resnick and Wolff, the fundamental class process and surplus labor appear wherever products are sold for a profit, while all other economic and social activity is supported by a redistribution of the surplus labor. As the relative size of these other activities grows much larger than the initial surplus-generating activities, the Resnick/Wolff approach relies on an evermore-fragile basis for interpreting the wide range of economic life.

Finally, the theoretical apparatus developed by Resnick and Wolff raises additional questions regarding the Marxian concept of exploitation. One of the "scientific" contributions for which Marx has been lauded is taking the concept of "exploitation" out of the realm of the subjective and giving it objective status and measurement capability. Exploitation is simply measured by the amount of surplus labor produced by the workers, and the rate of exploitation is simply the ratio of surplus labor to necessary labor (the latter being established by the socially determined material production required for the worker to live and reproduce him/herself).

While it is clearly the case that surplus labor is the source of the capitalist's profit within the Marxian framework, it is also true but often overlooked that it vastly exceeds that profit. The Resnick/Wolff framework has the virtue of making this clear, since the surplus must be the source of *all* the necessary conditions of existence for the fundamental class process to proceed. Thus, for example, the marketing, accounting, purchasing, security services, and so forth that are supported within the firm or the public services supported by the firm's taxes are all necessary conditions for the firm's activities to proceed. Most of the surplus labor/value goes to support these necessary conditions, while a relatively small residual constitutes the capitalist's profit. The vast majority of what is called "exploitation" then goes to pay for necessary support activities without which there could be no direct production in the first place. This is *not* a logical contradiction within the Resnick/Wolff framework, but it certainly serves to further dilute any potentiality for class struggle to play a central role in the process of social change.

Class structure in capitalist society

To understand the role of class in capitalist society it may help first to put the concept of class in its proper context. We first must acknowledge the legitimacy of Hindess's argument that classes cannot be "actors," which also implies that any role for "class consciousness" will be minimal at best. That is to say, in contemporary capitalism, it is not reasonable to expect that any large class will become aware of a common, transcendent interest, and then act accordingly. This is all the more true because of all the minor classes or subclasses or class fractions—however one chooses to categorize them—that characterize contemporary society in the industrialized states.

It does remain possible that a particular class or subclass group, such as farm workers in the US or janitors in a particular city, will become conscious of a common interest derived from its position in the division of labor, and express its understanding through the medium of a labor union, political party, or other organization. In such cases, however, it should be noted that it is the union or political party that is the social actor, not the class as such.

More generally, the interests of different members of a class are apt to diverge widely, so that to imagine a common interest and a consciousness capable of discerning that interest is fanciful. Thus, for example, farm workers, airline mechanics and shop clerks can be expected to have widely divergent interests, even though all are members of "the working class." Airline mechanics, like others working for large firms, are likely to have some form of health-care coverage through their employers, while farm workers and shop clerks may well have minimal coverage or none at all. In this situation, members of the latter groups might find some form of national health coverage a high priority, while those in the former group would not. Or airline employees might welcome a high cost of air travel as a means of supporting their high wages and benefits, while the other groups would find such high costs another factor reducing their standard of living. In like fashion, if high food costs raise the incomes of farm workers, they might be expected to favor them, while the other two groups most certainly would not. To assume that common class interests may form the basis for a unified working-class consciousness simply cannot stand the test of reasonableness.

As this discussion suggests, expectations for classes becoming the central actors in social change under capitalism must be scaled back. I would suggest that classes can most reasonably be thought of in terms of the roles people assume under different modes of production. In a capitalist social formation (that is, in capitalist society), a variety of modes of production exists, with the capitalist mode of production the dominant one. Thus as well as the capitalist MOP, one will find the individual MOP (the petty commodity MOP in Marxian terms), which could include an independent farmer selling his own produce, a physician with his own practice, or an artist selling his own works. One will also find the nonprofit MOP, the statist MOP (such as a city providing its own electricity or water services), and so forth. The classes defined by participation in these different MsOP will have common as well as conflicting interests, even where they form dualities such as the capital–labor one. This conception of class is essentially a structural one—it does not rely on consciousness—and finds class to be just one of the many factors that determine individual identity.

In this sense, the conception of class I am suggesting is not essentialist—it does not assume that class is the ultimate determinant of social reality, historical change, or anything else. An extensive range of individual characteristics, personal history and social processes determine individual identity—such as gender, cultural history, family background, ethnic identity, geographical location, type of job, and so forth. Class and class processes interact with all of these to shape individual identity, consciousness, and behavior. Under certain circumstances, which are overdetermined by all of these factors and all of the social processes that affect individuals, class or another factor can come to assume an especially critical place among these various determinants. During the early stages of the Industrial Revolution, when labor was frequently unskilled or low-skilled, wages minimal, and working conditions dramatically poor, class identity came to assume an especially prominent role. Under capitalism today it cannot ordinarily be expected to assume the same role.

Should we then return to the Resnick/Wolff theorization that focuses on class processes and avoids the problems inherent in specifying classes as distinct groups of people? I would suggest not, for the three main reasons I have indicated above: (1) there are cases where it is useful to think of classes in terms of specific groups; (2) the reallocation of the vast majority of surplus labor/value to individuals providing necessary conditions for the fundamental class process indicates that most of what is treated as the fruits of "exploitation" in the Marxian framework is going to support necessary activities; and (3) the very conception of the direct producers being responsible for producing the surplus on which the entire edifice of capitalist society is built becomes problematic when we consider the increasing role of professional workers in modern production—the modern pharmaceutical firm depends far more on its professional researchers than on the few workers at the production lines largely for reasons of quality control assurance.

If Marxian value theory and its derived conception of surplus labor and exploitation are unsatisfactory, does that mean we must do away with the concept of exploitation? I would suggest not. The term has a pejorative connotation, and I would suggest that we need not be ashamed of its normative implications. Exploitation can be thought of as reprehensible employer behavior, where workers are not paid enough to live decently, where they are forced to work under hazardous conditions, for excessive hours, or in ways that are likely to damage their health. Exploitation may also involve depriving employees of health care or disability protection, and so forth. The concept of exploitation will depend in large measure on community norms, but there is no reason to shy away from it for this reason.

Returning, then, to the question of class I would like to provide three examples of class analysis under capitalism: the robber barons or oligarchs who have appeared in contemporary Russian society; the professionals; and the minimum wage workers with limited skills. The Russian robber barons appeared in the early stages of the transition to capitalism (in the early 1990s) and proceeded through various means, generally unsavory, to accumulate vast holdings of privatized state enterprises (Kotz 1997). Often they were officials or worked with officials at these enterprises to obtain for a fraction of their true value the privatized shares distributed to enterprise employees, who had no familiarity with such financial instruments and in any event needed the pittances they received just to survive. Just as corruption and theft (including colonialism) played a major role in the early history of capitalism in the West, it played a major role in the early stages of capitalism in Russia as well.

One can understand that when the nascent capitalists play such a role they rely on the unsettled state of society to achieve their ends. Once the extraordinary concentration of ownership has been achieved, however, they become increasingly concerned with the emergence of a legal system to protect property rights. If such a system is not established, they could potentially fall prey to individuals just like themselves. Understanding the logic underlying the behavior of this class helps to understand the evolution taking place in Russia today, with the gradual "normalization" of life serving to secure the status and wealth of the oligarchs.[4]

If we think of the professional classes in the West, then it may be most useful to think of them as what they are and do, rather than in terms of the contradictory class location model proposed by Wright. Wright observes that when they are employed by corporations, the professionals (managers, those with advanced degrees, and so forth) are like the proletariat in being wage workers but like capitalists in having the ability to exercise power over others. This of course is true. But why start with the capital–labor opposition? The professionals tend to receive incomes well above average, much or most of which comes from the value that their training or experience brings to the enterprise—it does not depend on "exploiting" the direct producers, who may have a minimal role in the modern enterprise in any event.

The interest of the professionals is tied to a certain extent to the success of the enterprise, but they can typically move more or less readily to another enterprise, a nonprofit or a state agency—wherever their skills are in demand. They are often in a position to save and invest, or they may receive stock options, and if their holdings of capital become substantial then they may becomes capitalists themselves or move into the *rentier* class. Another possibility is that they may go into business for themselves, including becoming consultants. The very existence of these possibilities helps to shape their understanding of the world and their behavior in it. As individuals age, however, the possibilities for mobility may become constricted, altering their outlooks accordingly. Class does not have to be understood in terms of dualities, then, and interacts with a wide range of factors, as I have suggested, to shape individual identity.

Unskilled, minimum-wage workers in the United States typically fall into the category of exploited workers; again, we do not need a Marxian definition of exploitation to categorize them in this way. The national minimum wage remained below poverty levels for decades (see Chapter 3) and fell sharply over time in real terms. These workers can be considered as exploited because even when working full time they remained in poverty, a situation worsened by the common lack of health-care coverage for themselves and their families.

In response to this situation and the lack of legislative action on a national level, the "living wage" movement broke out across the United States during the 1990s.[5] Unfortunately, the scope of the movement was legally constrained. The movement could apply pressure on local governments to raise wages sufficiently to meet basic living requirements (with a lower wage acceptable when health benefits are included), but the workers covered include only those who work directly for the local governments or who work for contractors hired by the local governments. Thus a social movement has grown up to protect the interest of workers who are exploited, with the social (not class) consciousness generated by the movement possibly leading to broader social changes in the future.

In each of these examples class analysis provides some insight into the working of capitalist society. A final example of the potential usefulness of class analysis can be found in the political sphere. In European countries more than in the US, some left-of-center political parties have strong union support; in Germany, many legislators are actually union representatives. These politicians typically conceive of themselves as representing working-class interests. In the United States, the Republican Party by and large represents the interests of capital, as reflected by the Party's dominant thrust to limit social benefits and cut taxes, on both capital and high-income earners especially. It is of course possible to push this point too far; many Democrats represent the interests of trial lawyers or other special interests, and even among Republicans there is a wing of the Party (currently in serious decline) that espouses fiscal conservatism and a kind of *noblesse oblige* stance with regard to the welfare of less fortunate members of society. These qualifications notwithstanding, to think of the Republican Party as representing the interest of the capitalist class primarily, whether that comes in conflict with the interests of working women, of environmentalists in protecting the environment, or of workers receiving a living wage, is a useful approximation in understanding the dynamics of American capitalism.[6]

Class structure and surplus use

In thinking about the class structure in contemporary capitalist countries there are distinct advantages to dropping the assumptions that classes can be understood in terms of simple dualities, that classes are potential "actors," and that historical change can be understood essentially as driven by class conflict. Moreover, if Marxian value theory—built around the concept of direct laborers being responsible for all value creation, and thus for the creation of surplus labor/value—provides an unsatisfactory basis for understanding value creation in the contemporary world, it will be difficult to justify any class theory derived from it.

Given these considerations, how can class concepts be used to understand the dynamics of contemporary capitalism? Perhaps one can start with the observation that class is one of the multiple processes that shape individual identity and motivate behavior. Different classes may find some aspects of their relations mutually supportive and some aspects adversarial, and either aspect can emerge as dominant at different times. As social change takes place over time, classes change, their roles change, and other factors that interact with class to shape social behavior and outcomes may gain or lose significance. More specifically, as capitalism changes and repeatedly reinvents itself, classes are subject to change. Thus in early capitalism the merchant capitalist predominated, in the era of industrialization the industrial capitalist predominated, and in the current era of large firms and bureaucratic enterprises, the managerial/bureaucratic capitalist becomes the representative capitalist—although not of course the sole one.

Is it ownership or power, or a mixture of the two, then, that defines the position of capitalist in the modern era? To address this question it may help to return to the concept of the surplus. In any society, the elite class is the one that determines the use of the surplus, the share of national income that exceeds the (socially determined) subsistence requirements of the entire population. Under modern capitalism we can identify four distinct groups that have this capacity:

1 the owners of property (corporations, land and intellectual property);
2 certain providers of high-priced services (for example, top managers, certain doctors and lawyers, leading investment bankers and business agents, and so forth);
3 star athletes and entertainers;
4 other groups (for example, leading criminals).

The empirical evidence locating individuals within these four categories can be found in luxury consumption, high levels of saving, or (more usually) both.

For a group to constitute a class, however, more than high income is necessary. There must be a mechanism to transmit the capacity to sustain privileged status and unearned income intergenerationally. Under "communism" in the former Soviet Union this was carried out by the maintenance of the *nomenklatura* (literally, list of names), which provided a listing of individuals eligible for appointment to the highest positions in society; naturally the children of leading party members were always included on this list. Under capitalism, of course, inheritance is the primary mechanism for creating and sustaining class status intergenerationally.

Given the importance of inheritance in creating and maintaining class status under capitalism, those in groups 2–4 identified above must find a means of transforming their high incomes into capital; that is, into joining group 1. Thus, for example, we find many star athletes investing in businesses, or entertainers taking an ownership stake (including a percentage of the revenues earned) in the films, music, or other media they help to create (we also find criminal groups investing in real estate or other legitimate businesses). Under capitalism, then, the ownership of property plays a special role in *securing* class status, but power, talent, and other factors may play a central role in securing a disproportionate share of the surplus in the first place.

In any event, given this approach to class, we can see that class structure is always in flux to a certain degree, and that class can interact with a wide range of factors in shaping individual behavior and social outcomes. Under certain circumstances, the ownership of capital creates a class interest that conflicts with the interests of labor (for example, in paying wages that are as low as possible). Under other circumstances, capital may share the interests of labor (in an environment of robust demand, for example, capitalists may benefit from paying wages high enough to secure labor peace, labor force commitment to the enterprise, and so forth). Further, among the owners of capital, interests may diverge sharply, as between the owners of commercial property interested in maximizing their rents, and the enterprises renting the facilities, interested in minimizing their payments.

Under capitalism, control over the surplus can yield dramatically different results in different societies depending on the other factors that interact with property ownership to shape individual consciousness and social outcomes. Thus, in continental Europe the welfare state emerged, including national health insurance and many basic benefits widely considered to be the birthright of human beings. In the United States, by contrast, it is generally considered all right for poor people to lack medical and dental care so as to minimize the tax burden on high income and capital. There is no class explanation for this difference in types of capitalism; the difference must be understood in terms of the multiple forces creating individual (and thereby social) identity, forces among which class is only one.

In understanding the forces driving change within the capitalist system, then, it is a serious error to place class struggle at the forefront. Classes exist within capitalist society and class struggle does as well, but only as one of the numerous forces shaping individual identity and social behavior. To ascertain the primary contradictions driving change within the capitalist system it is necessary to take a more structural approach, starting with the accumulation imperative that drives the system forward. As I have emphasized in Chapter 1, a world with limited resources and limited pollution absorption capacity cannot sustain an indefinite increase in throughputs; that is, it cannot sustain an indefinite increase in production, consumption, and waste generation. Yet that is what capitalism produces. Barring systemic change, there are two possible ways in which this contradiction can play out. One is the end of human life on earth. The other, far more likely in my view, is the end of human life as we have known it, perhaps with the oceans turning increasingly into vast dead seas and human beings changing their living patterns so as to avoid the deadly rays of the sun as the protective outer ozone layer increasingly disappears from the earth's atmosphere. The contradiction between capitalism and the environment will be taken up in greater detail in Chapter 7.

7 Capitalism and the environment

In the 1960s, social movements against racial inequality and the Vietnam War gained traction on a national scale in the United States. The activist generation spawned by these movements soon turned its attention to feminist and environmental issues as well. And the "green" movement quickly spread throughout the industrialized world, with environmentally oriented green parties appearing in many countries, while nonprofit organizations devoted to environmental preservation proliferated. In economics, environmental economics emerged as a distinct subdiscipline, focusing for the most part on using the techniques of conventional neoclassical economics to address environmental problems. Although environmental economics sometimes extended its reach to include broader questions concerning the relationship between human beings and the biosphere, these more unorthodox concerns became the primary focus of ecological economics.

Starting from the 1960s, a substantial literature has emerged addressing environmental and ecological concerns. Whereas in its early years much of this literature dealt with pollution writ small—the disamenities associated with excessive noise, the pollution of local waterways, traffic congestion, and so forth[1]—the larger issues of environmental destruction soon began to receive increasing focus. The world became conscious of global warming, deforestation, desertification, the disappearance of species, the destruction of the outer ozone layer (leading to increased skin cancer), and other alarming environmental changes. Extensive writings, both inside and outside the realm of economics, brought these issues to the attention of the public. Within economics, however, relatively little attention was paid to the ways in which the capitalist economic system affects the environment. The journal *Capitalism Nature Socialism*, Martin O'Connor's edited volume, *Is Capitalism Sustainable?* (1994), and John Bellamy Foster's *Ecology Against Capitalism* (2002) are obvious exceptions, but most writings in environmental and ecological economics have tended to consider the issues they address outside the context of economic systems. My concern in this chapter is to consider environmental issues from the standpoint of the global capitalist system in which they are embedded.

At the outset, several disclaimers may well be in order. I am making no claim for the environmental superiority of the so-called socialist (actually "statist" is a more appropriate term) economies. Under Soviet-type economies, growth received even more emphasis than under their capitalist counterparts, and the fate of the managers charged with carrying out the economic plans was intimately tied to their ability to meet plan targets. Since most production consisted of intermediate products destined for other producing units, and since the absence of a market system generally precluded finding alternative sources of supply, the consequences of failing to meet one's target would reverberate throughout the economy. Under these conditions, and given the frequent rotation of senior managers, it is not surprising that environmental concerns were not a priority for most managers—or that environmental destruction in Soviet-type economies was even more virulent than it has been under capitalism.

I would also like to make clear that although I have definite ideas about how the environmental problem might be approached, the focus of my discussion in this chapter is meant to be positive rather than normative. That is to say, my intention is to clarify the ongoing role that capitalism plays in the destruction of the environment, and the reasons for which capitalism is compatible with neither preservation of the environment nor the perpetuation of human life on earth as we have known it. If, as I have suggested seems likely, capitalism persists for several more centuries, the challenge will be to minimize the damage until post-capitalist society can emerge.

Environmental destruction as the core contradiction of capitalism

In the writings of Marx, class conflict emerges as the central force driving historical and systemic change. As I have suggested in the chapters on the social structures of accumulation, however, capitalism has shown itself to be capable of repeatedly reinventing itself and recovering from contradictions tied to the social relations of production. The contradiction posed for capitalism by the environment, however, is an entirely different matter.

Conceptually, the contradiction is rather easy to visualize. The biosphere consists of the earth and all the species that inhabit it. The earth is almost "fixed" in its resources and capacity to absorb wastes. The principal exception to this is the ongoing potential for additional energy inputs stemming from the sun. A single species, humankind, cannot expand indefinitely in number and in throughputs (production, consumption, and the generation of wastes in both activities) in an essentially fixed environment. The end result can only be the destruction of that environment and of all the species that rely upon it.

Yet capitalism must expand to survive. Much as a bicyclist must keep going forward to maintain his/her balance, the capitalist system, with accumulation at its core, must continue to expand in order to exist. Capitalism is predicated on the pursuit of profit by individual capitalists and firms. Part of profit maximization involves minimizing costs, but these cannot be reduced below zero. Another part of profit maximization includes increasing output and revenues. On the surface, there is no apparent limit to this. Economic growth—the ongoing increase in throughputs—is thus central to the capitalist project. The contradiction emerges, however, because indefinite growth cannot be accommodated within the fixed environment defined by the limitations of the earth.

We would expect such a contradiction to be expressed in numerous forms well before it has reached its climax. Evidence that this is happening is already all around us. Consider, for example, global warming. As fossil fuels are burned, the amount of carbon dioxide in the atmosphere increases significantly. The result is a "greenhouse effect," in which heat from the sun that would ordinarily be reflected off the surface of the earth and dissipated in the solar system is retained in the atmosphere, leading to global warming.[2] As Richard Norgaard writes:

> Global climate change is expected to result in an average increase in temperature of between 1.5 and 4.5 degrees centigrade (2.7 and 8.1 degrees Fahrenheit) by the year 2030. Average temperatures during the last ice age were only 5 degrees centigrade lower than now . . . The increase will be much greater than average in the middle of continents and toward the poles . . .
>
> A 1.5 to 4.5 degree centigrade increase in temperature is expected to produce a sea level rise of 20 to 140 centimeters. A 50 centimeter rise would displace 16 percent of the population of Egypt and a comparable percentage in Bangladesh. Species in coastal ecosystems in many places will be severely stressed by the rapidity of the change.
>
> (Norgaard 1994: 13–14)

Norgaard goes on to detail a variety of other serious environmental problems. In many cases, environmentally destructive actions already carried out will continue to have consequences throughout the current century and beyond. Thus the impact of chlorofluorocarbons (CFCs) and other trace gases that deplete the outer ozone layer in the atmosphere will continue to do so for decades despite belated international agreements to phase out their production.

The problem with CFCs highlights a broader problem with environmental pollutants. It is often the case that the introduction of new substances or technologies creates long-term environmental consequences that are not well understood. At present, for example, a great deal of attention has been paid to the use of hydrogen as a potentially nonpolluting fuel that would yield only water as a by-product of its combination with oxygen. Were hydrogen to replace fossil fuels, it would appear as though the environmental benefits would be substantial. Recent research, however, suggests that the environmental consequences of such a switch might not be entirely benign.

If hydrogen were widely adopted, including for use as an automotive fuel, great volumes of the gas would have to be piped over long distances. Based on the experience with other gases, significant leakages would be inevitable. Further, if hydrogen becomes the energy of choice in the future for households as well as for cars (as seems quite likely to happen during the coming decades), widespread leakages from storage are likely as well. As molecular hydrogen enters the stratosphere it will interact with other gases to form water vapor and ice. This in turn will act as a catalyst to accelerate the destruction of the ozone layer.[3] Whether technological developments will lead in this direction is not the point. Rather, to support the growth process on which the viability of capitalism relies, new technologies are routinely deployed on a massive scale with little understanding of their environmental consequences.

Economic growth is essential for the capitalist system for social and political reasons as well as for firms' pursuit of rising profits. Economic growth diverts popular attention from existing inequalities in the distribution of income and wealth. Those who feel their material conditions are improving are less likely to begrudge the prosperity of the wealthy. Moreover, if they feel that they themselves or their children might have the opportunity to attain great material success—even if the actual probabilities are quite small—then they are more likely to support the perpetuation of capitalism. For this reason, some degree of mobility increases the legitimization and thus the stability of the system. On the other hand, the failure of economic growth would result, potentially, in massive unemployment, serious economic hardship, and delegitimization of the system.

For social and political reasons, therefore, as well as for the evident economic ones, capitalism without growth is unimaginable. At an ideological level, the idea of progress as open-ended, an idea that rose to prominence during the Enlightenment and gathered force during the Industrial Revolution, creates an intellectual climate within which the pursuit of economic growth goes largely unquestioned. Thus, capitalism's economic growth project is sustained by mutually reinforcing economic, social, political, and ideological elements. The problem raised by open-ended economic growth, however, is that ultimately it cannot be sustained in a constrained environment, that posed by an earth which is unlikely to expand at all.

Long-run possibilities

Dinosaurs lived on earth for some 165 million years—from approximately 230 to 65 million years ago. Modern human beings, by contrast, have been around for a few millennia and capitalism as the dominant social formation for about four and a half centuries. Yet in this comparatively short span of time we have wreaked havoc on our environment, engaging in a whirlwind of destruction that is if anything accelerating in intensity (despite limited national and international efforts at environmental preservation). One of three broad outcomes may emerge from the current situation. These include the self-destruction of the human species (together with many other species), human adaptation to ongoing environmental degradation, and the emergence of a modified stationary state (MSS).

Self-destruction, unfortunately, is not very difficult to envision. Despite efforts to contain the spread of nuclear weapons, such weapons have continued to proliferate since the United States first used them in the 1940s. Nuclear weapons provide just one example of the development of technology under capitalism accelerating beyond the capacity of the social system to control its use. The broader problem posed by competitive capitalism is the introduction of new substances and wastes into the environment without any clear idea of their long-term consequences. No one can predict with certainty whether global warming or other changes in the atmosphere associated with rapid economic growth will eventually render the earth uninhabitable. But if we compare the duration of modern human life on earth with that of the dinosaurs, and consider the amount of damage that has already been done, then the outlook for the very long term is anything but reassuring.

Perhaps much more likely than species self-destruction, at least over the next century or two, is adaptation to the ongoing degradation of the environment. Most of the world treats the oceans as a vast sewer, suitable for dumping wastes in every imaginable form. It is not difficult to envision the oceans a few centuries hence as vast dead seas, suitable for navigation and nothing else. With the development of inland aquaculture, fish can be raised in interior ponds, and that may well be the only source of fish in the future. Also looking out several centuries, with the destruction of the ozone layer, almost any exposure to the sun may simply become too hazardous. Human beings may then decide to carry out their activities exclusively at night, or simply to move human civilization underground. In that event, giant combines might be used in agriculture, with operators in secure cabs protected from the sun. These are of course extreme scenarios, but even if the extremes themselves are not reached, some degree of movement in their direction appears probable.

Over the medium term, such bizarre adaptations appear far more likely than species self-destruction. We human beings have already proven ourselves to be remarkably adaptable. We destroy the opportunities for outdoor recreation and build gymnasiums; we pollute the beaches and build swimming pools; we destroy the ozone layer and apply sunscreen; we allow extremes of poverty and employ private bodyguards; we pollute our drinking water and replace it with bottled water. The special concern here is that the marginal adjustments to ongoing environmental degradation can result in outcomes so unpleasantly bizarre that we would never choose them for ourselves. In effect, however, if we force future generations to avoid the sun (and in the extreme case to live underground), then through our current actions and inaction we may be condemning them to such a fate.

The third possibility for resolving the current contradiction between unbridled economic expansion and the limitations imposed by the capacity of the earth is the emergence of a modified stationary state (MSS). Under such a state, the focus of economic activity would be maximizing the quality of the capital stock, including all human beings, while minimizing throughputs—production, consumption, and the generation of waste.[4] Since the concept of an MSS is so alien to conventional economic approaches it requires some additional clarification.

The modified stationary state (MSS)

There is no evidence that, beyond a certain point, increases in material prosperity are associated with increases in happiness or satisfaction.[5] This of course is not the case with basic wants or needs, such as adequate food, shelter, security and so forth. The desire for most of the products and services consumed in the industrialized countries, however, does not fall within this category. Rather, for the most part we ascertain our own well-being in relation to the consumption standards of those around us. Sixteenth-century kings did not feel themselves deprived for lack of wireless phones or automobiles, and we do not consider ourselves deprived for lack of consumer products not yet invented.

As part of the growth process under capitalism, new products are developed and marketed. People begin to feel a sense of deprivation in response to the growing prevalence of these products around them, and to the conscious manipulation to which they are subjected by advertising and marketing. When they ultimately acquire the new item, the initial sense of deprivation is eliminated and they may feel better off for a time. The process then begins anew, however, as new products or old ones with new features are introduced. For this reason, economic growth may not yield increased satisfaction or happiness over time. It may also be argued that by misleading people into an emphasis on material concerns, which in the last analysis can never be fully satisfied, at the expense of all other sources of satisfaction, popular belief in economic growth and the idea of progress may actually lead to a diminution in happiness.[6]

To raise these considerations is to stray from the assumptions that underlie conventional economics. The doctrines of consumer sovereignty and revealed preferences take as their starting point the assumption that welfare is maximized by having the production system produce goods and services in accord with consumer decisions in the marketplace. If consumers and their preferences are understood in the context of the broader cultural forces that help to shape them, however, then the starting assumptions of modern economics can be regarded only as suspect.

The *modified* stationary state represents an alternative approach to human well-being. It can never come about under capitalism; it must come about in the post-capitalist era if human life even remotely similar to what we have experienced is to be perpetuated. It has several noteworthy implications. First and foremost, production must be undertaken for the use values it affords, rather than for profit. The focus of innovation would be on minimizing throughputs rather than on maximizing output. The point would not be to bring an end to scientific creativity and innovation, but to channel it in directions that maintain and hopefully improve the ecological balance on which the maintenance of human life depends. Research into improvements in health would of course continue. Even the introduction of new products that require less material throughputs would be encouraged; an example is the replacement of land-line telephones with wireless telephones.

It is of course true that under capitalism some innovations will have the same effect. It is also true that in many cases the price system itself will buttress this effect. For example, as minerals are depleted they tend to become more costly to extract, thereby spurring the search for substitutes. Thus as fossil fuels become depleted, more inaccessible sources are tapped at higher cost, making less-polluting alternatives such as solar or wind power more competitive. The same market logic, however, provides no assurance that the alternatives will indeed be less polluting. Thus as petroleum becomes more costly, there is a growing incentive to substitute the more highly polluting coal as an energy source.

The market system also fails due to the fact that perhaps the party most severely affected by environmental degradation is future generations. The market system works via people registering their preferences through their purchase and sale decisions. There is no way, however, in which future generations can register their preferences. Further, even if there were a way for them to do so, the existence of a positive interest rate implies that the further out we look into the future, the less the weight that can be accorded to the interests of future generations. Overall, therefore, there is no reason to believe that on balance the net effect of the price system will be to promote the use of substances and technologies that are more friendly to the environment.

This leaves regulation as the principal means of protecting the environment. There are several reasons for which regulation is unlikely to be adequate. Three of the most important ones include the growth imperative in capitalist economies, the difference between the beneficiaries and the victims of polluting activity, and the problem of the global commons. The growth imperative simply reflects the fact that regulatory limitations tend to be costly, lowering profitability and incentives to invest. This in turn diminishes employment opportunities and tends to intensify social conflict. The economic, social, political, and ideological factors that accord economic growth a preeminent place in capitalist societies tend systematically to weaken efforts at environmental protection.

A second major problem reflects the fact that the victims of environmental pollution tend to be spread out among the entire population, while the beneficiaries consist of more concentrated groups with stronger immediate interests. Since democratic politics in the industrialized countries more readily reflect the interests of such groups than the general good, their interest often tends to prevail. Thus the automobile industry—with the support of its workers—successfully resists efforts to increase the average gasoline mileage of the vehicles it produces, or the imposition of additional gasoline taxes that would encourage people to buy more energy-efficient cars and trucks. Of course it is true that the broad population tends to support the industry in these positions, reflecting the fact that most people, struggling to satisfy the material desires that the system generates and more concerned with their financial situation than they are aware of environmental problems, oppose higher taxes. In general, however, economic interest groups with more specific interests, such as the oil or timber companies and their employees, groups that can make major donations to the political parties or particular candidates, have a disproportionate sway over the political process, reducing environmental protections far below the optimal level.

The final major problem with regulation concerns the global commons. Garrett Hardin published "The Tragedy of the Commons" in 1968.[7] Hardin specifically criticized the

> dominant tendency of thought [after Adam Smith's discussion of the "invisible hand"] that has ever since interfered with positive action based on rational analysis, namely, the tendency to assume that decisions reached individually will, in fact, be the best decisions for the entire society.
>
> (Hardin 1973: 136–137)

Hardin's principal example to demonstrate the inadequacy of the "invisible hand" thesis concerns the tragedy of the commons. Suppose, Hardin explains, that there is a common grazing area open to all. Each individual herdsman will attempt to keep as many cattle as possible on the commons. The situation may work for an extended period of time, even centuries, as poaching, wars, and disease keep within check the number of herdsmen and animals. When social stability is attained, however, the numbers will increase and the problem emerge.

Since each herdsman receives the entire benefit of an additional animal, but pays only a fraction of the cost of overgrazing (since that cost will be shared by all the herdsmen) there is a powerful incentive for him to keep adding animals. This is true for all of the herdsmen. The result is overgrazing and the destruction of the capacity of the commons to support any animals at all. Each individual acts rationally, yet the result is a collective tragedy.

The problem of the global commons is analogous. The atmosphere and the oceans are shared by the entire world. The impact of any single country increasing its throughputs and discharges into these ultimate "sinks" may not be large. As countries throughout the world pursue economic growth, however, the collective damage increases disproportionately. Already severe overfishing and habitat destruction has depleted the stocks of many fish and marine mammals, while increasing toxins in those that remain. The discharge of harmful substances into the atmosphere has already damaged human health and threatens much more severe consequences over time. While regulation to limit pollution is already difficult within national boundaries, in the absence of world government, it is even more difficult to address the problems of global pollution through regulatory activity. There have of course been attempts to do so, but these depend on the voluntary commitment of all nations; and many have been unwilling to make such a commitment, arguing that economic development or growth must receive primacy, or simply reflecting the power of various interest groups, such as energy companies in the West. The 2003 refusal of the George W. Bush administration to classify carbon dioxide—the chief contributor to global warming—as a pollutant provides a clear example of private interest and the pursuit of political advantage trumping both science and the public interest.[8] Under capitalism, then, there are powerful forces that limit the likelihood of far-reaching environmental protection activities under either market-based or regulatory auspices.

Since an indefinite increase in throughputs is unsustainable, and since the continuation of capitalism is necessarily linked to such an increase, capitalism is not compatible with the continuation of life on earth as we have known it. The modified stationary state (MSS) emerges as the most desirable option to protect people and their habitat, but that will be possible only in post-capitalist society. Since post-capitalist society is unlikely to emerge for several centuries, there are a number of implications for public policy in the interim.

Even without knowing the precise conditions that might make possible a transition to an MSS in the distant future, it is possible to consider several preconditions. Since my purpose here is positive rather than normative analysis, I will attempt to refrain from anything resembling detailed prescriptions. There are two broad areas, however, where I think that something must be said. The first may be regarded as self-evident. While recognizing that economic growth and environmental destruction will continue as long as capitalism does, a transition to a sustainable human condition will be facilitated by preserving as much of the biosphere as possible. Hopefully, social, political, and economic policies will accord priority to this objective.

The second area has to do with the distribution of income and wealth. It is inconceivable that those who are on the short end of this distribution, either within particular countries or in less-developed countries, would support ending the pursuit of economic growth as national or international policy. For those living in poverty, or even for those not in poverty but feeling materially deprived compared to their neighbors, the promise of economic growth is a bright one. For the transition to an MSS to be feasible there must be a great diminution in inequality and a complete eradication of poverty. For this reason the entire world has an interest in the successful development of the Third World, as well as in measures that lead to a significant reduction in inequality within individual nation-states. This argument has been made previously on the grounds of social justice, but in fact it goes beyond that as a condition for the survival of the human species.

Spaceship earth

In 1966, Kenneth Boulding published a seminal article entitled "The Economics of the Coming Spaceship Earth" (reprinted in Lippit 1996). In this article, he likened the earth to a spaceship about to depart on interstellar travel. Just as such a spaceship could not expect to add supplies once it had departed, the earth cannot—with the exception of solar power—expect to be able to add resources to its current endowment. Moreover, just as unrecycled wastes would be expected to pile up within the spaceship, fouling its environment with potentially disastrous consequences, parallel consequences can be expected for the earth's environment as throughputs increase with economic growth.

Boulding uses a series of metaphors to develop his argument and his critique of the assumptions underlying conventional economic analysis. He imagines early man as thinking of himself as occupying a small portion of a limitless plain. As early man uses up resources and generates wastes in his immediate area, he simply moves on to a new one. As population and economic activity have increased dramatically in recent centuries, however, the viability of this option has diminished. In the future, a "closed" earth will require a different relation between human beings and their environment, and a different set of economic principles.

In the "open" earth of the past, the earth of the seemingly limitless plain, people were able to engage in the "reckless, exploitative, romantic and violent behavior ... which is characteristic of open societies" (1996: 362). In comparison, Boulding argues,

> the closed economy of the future might ... be called the "spaceman" economy, in which the earth has become a single spaceship without unlimited reservoirs of anything, either for extraction or pollution, and in which, therefore, man must find his place in a cyclical ecological system which is capable of continuous reproduction of material form even though it cannot escape having inputs of energy. The difference between the two types of economy becomes most apparent in the atti-

> tude toward consumption. In the cowboy economy, consumption is regarded as a good thing and production likewise; and the success of the economy is measured by the amount of throughput . . . If there are infinite reservoirs from which material can be obtained and into which effluvia can be deposited, then the throughput is at least a plausible measure of the success of the economy. The Gross National Product is a rough measure of this total throughput.
>
> By contrast, in the spaceman economy, throughput . . . is . . . to be regarded as something to be minimized rather than maximized. The essential measure of the success of the economy is not production and consumption at all, but the nature, extent, quality, and complexity of the total capital stock, including in this the state of the human bodies and minds included in the system. In the spaceman economy, what we are primarily concerned with is stock maintenance, and any technological change which results in the maintenance of a given total stock with a lessened throughput (that is, less production and consumption) is clearly a gain. This idea that both production and consumption are bad things rather than good things is very strange to economists, who have been obsessed with the income-flow concepts to the exclusion, almost, of capital-stock concepts.
>
> (Boulding 1996: 362–363)

The logic of Boulding's argument is, for the most part, quite compelling. Suppose that everyone lived in his or her dream house, and that the dream house did not depreciate or wear out. If the population were stable, there would be no new house construction and gross domestic product would fall sharply. Similarly, if all of us had an "ideal" wardrobe, with clothes for all occasions suited to our own tastes and remaining like new no matter how many times worn, there would be no need for significant additional expenditures on clothing, and GDP would fall further. Despite the lower GDP, we would all be far better off.

In a 1951 film, *The Man in the White Suit*, starring Alec Guinness, an inventor creates a white suit that never gets dirty and never wears out. He is delighted to have solved the problem of clothing humankind, and seeks to give his invention to the world. Unfortunately, the clothing manufacturers learn of his invention and he spends the remainder of the film fleeing for his life. Their interest in maximizing throughputs is at odds with the public interest in maximizing the quality, durability, and satisfaction provided by the capital stock. More generally, the capitalist system caters to the desire of producers to maximize profits, which requires ever-rising throughputs. Individuals may experience an increase in satisfaction when they consume desired goods, but since that may follow a sense of deprivation created by product marketing, it is not always clear that there is a net increase in satisfaction if the feeling after consumption is compared to that prevailing prior to the creation of the sense of deprivation. Moreover, to the extent that consumption satisfaction is tied to the levels of consumption of those around one, increasing consumption by some may generate dissatisfaction in others, with the net result indeterminable. It should also be kept in mind that people are social beings, and as such drive much of their satisfaction from their interactions with others in their families and communities, and among their friends. To the extent that people are driven by commercial culture to pursue material gains at the expense of these personal relationships, net reductions in satisfaction are quite likely.

Boulding was aware that certain production and consumption activities can yield satisfaction in themselves. Thus, for example, eating or growing one's own food may yield satisfaction in itself, a satisfaction quite distinct from the "stock" concept of feeling well fed. Boulding points out that if we could be fed intravenously while sleeping and always feel "well fed," we might still prefer eating or growing our own food. The problem with economics, in Boulding's view, is that it almost invariably treats throughput-maximizing activities as desirable, leading to more economic growth, while systematically ignoring the benefits to be gained from maximizing the quality, durability, and satisfaction-providing capacity of the capital stock, failing to even begin to explore how to provide ways to measure the contributions made to human existence by a high-quality capital stock.

Boulding's article appeals to our reason, but it does not attempt to set the ecological problem in the context of economic-systems analysis. It is clear, as Boulding argues, that we are in the midst of a necessary transition from a "cowboy economy" to a "spaceman economy," and that economics as a discipline has yet to make the appropriate adjustment. It is also clear that this transition cannot be accommodated within the context of the capitalist system. That system has been responsible, in large measure, for the great increases in income, wealth, and well-being that at least part of the world has experienced over the past four-and-a-half centuries. The rapid growth of the "middle class" in countries like China and India over the last several decades suggests that it still has contributions to make. Nevertheless, the costs of continued unchecked growth are beginning to become palpable, and in the long run such growth cannot be sustained. That is to say, capitalism is incompatible with the continuation of human life on earth as we have known it. As I have indicated, the core contradiction in capitalism may well be its requirement that the earth provide a virtually unlimited source of inputs for ever-expanding production, and a limitless repository for the wastes generated in production and consumption. Since the earth is incapable of filling either of these roles, the accumulation process at the core of capitalism can lead only to the destruction of the system. The challenge for human society is to recognize this contradiction and take action to facilitate the transition to post-capitalist society, a process that is likely to take centuries to complete.

Neoclassical treatments of the environmental problem

Conventional economic approaches to the environmental problem fall into two broad categories. The first relies on the price mechanism to solve the problem. As resources become more scarce, their price rises and alternative resources or production methods become more attractive, mitigating the scarcity problem. Thus, for example, as oil prices rise, other energy sources—ranging from nuclear to wind power—that were initially more costly begin to become competitive. As this takes place, research into improving the alternative sources tends to pick up, bringing relative costs down even further. The same mechanism may also affect waste disposal. Thus, for example, as landfills fill up, wastes must be transported longer distances at higher costs, thus spurring recycling in various forms.

The second conventional approach recognizes the presence of market failure in many activities that have an impact on the environment. This approach often sanctions regulation as a last resort, but typically seeks to establish market-based rewards and sanctions to achieve public goals. Thus, for example, in preference to rationing gasoline or limiting the number of vehicles that may be in use, this approach might favor high taxes on gasoline to limit driving or to encourage the development and purchase of fuel-efficient cars.[9] Whenever there are (negative) externalities present—that is, whenever the activities of an individual or company cause damage to others who are not involved in the activities—intervention by the state may be appropriate. In the case of motor vehicles, they contribute to smog that makes breathing the air less healthy for the residents of a particular region, and to global warming through the emission of carbon dioxide. Besides discouraging activities (driving) which have this effect, high taxes on motor fuel may provide public funds to support research into less-polluting motor vehicles, to provide medical care to those whose health is affected adversely, or to finance mass transportation infrastructure that will lower emissions by providing alternatives to private car use.

Conventional economics is certainly correct in its understanding of the way in which the price mechanism may contribute to overcoming resource or waste-absorption deficiencies. It is also correct in its understanding of the numerous ways in which externalities can in principle be internalized (this is what happens when the driver of a car is forced to pay the true social cost of his or her activity via sharply higher gasoline taxes). Ultimately, however, neither unfettered markets nor government measures are likely to address satisfactorily the environmental destruction that has been associated with economic growth.

Consider first the impact of resource depletion, potentially combined with technological change. A good example is provided by hydrocarbons and especially petroleum products replacing whale oil as a primary source of fuel, especially for lighting. This change, which took place in the nineteenth century, reduced the cost of energy and made it far more plentiful, encouraging additional usage. With global warming accelerating as a consequence of the vast increase in the use of fossil fuels that ensued, however, the consequences for the environment have been far from benign. And with various whale species being hunted to the verge of extinction, the shift has not even ensured their preservation. The point to be emphasized in this example is that there is no reason to assume that a new product or technology will necessarily be more benign environmentally than the one it replaces. While the price mechanism does render running out of basic resources less likely, as new resources and technologies come into use, it does nothing to ensure that the wastes generated will be less harmful to the environment.

The problem in dealing with the externalities associated with market failure is somewhat different in nature. It is certainly true that within limits the market system can be manipulated to discourage environmentally damaging activities. The question remaining concerns the extent to which it is likely that it will be used in this way. There are a number of problems in this regard. First, there is the tragedy of the commons issue on a national scale. If the United States restricts the burning of fossil fuels, thereby restricting economic growth and its standard of living, there is almost no likelihood that that will restrict the burning of forests in Africa or Brazil to clear land for agriculture or grazing. With the impact on other greenhouse gases apt to remain negligible as well, the US would simply be acting like the herdsman who responds to overgrazing by limiting his own use of the commons. It would neither maximize its own welfare in the short run nor solve the problem of the commons in the long run. At the same time, those who would be inconvenienced by the cutting back on fossil-fuel use—a broad swath of the population ranging from manufacturers to car and truck drivers—are unlikely to accept the deprivation, voting out of office any government that sought to implement such a policy.

This example introduces a second broad problem that is associated with regulatory efforts to make polluters bear the full cost of the externalities they impose on the wider community. In many cases the interest of the polluters is more concentrated than that of the victims, making them a more potent source of financial and political support for limiting taxes or regulations that would force them to bear the full cost. It is of course true that where the externality is concentrated in a particular city or region, public opposition may prevent it. Thus, opposition to nuclear or other power plants in a particular region can often prevent them from being located there. In many cases, however, the special interests that benefit from polluting activities are more powerful. This can even be the case in the affected region, when, for example, employment in a timber-producing region depends on the absence of logging restrictions.

In many cases, moreover, the benefits from environmental preservation may not be immediately evident while the costs are, limiting popular support for environmental measures. Much of the United States, for example, has grown up around the use of the private motor car, which has become essential in most of the country for access to jobs, shopping, medical care, and entertainment. Anything which restricts automobile use—such as high taxes on cars or gasoline—tends to be highly unpopular. On the other hand, environmental damage is not always visible and may take place over many decades, as in the case of global warming. The tendency of the public to favor the evident benefit over the environmental one is further strengthened by spurious claims by politicians and business interests questioning the scientific basis for global warming.[10]

A third factor contributing to political inaction in the realm of environmental protection is the market failure associated with the lack of representation of the interests of future generations. Adam Smith's invisible hand assumes that the interested parties make market decisions in their own interest, thereby contributing to the general interest. However, future generations have no way in which to express their preferences. Thus, in the extreme case, decisions made today may render the earth extremely inhospitable or even uninhabitable for future generations; but those severely impacted generations can have absolutely no input on the decisions that affect them.

The difficulty in making arrangements to protect the environment is evident in the environmental degradation that is continuing throughout the world. Overfishing has severely depleted the world's oceans, making questionable the very survival of various species. Deforestation is continuing throughout the world at a fierce pace.[11] International efforts to limit greenhouse gases and thereby global warming have thus far failed to make a significant impact. The analytical approaches fostered by neoclassical economics, itself a form of ideology spawned by the capitalist system to justify its social and economic arrangements, are unable to deal adequately with the long-term devastation wrought by economic growth.

Coevolution and indeterminacy

In *Development Betrayed* (1994), Richard Norgaard adds important new dimensions to our understanding of the environmental problem, and although his focus is not on the capitalist system *per se*, the logic of his argument can readily be extended to consideration of the relationship between capitalism and the environment. In biology, coevolution refers to "the pattern of evolutionary change of two closely interacting species where the fitness of the genetic traits within each species is largely governed by the dominant genetic traits of the other" (Norgaard 1994: 26). An example is provided by certain hummingbirds having curved beaks that provide unique access to the flowers on which they feed; both the flowers and the birds have evolved in a mutually advantageous way.

Norgaard expands the concept of coevolution to include not only biological entities, but also interactions between the environment, social institutions, belief systems, values, and technology. According to his argument, each of these elements affects the evolution of all of the others in an ongoing, coevolutionary process. In his vision, these various elements—and others as well—are mutually determinative, helping to shape the evolution of all of the others over time. He cites the development of pest management in American agriculture as an example.

DDT was discovered in 1939 and, together with other organic chemicals, became widely applied in the postwar years. These chemicals were highly effective, but their very effectiveness created new problems. Since only the most resistant insects in the target populations were able to survive the new insecticides, succeeding generations contained increasingly disproportionate numbers of insects not susceptible to them. Other problems were raised in some circumstances when other harmful insects moved in to take the place of the target population, or when their predators were also killed off.

The emergence of increasingly resistant insects led to efforts to deal with the problem by increasing the frequency and intensity of spraying. This of course intensified the problems. Meanwhile, the increased introduction of toxins into the environment was proving harmful to farmworkers, bees, birds, and other forms of wildlife. Since farmworkers and bees are essential to agriculture, and since environmentalists were able to raise widespread concern over the use of DDT, legislation was passed prohibiting its use in the United States. At present, biological controls over pests and integrated pest management are increasingly used in American agriculture, but the usage of insecticides remains quite high and crop losses to insects "are about the same as they were before the use of modern insecticides" (Norgaard 1994: 26).

Underlying this history of pest management is a widespread social belief in science and progress as capable of solving all problems; in individualism and the market system as providing the appropriate guidelines; in the development and application of technology without a clear understanding of its full ramifications; and in the ongoing evolution of specific institutions such as agricultural extension services. In Norgaard's view, evolution itself is overdetermined by the myriad impacts not only of other species but also of human culture, institutions, and technology.

The belief in progress, in an ever-improving future, is a hallmark of capitalist ideology. It legitimates the ongoing pursuit of profit through expanded throughputs and minimizes concerns with unexpected externalities. Yet the very nature of coevolution, essentially another term for overdetermination but applied specifically within an evolutionary framework, suggests that the future is indeterminate. The idea of coevolution also tends to confirm the response to deepening environmental degradation that I have indicated appears to be most probable: human society will, at least in the first instance, adapt to a deteriorating environment. This may mean that many wild animals survive only in zoos, the oceans become increasingly depleted of living organisms, everyday life changes in ways that enable people to avoid the sun, or other bizarre adjustments become prevalent. There is no way to know with certainty precisely what will come about, but the direction of change is apparent. Ultimately, of course, human self-extinction cannot be ruled out either.

A response to the contradiction between capitalism and the environment

One of the most thoughtful analyses of the contradiction between capitalism and the environment appears in an essay by Thomas Weisskopf (1996) entitled "Marxian Crisis Theory and the Contradictions of Late Twentieth-Century Capitalism." The first part of this essay considers the various interpretations of Marxian crisis theory and concludes that none apply to contemporary capitalism. The second part focuses on social and especially environmental contradictions as the core contradictions of contemporary capitalism.

Of particular interest, Weisskopf goes beyond identifying the core contradictions to analyzing the ways in which they could potentially play out. With regard to the environment, he focuses first on the depletion of environmental assets. Suppose—and this is not Weisskopf's example—a country's sole asset is a forest, and its sole income comes from cutting and selling 10 percent of its (initial endowment of) trees each year. At the end of ten years its income would fall to zero. Treating its income in the preceding ten years as an indicator of the welfare of its people would be grossly misleading. In calculating national income or output, Weisskopf argues, allowance should be made for the depletion of "environmental assets." If this is done, then sustainability becomes part of the measure of the welfare-effects of production (in parallel fashion, net domestic product or NDP provides a better measure of the welfare effects of national output than gross domestic product or GDP, since it subtracts from output a measure of the capital stock used up in the production process). Weisskopf goes on to observe that

> Although it is currently still impossible to get even a rough quantitative estimate of the net depletion of environmental assets in a given society, it is not so difficult to evaluate the general direction of change. The kind of evidence cited . . . leaves little doubt that in much of the capitalist world today . . . the trend in the quality of the natural environment is downward. The last decade has witnessed increasing depletion of the atmospheric ozone layer, gradual warming of the earth's temperature, increasing destruction of tropical rainforests, major oil spills, contaminated beaches, polluted harbors and acid-rain-impacted forests and lakes, the depletion of fossil fuel reserves, the

> loss of arable land and green belts to urban and industrial expansion and waste disposal sites.
>
> All of these trends cast increasing doubt on the validity of conventional measures of macroeconomic performance as indicators of the true prosperity of contemporary economies.
>
> (Weisskopf 1996: 381)

On the one hand, conventional national income accounts fail to take into account the depletion of environmental assets. On the other, activities undertaken to prevent such depletion are treated as net increases in output, as when "scrubbers" are inserted in power plants to limit sulfur dioxide emissions and thus acid rain. In general, even while environmental assets are being depleted, environmental maintenance activities are increasing in contemporary capitalist development.

Weisskopf then turns to the question as to how these trends might be expected to impact the normal functioning of a capitalist system, and in the extreme case to threaten its viability. In this case, he raises the possibility of technological *regress* (the precise opposite of the technological progress that is ordinarily associated with capitalism). When technological progress prevails we expect more output from given inputs of capital and labor. When technological regress prevails it will require more capital and labor to attain a given amount of output. If, for example, overfishing depletes the fishing stock, more boats and crews will be required to catch a given number of fish. Alternatively, if warming of the earth's atmosphere makes farmland less productive, then more inputs of labor and capital will be required per unit of output.

Weisskopf observes that while adjustment to technological regress would be difficult in any society, it would be particularly difficult under capitalism, since the "long-run growth of material production and consumption has been an especially important vehicle for managing the social and economic tensions that would otherwise arise from the uneven and unstable pattern of economic development so characteristic of capitalism" (1996: 383). To extend Weisskopf's argument one step further, even if technological regress is not predominant but simply slows the growth of material output markedly, social and economic tensions could still be expected to grow.

If capitalist societies shift an increasing portion of their output to environmental maintenance activities, similar problems would emerge, even though the environment would be healthier as a result. Such a shift would detract from the output available for popular consumption, intensifying social and economic tensions. Moreover, since both results would be likely to decrease profitability, both would decrease the incentive to invest, lowering the accumulation rate. This in turn would raise unemployment, increase the likelihood of recessions or sluggish economic growth, and undermine the legitimacy of the capitalist system as well as its functioning.

The third response to a deteriorating natural environment that Weisskopf considers is a scenario in which few production constraints emerge, but little or nothing is done to check the deterioration. In this case the legitimacy of the system might come under question as people perceive the decrease in their well-being caused by the deteriorating environment around them. If people feel that they cannot safely swim at the beach, breathe the air, or drink the water, their support for the capitalist system might well be undermined.

In my own view, these environmental contradictions are unlikely to threaten the capitalist system in the foreseeable future. They are valuable primarily in providing ways of thinking about the system and its core contradictions. Since capitalism appears likely to persist for centuries to come, however, the effects to which Weisskopf points are likely to become more significant over time. And in the last analysis, since unlimited economic growth cannot take place within a limited space such as the earth, the human species, if it is to survive, will have to find an alternative social formation to replace capitalism.

Conclusion

It may appear that the problems I have noted are long range in nature and not likely to have a significant impact for generations. In response to this I believe that several things need to be noted, starting with the thoughtful observations of Kenneth Boulding:

> It may be said, of course, why worry about all this when the spaceman economy is still a good way off (at least beyond the lifetimes of any now living), so let us eat, drink, spend, extract and pollute, and be as merry as we can, and let posterity worry about the spaceship earth. It is always a little hard to find a convincing answer to the man who says, "What has posterity ever done for me?" and the conservationist has always had to fall back on rather vague ethical principles postulating identity of the individual with some human community or society which extends not only back into the past but forward into the future. Unless the individual identifies with some community of this kind, conservation is obviously "irrational." Why should we not maximize the welfare of this generation at the cost of posterity? "*Après nous, le déluge*" has been the motto of not insignificant numbers of human societies. The only answer to this, as far as I can see, is to point out that the welfare of the individual depends on the extent to which he can identify himself with others, and that the most satisfactory individual identity is that which identifies not only with a community in space but also with a community extending over time from the past into the future... and there is a great deal of historical evidence to suggest that a society which loses its identity with posterity and which

> loses its positive image of the future loses also its capacity to deal with present problems, and soon falls apart.
>
> (Boulding 1996: 364)

A second consideration involves the appropriate time-frame. From one perspective the four and a half centuries or so since capitalism became the dominant social formation, and the roughly half that time since the start of the Industrial Revolution, both seem like lengthy periods, extending back many generations. Yet these few hundred years are as nothing compared to the 165 million years during which dinosaurs roamed the earth. Did they know something that we do not? That of course is highly unlikely. The dinosaurs survived as long as they did because the various species among them simply adapted to the environment in which they were placed. Human beings, by contrast, are engaged in a Herculean effort to raise throughputs as rapidly as possible, with little consciousness of the speed with which we are destroying the very environment that serves as a basic condition for the continuation of human life on earth.

Since the advent of capitalism, the speed of economic growth has increased enormously. This has created comfortable living standards for an unprecedented number of people in the industrialized countries and creates comparable possibilities for large sections of the less-developed countries that are currently in the midst of their own industrial revolutions. The dynamic character of the capitalist world economy, with accumulation and innovation at its core, is likely to sustain this process and extend the benefits of development to much of the rest of the world in the centuries to come. Equally likely is an accelerated destruction of the environment on which human life depends, ultimately requiring bizarre adjustments in the way in which we live or, in the extreme case, bringing an end to human tenure on earth.

If human life in anything resembling its current form is to be preserved, the mindless pursuit of economic growth as an end in itself will have to cease. That suggests that capitalism will have to end and be replaced by some form of post-capitalist society. It does not mean that all innovation and change must end, only that the pursuit of profit and personal gain as the driving force behind human activity will have to be replaced at some point; the sooner this is done, of course, the more there will be left to preserve.

Since capitalism both generates and is sustained by uneven development and inequality, the preparation for post-capitalist society must take this into account. The preparation for post-capitalist society, therefore, requires intensified efforts to reduce inequality and to eradicate poverty—both within and among nations. Further, since the speed of environmental destruction is accelerating, intensified measures to protect the environment are in order if anything is to be left to protect. Such measures will require multi-pronged efforts at both the national and international levels, and can range from market-related measures (like fossil-fuel taxes) to enforced regulations, such as limitations on deforestation, dumping effluents into the oceans, and so forth.

I am not arguing that such actions are likely or will prove sufficient to prevent catastrophe. I am saying that capitalism is unsustainable because it destroys the very environment on which all human life depends. Over the next few centuries human beings will have to make a choice; inaction will also involve a *de facto* choice. In the final analysis, despite all the creative capacity that human beings have displayed, the capitalist world economy cannot overcome the ultimate contradiction posed by environmental constraints. If preparations for post-capitalist social formations are not set in motion, and if measures to limit environmental destruction in the interim are not accelerated, then the long-run outcome can only be catastrophic.

8 The future of capitalism

In thinking about the future of capitalism, it is perhaps most appropriate to consider the capitalist system in its historical context, and to evaluate its probable evolution in the light of its basic dynamics and internal contradictions. All of these elements were touched upon in Chapter 1, but a more fully developed assessment becomes possible following the explorations pursued in the following chapters. The core dynamic of the capitalist system is the accumulation process, a process in which a portion of the profits reaped through the sale of goods and services is reinvested, swelling the capital stock, incorporating new technologies in the process, and permitting larger sales and profits in the future.

One of the consequences of this dynamic is the significant rise in average living standards in the industrialized world, especially since the start of the Industrial Revolution. Starting in the late nineteenth century, Japan proved that successful capitalist development was not restricted to Western Europe and its New World colonies, that countries with quite different social systems could aspire to capitalist development as long as they were able to create appropriate sets of institutions. In the second half of the twentieth century, the Asian "tigers" joined the group of developed nations, and by the beginning of the twenty-first century, China was clearly on a similar path, stimulating growth throughout East Asia in its development upsurge.

While the outlook for other parts of the less-developed world remains less clear, it appears highly likely that the transformative power of the capitalist world economy will in time do its work there as well, perhaps over a period of several centuries. Since capitalists or firms are always searching for new markets and investment outlets, and for ways to limit or lower costs of production, there is a natural tendency for them to incorporate the entire world in their purview. The issue for less-developed countries is whether they will create the institutions that favor the creation and expansion of domestic firms, and attract foreign direct investment. Such institutions can range from the establishment of public education to the creation of special export zones and the provision of personal security and property rights.[1] There is no single set of institutions that is required; what is appropriate for each nation will depend on its own culture and initial conditions, as well as the current state of the capitalist world economy.

If we consider the state of the Third World early in the twenty-first century from this perspective, then it is clear that China has already launched itself on a trajectory that promises rapid capitalist development, and it appears likely that it will pull along in its wake the Southeast Asian countries that structure their institutions appropriately. Although India is well behind China in the process of economic reform and has distinctive institutional problems, many of which are tied to an excess of bureaucracy and regulation, India did set out on a reform path in 1991 and may prove capable of fulfilling the role in South Asia that China is filling in East Asia.

Latin America has its own distinctive problems. Although average gross domestic product is comparatively high in the major economies of Mexico, Brazil, and Argentina,[2] an excess of populist policies, combined with great inequalities in the distribution of income and wealth, creates unique regional barriers to rapid development. These conditions in turn have contributed to breakdowns in personal security, ongoing battles with inflation, and other ills that create an inhospitable environment for capitalist development. Nevertheless, with some of the countries enjoying favorable natural resource endowments and some capable of benefiting from free trade agreements with the United States and other countries (both in the hemisphere and outside it), and with struggles for institutional reform an ongoing feature of national life, it is not unreasonable to imagine that in time Latin America, perhaps led by countries like Brazil and Mexico, will also set out on a path to sustained development.

In other parts of the Third World, especially in Africa and the Middle East, ethnic, religious, and tribal divisions, as well as kleptocratic governments, create special difficulties in establishing conditions for successful capitalist development. Even so, if development does proceed in South Asia, if Turkey is able to join the European Union, and if political and institutional reform proves possible in the states of Africa and the Middle East, there is every reason to believe that the capitalist world economy can ultimately incorporate even these regions within its embrace. It should always be kept in mind that there is an ongoing tendency for the capitalist world economy to be outward looking, to search for new sources of low-cost labor or raw materials, as well as for new markets, so the challenge for the less-developed countries is essentially to restructure themselves in such a fashion as to accommodate the capitalist world's quest. From the perspective of the year 2300 (more or less) then, it may be possible to look back on underdevelopment as an historical phenomenon, with the capitalist system responsible for elevating and transforming living standards on a worldwide basis. It is then possible that despite all the cruelty associated with primitive accumulation under capitalism, and despite all the inequality and social injustice that the capitalist system has engendered, the historical role of capitalism will prove to be one of transforming mass subsistence into mass prosperity.

If we regard the capitalist system from this historical perspective, we can think of its precursors as lying in the acquisition of goods and provision of services for sale in the market. In the sixteenth century, merchants began to do this in a systematic and large-scale fashion, to search out new sources of supply, and to reinvest in ships, warehouses, and other capital on a significant scale, expanding their operations accordingly. The period of "merchant capitalism" came to an end with the Industrial Revolution, when capitalists themselves began to produce on a large scale for sale on the market. The development of the market system is part and parcel of the development of capitalism, with markets in labor and the means of production becoming intrinsic to the system.

Even as the capitalist system has given rise to mass prosperity in portions of the world and promises to extend that prosperity to much or possibly all of the remainder in the centuries to come, it continues to be marked by extremes of poverty, inequality, social injustice, exploitation, and personal insecurity. Since capitalism is likely to persist as the dominant social formation for the foreseeable future, one of the challenges faced by all countries experiencing capitalist growth or development is to minimize these side-effects. Unfortunately, there are certain systemic tendencies associated especially with the interaction of globalization and technological change that can be expected to magnify them, making the challenge all the more intense.

As Chapter 4 shows, globalization and technological change have numerous consequences, one of which is the strengthening of capital relative to labor on a worldwide basis. Other things being equal, this tends to make jobs less secure and to increase the returns to property, especially capital, relative to the returns to labor. Further, the more humane forms of capitalism, especially those established in the welfare states of continental Europe, are confronted by aging populations and rising dependency ratios, including especially an increase in the number of retirees relative to each active participant in the labor force. Since these welfare states rely primarily on payroll taxes to fund transfers to retired workers, they face unsustainable tax increases just to maintain existing benefits (pensions, health care, and unemployment insurance especially). Not only would the required tax increases create onerous burdens on their active working populations, the intensification of globalization and technological change have facilitated outsourcing or the "export" of jobs, so that even the maintenance of existing taxes threatens to drive firms abroad. The challenge these countries face, then, is to find ways to reduce taxes, reform labor markets, and sustain competitiveness, while preserving as much as possible the principles of social democracy, which provide a partial amelioration of the harshness of the capitalist system.

To understand more fully the dynamics of capitalism, however, it is necessary to come to grips with its core contradictions. The persistence of poverty and insecurity in the face of unprecedented productive capacity is of course one of the core contradictions of the capitalist system. These may contribute to the rise of crime and terrorism, sometimes to such an extent that the conditions for the carrying on of business activity and accumulation are hindered greatly. Social contradictions are also reflected in workplace conditions, which can be so dangerous or unpleasant as to give rise to large-scale conflict between capital and labor, especially when long hours and inadequate wages are also prevalent; this of course is what writers in the Marxian tradition have focused on. There are other contradictions that affect the evolution of capitalism as well, however, both in the intermediate term and over the long run.

The contradictions of capitalism

The intermediate-term contradictions characteristically arise in the context of social structure of accumulation (SSA) formation. Chapters 2 and 3 explored the factors underlying the tendency within capitalist countries for extended periods of relative prosperity to alternate with extended periods of stagnation or sluggish economic growth. During the periods of prosperity, contradictions arise that, interacting with "external" factors, ultimately lead to their demise. In this context, a contradiction can be thought of as something that maintains the momentum of capitalist expansion, but over time comes to undermine the very basis of that expansion. In the United States, during the post-World War II period, for example, US economic hegemony was associated with the wartime devastation experienced by potential rivals and the adoption of the US dollar as a reserve currency for the entire capitalist world. Over time, however, the strong US economy provided capital and markets for Europe, Japan, and the Asian tigers, creating conditions for them to grow rapidly and emerge as US competitors. In this way, US hegemony contributed to the emergence of conditions that would ultimately undermine it.

In general, SSAs emerge when a set of institutions that favor the accumulation process are established. Once established, SSAs tend to endure, in part because institutions are by their very nature slow to change, in part because the various institutions that comprise each set are mutually supportive, and in part because SSAs create groups of beneficiaries who seek to maintain them. All of these features were clearly present in postwar Japan, for example, where the systems of seniority and lifetime employment, the family system and the educational system interacted among themselves and with other characteristic institutions to create a period of rapid and sustained economic growth. Ultimately, however, all SSAs develop internal contradictions that undermine them, contributing eventually to their collapse and the ensuing period of more or less extended stagnation that follows.

These contradictions typically vary among countries according to the nature of their SSAs. Thus, for example, the difficulty that firms in Japan and most of Europe have in firing workers, even when they are unneeded, is not generally a problem for American firms. When the capitalist world economy was experiencing its post-World War II boom, inflexible labor markets were not a problem in Japan and Europe, since the growing demand for labor could be accommodated at modest wage rates and minimized problems of surplus labor. By the 1980s and 1990s, however, as international competition increased with the intensification of globalization and technological change, and as both the number of workers and the skills required changed accordingly, the competitive advantages a committed, skilled labor force had once provided became disadvantages. This came about as firms were forced to retain employees in excess of their needs, employees who often lacked the newly required skills and who were paid at higher-than-market wage rates. This in turn contributed to an era of sluggish economic growth in both Japan and the leading countries of Europe.

When SSAs break down, as they have in continental Europe and Japan, a more or less extended period of intensified conflicts ensues, made sharper by the very economic sluggishness that characterizes such periods. The key issue in the European countries is how to bring about economic reforms—especially reducing tax rates and reforming inflexible labor markets—while retaining the core benefits of the welfare state, benefits that ease the inherent harshness of the capitalist system. If the reforms prove inadequate, then firms will move their activities abroad or weak economic growth will deprive them of reasons for expansion. This in turn will further weaken the financial underpinnings of the welfare state.

Yet any move toward reform tends to generate widespread political opposition, since the beneficiaries of the welfare state have (in many cases) come to regard their benefits as entitlements that are independent of the capacity of the state to pay for them. As long as the opponents of reform prevail, the financial conditions of the welfare states of Europe will continue to weaken, threatening a much more severe breakdown of state financial protection in the future. The challenge facing Europe is to find a way to adjust to the economic demands created by aging populations in the era of globalization and technological change, while at the same time maintaining to the extent possible the benefits associated with the most humane form of capitalism the world has seen.

In the case of Japan, far deeper changes will be necessary. First, the Japanese population is aging even more rapidly than the European populations. Of greater importance is the fact that the institutions that sustained exceptional economic growth over the course of the twentieth century are no longer well suited to the conditions prevailing in the twenty-first century. The *keiretsu* system of industrial groups and interlocking shareholdings no longer creates particular advantages for the Japanese economy. This system worked well when economic growth could be taken for granted and securities prices were generally rising. When many members of the groups, are struggling, however, and their banks "required" to continue supporting them, the result is financial distress for the banks, the groups and the economy as a whole. Further, in an age of intense international competition and accelerated technological change, the system of offering "lifetime" jobs to generalists and making raises dependent on longevity rather than value added is no longer functional. Moreover, a household division of labor that systematically discriminates against women, and an educational system oriented largely toward slotting individuals into the corporate system, both become unsustainable when the requirements of the corporate system change.

However gradually, Japan has been adjusting to its changed circumstances, with, for example, banks beginning to merge and to sell off the shares of group members to strengthen their finances. Hostile takeover bids are also beginning to appear in Japan's banking industry, something that would have been unthinkable under the old system. The struggle for change is likely to remain a difficult one, nevertheless, as the beneficiaries of the traditional institutions, as well as those who have sacrificed to attain the benefits they promised, seek to limit change. As in Europe, the changes that come about in Japan will reflect the ongoing class struggles between capital and labor, but they will reflect as well the full range of social struggles that characterize contemporary societies, including, among others, struggles between urban and rural residents, the young and the old, men and women, independent proprietors and big capital, and those seeking to protect the environment and those seeking to exploit it.

In both Japan and Europe, there are strong grounds for expecting that new SSAs will in time be established, with economic growth once again becoming vigorous. The favorable factors include: (1) the thrust of capital to reestablish favorable conditions for reinvestment and expansion; (2) the dependency of the population on capital for employment and transfers (even though the transfers come via the state); (3) the presence of strong firms capable of competing internationally; (4) the presence of government institutions that have supported the accumulation process in the past and (with some limited changes) could well do so in the future; and (5) the existence of favorable international prospects for the world economy in the era of globalization and technological change—prospects enhanced for Japan by the emergence of China as a regional force driving accelerated growth throughout East Asia and for Europe by the ongoing expansion of the European Union (now including twenty-five countries).[3] Given these conditions, it appears quite likely that both Japan and Europe will in time be able to establish new SSAs, although the exact timing of their doing so remains open to question.

When Japan and Europe do establish new SSAs, each will involve a reinvention of their respective capitalisms. Japanese capitalism will still be distinct from European capitalism, probably with greater state involvement in the economy, while in Europe sufficient elements of the welfare state are likely to be maintained to give European capitalism a distinctive hue. At the same time, however, the new stages of capitalist development in each region will be distinguished not only from each other but from the prior stages from which each has emerged. That is to say, capitalism will once again be reinvented in both Japan and Europe, with results differing in both instances from their postwar forms.

In thinking about the future of the United States and China, both of which have established new SSAs, the most helpful approach involves considering the contradictions that, interacting with exogenous conditions, might serve to undermine them. In the case of the United States, for example, limited government has meant limited taxation, increasing incentives both for firms and individuals. It has also meant skimping on education and infrastructure, which in the long run are basic requirements for economic prosperity. Education is of special importance in the current age given the speed and scope of technological change. At some point, the contradiction between limited government and the need for education and infrastructure can be expected to have increasingly serious repercussions.

Another contradiction affecting the American economy is reflected in the loss of "good" jobs, and the growing polarization of income and wealth. This did not affect the economy as strongly as might have been expected during the decade that began in the mid-1990s because falling and low interest rates helped sustain consumer demand, with mortgage refinancing (at lower rates) playing an important role in making funds available for the full range of consumer goods and services. Interest rates cannot go down forever, though, and large and growing budget deficits in the US make the next major move likely to be upward. When that happens, it will worsen conditions for business expansion even while limiting consumer demand.

In the case of China, the primary contradictions may well be social and environmental. Successful entrepreneurs and highly educated individuals are the principal beneficiaries of China's new capitalist economy, with bribery and corruption also benefiting local officials especially. People who live in the more remote rural areas, especially in the western part of the country, have not benefited commensurately, as is the case with the floating population of perhaps 100 million people who travel from their home places to seek work. The number of underemployed in the agricultural sector may reach 150 million, and many people in the old industrial sector have lost their "lifetime" positions as old state firms, unable to compete, have been forced to cut back or close down. One of the prime imperatives of the Chinese government has been to sustain a sufficiently high rate of growth, thereby generating enough new job opportunities to keep social tensions under control. The transition to an economy capable of fully employing the population is apt to take decades, however, and the growing inequalities between those benefiting from the new economy and those still trapped in the old could intensify social tensions, requiring greater expenditures for maintaining public order or, alternatively, greater financial support for those who are presently excluded. In either event, cutbacks in the pace of investment may be required.

Another contradiction in China is reminiscent of one that marked America's postwar SSA. Rapid economic expansion is often taking place without conscious attention to the environmental disasters it is creating. High levels of pollution in China's cities and waterways, severe air pollution, and the lack of sufficient water in various regions to sustain ongoing urban growth are creating conditions that could easily undermine future growth, especially if firms are made responsible for the environmental damage they create. Once again, this is a contradiction that is continuing to evolve over time and its resolution cannot be anticipated in any specific time-frame, but it remains clear that at some point China will have to pay much greater attention to the preservation of its environment, curtailing economic growth accordingly.

The medium-term contradictions within capitalist societies are typically associated with the collapse of their social structures of accumulation. When a country's SSA collapses, a more or less extended period of intensified social strife ordinarily ends with the emergence of a new stage in its capitalist development, with the reinvention of its capitalism. The longer-term contradictions of capitalism, by contrast, are not necessarily amenable to resolution within the capitalist system. This is most certainly the case with regard to the long-term contradiction between capitalism and the environment.

The environmental contradictions of capitalism

As a general rule, when thinking about the sources of change within any system, it makes sense to begin with a consideration of its internal contradictions. Once those have been identified, attention can be diverted to the things going on in the world outside that system that are capable of interacting with it, and especially with its evolving contradictions. In the case of the capitalist system, various contradictions have been identified. The entire Marxian tradition has focused on the contradiction between capital and labor, between capitalists (or firms) and workers. In this tradition, class struggle becomes the dynamic underlying systemic change. The Monopoly Capital school, after Baran and Sweezy, has focused on the contradiction posed between a growing surplus and the inability of the capitalist system to absorb that surplus productively. In this tradition, underlying stagnationist tendencies within capitalism foretell its demise, although the actual mechanisms that will bring that about are not spelled out.

In this book I have argued, in effect, that although class contradictions are manifest, they are only one (albeit a prominent one) of numerous social contradictions, and that there is neither reason nor evidence to support the belief that stagnationist tendencies will prevail in the long run, even though they become prominent during periods of SSA collapse. In both cases—whether the contradictions are associated with class struggle or a rising surplus—the almost astonishing ability of the capitalist system to revive itself, in essence by reinventing itself with the formation of new SSAs, suggests that these contradictions play a greater role in shaping the evolution of capitalism than in determining its long-run viability. As Chapters 5 and 6 have shown, moreover, classes have become less clearly demarcated in contemporary capitalism, and the surplus may well be better characterized as having a long-run tendency to diminish than to rise. Both of these factors support the finding that class struggles and rising-surplus tendencies are unlikely in themselves to bring about the termination of capitalism as a social and economic system.

The search for fundamental contradictions in capitalism, however, has received new energy from the outpouring of environmental literature over the last four decades, and especially from the 1970s. Perhaps because much of this literature has been produced by scientists, environmentalists, and social critics with a reformist bent, the systemic ties between capitalism and environmental degradation remain under-explored. The sub-text underlying much of this literature is that abstract reason and good will can bring about remediation of the environmental problem, that the proper political policies can enable human beings to live in harmony with the ecosphere. My argument, to the contrary, is that for all the material progress that capitalism has created, it is not possible in the long run for capitalism to continue without profoundly transforming the natural world and ultimately destroying its capacity to sustain most life forms, including human life.

The worldwide environmental movement dates to the 1960s. It has resulted in some successes, such as the banning of DDT, the cessation (with some exceptions) of atmospheric nuclear testing, and sharp reductions in atmospheric lead pollution following its discontinued use in gasoline manufacture. At the same time, the overall condition of the environment has continued to deteriorate. This is true of both local pollution, such as the smog that now envelops practically all American cities of any size, and of global environmental problems, such as deforestation, global warming, and the depletion of ozone in the stratosphere. As capitalist development continues in the industrialized countries, and as it spreads over China, India (both with populations over one billion), and the rest of Asia, the prospect can only be one of intensified environmental deterioration.

Although proper policies can ameliorate and retard environmental destruction, they cannot forestall it indefinitely. Capitalism as a system requires continued expansion of throughputs, and it is not possible for the earth, which is not expanding at all, to accommodate this. The problem is unlikely to be one of running out of resources, since scientific ingenuity, combined with the profit motive, has shown that it has been capable of great feats in the past and may well continue to display the same capability in the future. From finding and extracting petroleum from inaccessible sites and developing alternative (to fossil fuels) energy sources to developing plastics and new composite materials, researchers in capitalist countries have proved themselves to be highly adept at discovering or replacing essential raw materials. It is not difficult to imagine even the creation of factory-produced, semi-synthetic foods. Changes such as these may eventually transform human life in grotesque fashion, but would not necessarily be incompatible with its perpetuation.

It is more difficult to imagine the capitalist system addressing the problem of waste absorption. In part this is because of the system's requirement that firms do everything in their power to use cost-reducing processes, and to introduce to the marketplace new products long before their environmental consequences are known, or even knowable. This results both from their pursuit of profit and the pressures of competition. The most immediate global threat resulting from these pressures is that of global warming, with the depletion of the stratospheric ozone layer (which absorbs harmful ultraviolet radiation from the sun) perhaps a close second.

There are numerous uncertainties concerning the precise consequences of global warming, as well as their precise timing, but there is no question but that they will be severe. They are likely to include the melting of polar ice caps and the rising of sea levels, flooding large parts of low-lying countries; new patterns of severe weather conditions; and intense disruptions in agriculture (the American Midwest might become a dust bowl and California akin to Death Valley, with extreme heat prevailing much of the year). The "great conveyor" current, which originates in the tropics and flows northward in the Atlantic, warms North America before heading east to warm northern Europe and then looping back, might loop back much earlier, bringing a new ice age to North America and northern Europe, with the United Kingdom conceivably surrounded by ice on a year-round basis.[4] Even without knowing the precise consequences and the precise sequencing of events, we already know enough to realize that, unambiguously, global warming poses a severe threat to human life.

The response to this threat, or rather the lack of a response, is instructive. Consider, for example, the situation in the United States, where the George W. Bush administration has refused to even acknowledge the seriousness of the threat. This lack of political will reflects in part a lack of political pressure. This is turn reflects partly popular ignorance, but probably to a much greater degree the tenuousness of people's lives even under a thriving capitalism. American lives and culture are built around the automobile, which we need, in most parts of the country, for access to jobs, medical care, shopping, visits with relatives and friends, and recreation. Even with the visual evidence of smog and the knowledge of its detrimental health effects, people have accepted the repeated pushing out into the future of requirements for clean air.[5] At the same time, the American automobile industry—as well as its workers, the firms that depend upon it and their workers—lobbies successfully against measures that would diminish the production of smog and greenhouse gases meaningfully.[6] American capitalism is incapable of taking action in a timely fashion to forestall calamity.

Although green movements have greater political clout in Europe, the story is broadly the same. People's livelihood depends on the continuity of employment and the creation of jobs, and that remains true even when they retire, since the payroll tax is the source of most of their benefits. Above and beyond strictly material dependency, people's psychology under capitalism revolves around aspirations for higher income, creating a climate of support for economic growth. In addition to the marketing and advertising pressures tied to commercial culture, this is quite likely tied to the diminished opportunities for deriving satisfaction from interacting with family and friends, as the pressures for work and income tend to dominate individual existence. In disciplines such as economics, it is interesting to note that enormous attention has been devoted to economic growth, its measurement and its causes, while practically no attention has been paid to the quality of the capital stock, including human beings, and the sources of satisfaction that might well be derived from maximizing its quality.

Like all social formations, then, capitalism tends to incorporate mechanisms and institutions that serve to perpetuate it. These become especially powerful because even when the system enters one of its periodic spells of stagnation, it has mechanisms of recovery through self-reinvention—the creation of new social structures of accumulation that reestablish favorable conditions for accumulation to proceed. The various systemic contradictions that afflict capitalism can for the most part usually be overcome each time capitalism reinvents itself and moves on to a new stage, albeit often with great human suffering. The contradiction between capitalism and the environment, however, is ultimately unresolvable. A system that is based on ongoing expansion may thrive in its early stages in a fixed environment, but is ultimately incompatible with it.

The future of capitalism

Since capitalism is not compatible with the continuity of human life on earth—at the very least not with the continuity of human life as past and present generations have experienced it, and quite possibly not with any human life at all—the question quite naturally arises as to what might be done about this. One can imagine three broad scenarios. These include (1) the replacement of capitalism with a social formation, probably some variation of socialism, in which production is for human need rather than profit, broad equality in the distribution of income and wealth prevails, the expansion of output would continue only until a modicum of prosperity is possible for the entire planet, and a commitment to make human technologies and economic activity generally consistent with environmental preservation becomes taken for granted. They also include (2) muddling along as we have been, responding belatedly to environmental threats as we perceive them but generally accepting a deteriorating environment as an unfortunate but inevitable accompaniment to human "progress," and (3) preparation for a modified stationary state (MSS). Consideration of each of these alternatives in turn should help to clarify the possible futures for the capitalist social formation.

The first possibility could be realized only if social systems were created on the basis of rational, humanist thought. This is not, of course, the way in which the world works. It is somewhat akin to the utopian socialists early in the nineteenth century who thought that envisioning their ideal societies and putting their visions into words could help bring about their realization. People in capitalist countries are insecure, and their aspirations are shaped by the system toward material goals. People who live in or near poverty, including those in the Third World, have legitimate aspirations for material progress. Capitalists and firms, who both create capitalism and are its products, cannot have their conduct transformed by abstract thought. Workers who depend on capitalist expansion for their jobs and benefits are not in a position to support systemic change. In short, there is no prospect of the first alternative being realized under any circumstances.

The overwhelming probability is that the second scenario will continue to prevail. The capitalist system creates both the expectation and the necessity of ongoing economic growth. People anticipate improved lives from the ever-increasing production of goods and services that capitalism promises. In Third World countries and among the poor in industrialized countries this promise is a meaningful one. Among the "middle" classes and the well-off in industrialized countries, there is limited awareness that greater material prosperity has not been associated with increases in happiness. Probably for most people there is some environmental concern, but just as urban residents increasingly take smog for granted, environmental concerns are rarely the basis for forceful action. In the United States, even such obvious measures as a carbon tax are not even debated.

If environmental protection measures continue to be accorded low priority and continue to be taken belatedly, as is the overwhelming probability, then we can certainly anticipate ongoing environmental deterioration. People will continue to adjust to this until some form of calamity strikes. From the perspective afforded by conditions early in the twenty-first century, it appears most likely that this will take the form of drastic climate change associated with global warming. At that point, the strength of public opinion may lead to some changes in environmental policy, but it may be far too late. Although reforestation would reduce the carbon dioxide in the atmosphere over centuries, remedial policies would be incapable of replacing the polar ice caps, and there is no known way to replace ozone in the stratosphere. Moreover, if the destruction experienced by civilization is severe enough, there may be no political authority capable of bringing about the required changes.

Disaster scenarios are, of course, always speculative. Even without calamity striking, however, ongoing environmental deterioration promises to transform human life in future generations, and to do so in ways that the current generation would be unlikely to choose for itself. The dual images I have presented as extreme cases, of the oceans as dead seas and of human beings forced to limit to an extreme degree exposure to the deadly rays of the sun, are merely two of the possible destinations toward which capitalist civilization is heading. None of them are attractive, even if the road is traveled only part of the way. Every other species adjusts to its environment; only human beings transform their environment in ways that are ultimately self-destructive.

The third option for the future of capitalism lies somewhere between the first two. It involves envisioning some form of modified stationary state (MSS) as the successor to capitalism, and doing everything possible to minimize the environmental damage that an ongoing capitalist world economy will inevitably create. It also involves acting forcefully to create the preconditions for a post-capitalist world. Since this scenario, like the first one, involves conscious intervention in the capitalist process, and since I have already indicated the reasons for viewing such interventions skeptically, let me first spell out my reasons for treating this one seriously.

The second scenario—letting the capitalist process play out on a worldwide basis as we are currently doing, making minimal and belated efforts to contain the damage we are doing to the environment—will lead ultimately to the transformation of human life in ways that are unacceptable, or, in the extreme case, to the self-destruction of humanity. The first scenario, for the reasons I have indicated, lacks plausibility. However limited the prospects may be for realizing the third scenario, it is, in my view, the only hope humanity has for surviving capitalism and the environment-destroying orgy of throughputs that accompanies it.

There are, moreover, reasons to believe that there is at least some possibility, however small, that humanity might embark on the road toward a modified stationary state. First of all, this path does not envision the immediate end of capitalism, with all the resistance and conflict that would entail. Rather, it envisions additional centuries of capitalism, possibly even as long as the four and a half centuries for which capitalism has already existed. It incorporates an appreciation of the role that capitalism has played in transforming mass subsistence into mass prosperity, and capitalism's potential to continue this role until the entire world has been affected by it. In short, it views capitalism as a social formation that like its predecessors has a distinct beginning and end. The only way in which capitalism will mark the end of history is by allowing the destruction of the environment to play itself out fully, in which case history will end as the human race disappears from the face of the earth.

An additional reason for believing that movement along the path toward a modified stationary state is possible is the strength of environmental movements that have already appeared across the globe, and the limited efforts at environmental preservation that have already been undertaken. As the inadequacy of these efforts becomes more evident over the decades, people's lives will increasingly be affected adversely, swelling support for environmental reform. New industries that profit from reform will arise, and existing ones will grow, expanding the capitalist constituency in favor of reform.[7]

Another part of preparation for an MSS involves global measures to eliminate poverty and reduce inequality, both within and among nations. This is not a new task, either within nations or internationally. The United Nations has established a set of Millennium Development Goals for Third World development between 1990 and 2015, and has set a standard of 0.7 percent of GDP for each wealthy nation to set aside for development assistance (*The Economist*, 9/11/04: 72). Of course the actual levels are closer to 0.25 percent, but if 3 or 4 percent of developed country GDPs were set aside in development aid, a not intolerable level, and the necessary institutional reforms in Third World countries undertaken, the elimination of underdevelopment worldwide would be a feasible task, and one that could be accomplished without creating onerous burdens for the industrialized world.

Support for development aid within the industrialized countries has not been particularly great, with the possible exception of the Scandinavian countries, but that is essentially a reflection of the inequality and insecurity that prevail within them. When people feel that their own jobs, pensions, and medical care are insecure, that their own infrastructure is decaying, that their own educational systems are inadequate, and that other social institutions lack adequate funding, they are unlikely to support foreign aid. To address this situation requires a substantial commitment to domestic reforms. Just as there are substantial environmental constituencies within each industrialized country, there are substantial reform constituencies as well, so at least a modicum of support for the necessary changes would be present from the outset.

Another concern about creating the preconditions for a stationary state is related to the possibility of a diminishing surplus. In Chapter 6, I explored the concept of an expanding surplus as one of the potential core contradictions of the capitalist system. My finding there was that, contrary to the Monopoly Capital school argument, the economic surplus can be expected to shrink over time, diminishing the discretionary funds of the industrialized countries accordingly. This means that extended postponement of measures to promote domestic reforms, environmental preservation, and foreign aid will lead to growing funding difficulties in the future.

There is even greater reason, then, to make an early start on such measures.

In Chapter 1, I indicated that a particular vision of capitalism informs this book. Capitalism is a system that has brought with it great prosperity for parts of the world and promises to extend that prosperity over its remainder. It is a system that has created the conditions for a great flowering of science and the spread of democracy, among its many benefits. It is also a system that has demonstrated great vitality over the centuries, addressing its social and economic contradictions especially by repeatedly reinventing itself, creating new stages of capitalist development—new SSAs—in each country where it flourishes.

At the same time, capitalism generates various long-term contradictions, both social and natural, that are not amenable to resolution through the emergence of new SSAs. At its core, the capitalist system is based on self-seeking, with its social justification deriving from Adam Smith's observation that self-seeking behavior ultimately benefits the entire community. We know this to be true in certain respects, but we know just as firmly that it fails in others. One evident result is the perpetuation of poverty and inequality in the midst of plenty on both a national scale and internationally. Another is the ongoing destruction of the natural environment.

Globalization and technological change are shrinking the world, increasing consciousness of social injustice and magnifying the damage that those who react against it in distorted fashion are capable of doing. Terrorism has been transformed from a local condition to a global one. Terrorism of course also has its roots in long-standing religious, ethnic, and tribal rivalries, but these assume a new dimension in the era of globalization and technological change. As long as the capitalist principle of pursuing one's own interest without requiring commensurate regard for that of others continues to prevail,[8] a world rife with social injustice is likely to persist. Such a world provides a fertile breeding ground for terrorism. The damage that may emerge from social injustice and the strife to which it contributes—including that associated with terrorism—is potentially enormous, but not likely to threaten the capitalist system fundamentally. Not so the contradiction between capitalism and the environment.

In the last analysis, a fixed world cannot accommodate the indefinite expansion of throughputs that capitalism requires. This is the ultimate contradiction of the capitalist system and one that the repeated reinvention of capitalism in the form of new social structures of accumulation cannot overcome. If capitalism is allowed to play out its "natural life" without conscious intervention it will ultimately wreak such havoc on the ecosphere as to make the continuation of human life possible only with extreme distortions, or in the extreme case not possible at all.

If the destruction of civilization can be avoided and a post-capitalist world proves feasible, it will be made possible only by humankind making the same kind of adaptation to its environment that all other species have made. This in turn means that the establishment of a modified stationary state will be necessary. Accumulation can no longer be the driving force behind human activity, as a cyclical harmony comes to define the relationship between human beings and their environment. Human inquiry, scientific research, and economic innovation could proceed in such a context, subject to the constraint that preservation of the environment is a fundamental requirement. Economists and others will no longer focus on means to raise the rate of economic growth, but on enriching the quality of the capital stock, including above all that of the human beings who are a part of it.

This is the vision that informs this book. To make possible the arrival of post-capitalist society, steps must be taken as soon as possible to limit destruction of the environment, to reduce inequality and poverty, and to create the conditions of individual security and satisfaction that will enable people to consider more seriously the welfare of posterity. Half-measures are likely to prove inadequate, as they have proven themselves to be to date. The challenge for the twenty-first century is to establish the preconditions for post-capitalist society, for a modified stationary state. To continue on our present course—unfortunately the most probable outcome by far—will ultimately lead to a collision between the capitalist world economy and its natural environment that can only be catastrophic.

Notes

1 The capitalist system

1 "Liverpool employed in the slave trade in 1730, 15 ships; in 1751, 53; in 1760, 74; in 1770, 96; and in 1792, 132" (Marx, 1961–62: v.1, 759). See also Mantoux (1961: 105–108).
2 The US minimum wage rose from $1.25 (in current dollars) in 1963 to $5.15 in 2003. Adjusting for inflation, however, the real value of the US minimum wage *decreased* from $6.37 to $5.15 (in real 2003 dollars) over this period. (Economic Policy Institute, "Table 4: Historical Values of the US Minimum Wage, 1960–2003"; www.epinet.org/issueguides/minwage/table4.gif). For someone working every weekday of the year at the minimum hourly wage in 2004 (it was last increased in 1997), annual income would be $10,712. This compares to the 2003 official poverty threshold of $14,824 for a family of three. (Economic Policy Institute, "Minimum Wage Facts at a Glance"; www.epinet.org/content.cfm/issueguides_minwage_minwagefacts).
3 Center for Strategic and International Studies: www.csis.org/press/pr03_14.htm
4 The $802 million is from a widely cited 2001 study by the Tufts Center for the Study of Drug Development. A 2003 study by the consulting firm Bain & Co. indicates a figure of $1.7 billion. The two studies use different methodologies and thus are not directly comparable. It is of interest to note, however, that the Bain & Co. study finds an increase from a 1995–2000 average of $1.1 billion, when clinical trials were less costly and one in eight drugs that started out in animal testing made it to market, versus one in thirteen drugs more recently (*Wall Street Journal*, 12/8/03: B4).
5 Except for the very largest state-owned enterprises (for the time being), the Chinese government has been following a policy of encouraging their gradual privatization.
6 Brenner (1977: 25–92); Wallerstein (1976).
7 "A Survey of South Korea," *The Economist*, 4/19/03, p. 10.
8 It must nevertheless be acknowledged that in countries with a history of state economic leadership, the effort is being made. Both Singapore and South Korea, for example, are trying to establish major biotechnology industries. In South Korea, "The government wants Korea to become an important player in the global biotechnology industry by 2012," capturing "10% of the world market by that date, up from 1.4% in 2002. It projects biotechnology exports to go to $10 billion from $700 million over the same period" (*Wall Street Journal*, 3/10/04: B4C). The chances for success in this venture are remote, however. Money for research and development—from public sources as well as private—remains scarce, and the country lacks the infrastructure to support rapid devel-

opment in biotechnology. Given the vast array of public needs in modern states, it will be difficult for governments to justify devoting enormous funds to what ultimately are speculative ventures.

9 In *An Inquiry into the Nature and Causes of the Wealth of Nations* (1937: 14), first published in 1786, Smith published his well-known observation that "It is not from the benevolence of the butcher, the brewer, or the baker, that we expect our dinner, but from their regard to their own interest."

10 Marx (1961, vol. 1) uses "C" and "M" in *Capital*, but he does not actually use C′ and M′. Nevertheless, I have used these terms here to reproduce the logic of his argument with enhanced clarity.

11 Weisskopf (1996: 369–370) presents a brief, elegant exposition of the various contradictions, including this one, which Marx perceived in the capitalist system.

12 All of Ricardo's writings have been collected in Sraffa (1951), but an exposition of his core ideas appears in much more accessible form in Heilbroner (1986: 94–104).

13 I have used (and will again use) these examples as symbolic representations of the dramatic impact environmental change is bound to have on human life. Even if these particular outcomes do not emerge, the point is that human society is quickly approaching a point of no return. In 2004, world consumption of oil was about eighty million barrels per day. According to the International Energy Agency, it is expected to hit 120 million barrels per day by 2030 (*Wall Street Journal*, 8/17/04: A1). If another 50 percent increase takes place in the following twenty-six years, we would reach 180 million barrels per day in 2056. These projections suggest that global warming is likely to continue and intensify despite our knowledge of the dire consequences.

2 Social structures of accumulation: the theoretical issues

1 The case of Peregrine Investments Holdings, a company based in Hong Kong, provides an instructive example. Peregrine was the largest Asian investment bank outside Japan. On January 12, 1998, it announced that it was filing for liquidation after an Indonesian transportation firm, Steady Safe, to which it had loaned US $265 million, defaulted on its debt (washingtonpost.com, 1/13/98: A12). What is of interest here is that Peregrine was forced out of business with no recourse to the assets of Steady Safe, while Steady Safe was able to remain in operation.

2 Gordon, Edwards and Reich (1994: 15) define "the capital accumulation process to be the microeconomic activity of profit-making and reinvestment." This activity takes place "within a given institutional environment." An SSA consists of those institutions "that directly and demonstrably condition capital accumulation and [excludes] those that affect it only tangentially. Thus, for example, the financial system bears a direct relation whereas the character of sports activity does not."

3 David Gordon's 1978 essay, "Up and Down the Long Roller Coaster," is one of the precursors of SSA theory. In it, Gordon examines the quantitative evidence for long cycles in the United States since the beginning of the nineteenth century, ties the long cycles to institutional structures that support (or fail to support) the accumulation process, and links them logically to Marxian theories of contradiction and crisis. The essay appears in Union for Radical Political Economics (1978).

4 For an exploration of the struggles between capital and labor that contributed to the reinvention of American capitalism at the start of the twenty-first century, see Lippit (2004: 336–343).

5 David Kotz, Terrence McDonough, and Michael Reich (1994) raise and address most of these issues in their own essays that appear in their edited volume. My own response to these questions (which follows in the text), however, differs quite markedly from theirs.

6 Stephen Resnick and Richard Wolff (1987: 81–99) discuss Althusser's use of the term "overdetermination" as a basis for understanding Marxian epistemology. My own interest in the concept, however, lies in its capacity to clarify the manner in which social processes and social outcomes generally must be understood as the result of the interaction of multiple forces.

7 In the 1950s and 1960s, (before tax) corporate profits as a share of US national income were typically in the 11–13 percent range (US Bureau of Economic analysis website: www.bea.gov), but in the 1970s and 1980s were more typically in the 8–10 percent range. The corporate profits reported in the national income accounts have a number of flaws in that they are influenced by accounting conventions and laws that are somewhat arbitrary (assumptions as to the useful life of capital equipment and structures, for example, influence depreciation charges and therefore reported profits). Moreover, corporate profits exclude "proprietors' income," a large part of which represents profits. Even so, the ability of companies to maintain profits in the 1950s and 1960s, and the drop in corporate profit rates in the 1970s and 1980s compared to the 1950s and 1960s, are significant.

8 "Remarks by Chairman Alan Greenspan Before the HM Treasury Enterprise Conference, London England (via satellite), January 26, 2004" (www.federalreserve.gov/boarddocs/speeches/2004).

9 Like the firing of the air traffic controllers, the significance of the Caterpillar strike was widely recognized at the time. Starting on Sunday, May 14, 1995, the *Los Angeles Times* ran for five consecutive days a series of lengthy, page one articles concerning the strike.

10 The twenty Fortune 500 companies that filed a legal brief in support of the University of Michigan included such well-known firms as Microsoft, Intel, Texaco, Kodak, Dow Chemical, and Procter and Gamble (http://acad.english.ucsb.ed/docs/unlikely.html). According to testimony before the Supreme Court, all military academies except the Coast Guard have racial preferences (www.uwm.edu). The friend-of-the-court briefs filed by the military officials stated that "compelling considerations of national security and military mission justify consideration of race in selecting military officers . . . In the 1960s and 1970s, the stark disparity between the racial composition of the rank and file and that of the officer corps fueled a breakdown of order that endangered the military's ability to fulfill its missions" (Christian Science Monitor, 3/28/03 (www.csmonitor.com)).

11 The Ministry of International Trade and Industry (MITI) is now the Ministry of Economy, Trade and Industry (METI).

12 A number of opposing pressures, however, should be recognized, pressures that may well strengthen the tendency of Japan to attempt to muddle through its present predicament. Foremost among these, perhaps, is the positive impact demand from China is having on the Japanese economy in the early twenty-first century. As of 2004, Japan's exports to China were running at an annual rate of about US $80 billion, up from about $20 billion six years earlier (*Los Angeles Times*, 10/17/04: C1). These figures do not include the indirect impact of China's rapid growth, which is sparking all of East Asia, thereby increasing the demand for Japan's products—especially technologically sophisticated ones—throughout the region. To the extent that Japan is able to improve its economic performance even modestly—even though that performance is far

below its potential—the opposition to reform will be strengthened and the period of muddling through is likely to be lengthened.

3 Social structures of accumulation: the reinvention of American capitalism

1 In August 1953, the US Central Intelligence Agency, acting in concert with the British Intelligence Service (M16), organized a coup to oust Prime Minister Mossadegh of Iran and restore the Shah, who had fled the country, to his throne. Mossadegh was a strong nationalist, and the US and UK feared he would nationalize the country's oil (*New York Times* website, 4/16/2000; www.angelfire.com/home/iran/1953coup.html). It can be argued that by maintaining repressive and corrupt regimes in power to secure access to oil in the short term, the Western governments have played a key role in forestalling the development and modernization of the Middle East. The long-term results of such policies may well have contributed to the Iranian revolution in 1979, and more recently to the rise of religious fundamentalism and terrorism in the region. The point is not that US policy "caused" the Iranian revolution, merely that it played an important role in creating the conditions that led to the revolution. From this vantage point, treating events like the Iranian revolution and the tripling of oil prices to which it led as "exogenous" events is admittedly imprecise, and I have treated it as such purely to make the analysis manageable.

2 A listing of the major environmental laws can be found on the Environmental Protection Agency website under www.epa.gov. Other major environmental acts included the Resource Conservation and Recovery Act of 1976 which sought to maintain ongoing monitoring of hazardous wastes, the Toxic Substances Control Act of 1976 which sought to track, monitor and control the 75,000 industrial chemicals used in the US (as well as the thousands of new chemicals introduced each year), and the Superfund Act of 1980 that gave the EPA authority to require polluters to pay for the hazardous wastes they had dumped over the decades.

3 These remaining businesses are now part of the media giant, Viacom.

4 *The Machine that Changed the World: The Story of Lean Production* provides a comprehensive account of lean production (see Womack, Jones, and Roos (1991)).

5 In referring to the US firm as an effective global competitor I am not of course focusing on the trade balance, which has shown enormous and increasing deficits over time (as of the time of this writing in 2004). The ability of US firms to raise profits by assuming a pioneering role in new industries, by outsourcing, and by establishing their own facilities abroad has raised productivity and corporate profitability quite rapidly over the last decade, and this plays a central role in the international competitiveness of the larger firms.

6 The 264 firms listed on Germany's *Neuer Market*, for example, lost 96 percent of their value between early 2000 (when the Internet bubble began to deflate) and September 2002, when the closing of the exchange was announced (http://news.bbc.co.uk/1/hi/business).

7 This was one of the outcomes of the Southern California supermarket strike of 2003–04. The strike was triggered by the imminent arrival of Wal-Mart superstores in the region (Wal-Mart is well known for its anti-union stance, low wages and poor health-care benefits [Lippit 2004]). The strike was eventually won by the companies when their workers were forced to accept a two-tier wage system and diminished health-care benefits.

8 "In 2003 China consumed 7% of the world's crude oil, 31% of its coal, 30% of its iron ore, 27% of its steel, 25% of its aluminum and 40% of its cement—in all cases a large leap from two years before" (*Forbes*, 5/24/04: 188).

9 In 2003, for example, personal consumption expenditures on goods (both durable and nondurable) amounted to $3,150.8 billion, while personal consumption of services amounted to $4,610.1 billion (http://www.bea.doc.gov).

10 See, for example Jim Chappell, "Deregulation, Re-Regulation and California's Energy Future" (http://www.spur.org/documents/030801_article_05.shtm).

11 In 2003, some $25 billion was expected to be committed to US venture capital funds. This was down from the peak of $99.8 billion in 2000, but would still be one of the industry's best years ever and put the total raised above its 1997 level—prior to the Internet boom (*Business Week*, 3/3/03: 114). Even major pension funds are increasingly allocating a small portion of their investments, often 5 percent, to private equity.

4 Capitalism, globalization, and technological change

1 See, for example, Wallerstein (1976).

2 For a provocative discussion concerning the possibilities raised by the GNR technological revolution, see Bill Joy's essay in the April 2000 *Wired* online magazine (http://www.wired.com/wired/archive/8.04/joy_html).

3 According to the US Census Bureau, the number of Americans without health-care insurance grew to a record 45 million in 2003; and in 2004, health-care insurance was offered by five million fewer jobs in the United States than in 2001 (*Los Angeles Times*, 9/10/04: A1).

4 Over the five years to 2004, economic growth in Germany, France, and Italy averaged only 1.6 percent (*The Economist*, 5/1/04: 25). In May 2004, the unemployment rate was 10.3 percent in Germany (http://www.dw-world.de/english) and 9.8 percent in France (Matthew Lynn, 7/15/04, in Bloomberg.com: Bloomberg Columnists).

5 Foreign direct investment in China averaged US$11.7 billion per year between 1985 and 1995, rising to $43.8 billion in 1998 and $52.7 billion in 2002 (Bank of China web site: http://www.tdctrade.com/econforum/boc/boc030101.htm).

6 The pressures are likely to be intensified in countries like China that have brought their population growth rates down dramatically. China's population will be aging more rapidly than that of other countries in developing Asia, raising the dependency ratio and making more costly the provision of a social safety net covering pensions, health care, and unemployment insurance.

7 For supporting data, see the discussion on pp. 81–83 of institutional reform in China and its impact.

8 The disinflationary forces are associated with firms' ability to take advantage of low labor costs in developing countries, and for those in industrialized countries to put pressure on their domestic workforces to accept lower wages and benefits when confronted with the real possibility of job loss. These forces are intensified by the difficulty firms have in raising prices when faced with global competition. It should also be recognized, however, that there are countervailing forces: as economies in the developing world reach critical mass—and this is already evident in the case of China—the world demand for commodities rises, pushing up their prices. Nevertheless, on balance the disinflationary forces have been more powerful to date (2004), and this situation appears likely to be maintained.

9 At the end of 2003, the two countries holding the world's largest foreign exchange reserves were Japan, with US$673.5 billion (up 43 percent from

2002), and China, with $403.3 billion (up 41 percent from 2002). Most of these reserves are invested in US Treasury securities (*Wall Street Journal*, 2/11/04: C4).

10 See, for example, Brian Carnell, "Monsanto to Give Genetically Modified Rice Away" (8/8/2000: http://www.overpopulation.com/discussion).

11 The health benefits of eating even farm-raised salmon as part of a diversified fish diet are still considered to be positive on balance at the time of this writing (http://healthletter.tufts.edu/issues/2003–11/salmon.html).

12 Chapter 3 provides the data on productivity growth rate changes.

13 Since the 1970s the total value of world exports has been growing much faster than gross world product (GWP). Just between 1990 and 2001, GWP was up less than 30 percent while world exports rose by close to 80 percent (http://www.globalpolicy.org/globaliz/charts/tradecomp.htm).

14 It is of interest to note that the Indian government, starting in 2001, has been trying to emulate China's special economic zones (SEZs) as a means of attracting foreign direct investment (FDI). Like China, India has an abundant supply of low-cost labor, but an excess of bureaucratic regulations, poor infrastructure, and other impediments have limited FDI. The Indian SEZs are trying to remove these obstacles (*Wall Street Journal*, 5/1/03: A16).

15 Factory employment has in fact been falling worldwide. Even in China, manufacturing employment fell from 98 million to 83 million between 1995 and 2002, a 15 percent fall that exceeded the 11 percent fall in the US over the same period (most of China's drop was concentrated in the older, state-owned enterprises; *Wall Street Journal*, 10/20/03: A2). Competitive pressures to raise productivity and the development of technologies to make that possible suggest that manufacturing may be in the midst of a global employment decline paralleling the decline in agricultural employment that the industrialized countries experienced in the twentieth century.

16 Sales of locally made cars in China increased by 50 percent in 2002 and by 75 percent in 2003, reaching 1.97 million. The Chinese market passed the German market in 2003 and could pass Japan's (second only to the US market) within a few years (*The Economist*, "A Survey of Business in China," 3/20/04: 6).

5 Capitalism and the economic surplus

1 Technological progress can be distinguished conceptually from accumulation (the increase in the capital stock), but new technology is characteristically embodied in new investment. Thus when I maintain that accumulation is at the heart of the growth process, I mean to include technological progress.

2 The major work in which they pursue this project is *Monopoly Capital* (New York: Monthly Review Press, 1966).

3 See, for example, Davis (1992).

4 In "Reevaluating the Concept of the Surplus," in Davis (1992), I provide my own estimates of the size of the US surplus (much smaller than Baran and Sweezy's estimates), and indicate reasons for which it may well continue to shrink over time.

5 For a sophisticated, in-depth analysis of the relation between income and happiness, see Lane (2000).

6 Continuing rapid urbanization appears to be in store for the entire world, but especially in developing Asia in coming decades. In the East Asia and Pacific region (excluding Japan), for example, the urban population is expected to increase by 3.75 percent annually, almost doubling from 665 million to 1,230 million between 2000 and 2030, accounting for 130 percent of the region's

population growth in that period (as the rural population experiences an absolute decline). The urban share of the population will increase from 35.4 percent in 2000 to 53.4 percent in 2030 (World Bank 2003: 2).

6 Capitalism and class

1 Marx's actual words (in translation) are as follows: "The sum total of these relations of production constitutes the economic structure of society, the real foundation, on which rises a legal and political superstructure and to which correspond definite forms of social consciousness. The mode of production of material life conditions the social, political and intellectual life process in general. It is not the consciousness of men that determines their being, but, on the contrary, their social being that determines their consciousness" (Marx and Engels 1958, vol. I: 363).

2 In *American Capitalism: The Concept of Countervailing Power* (1952), John Kenneth Galbraith develops this point at some length, arguing that the prevalence of oligopoly pricing and the higher-than-competitive profits it brings spurs (often successful) efforts by labor to obtain a share of these excess profits for itself.

3 Resnick and Wolff (1996, 2002) provide a trenchant critique of these approaches.

4 Normalization in Russia does not, unfortunately, preclude increasingly authoritarian rule. It does appear, however, that the oligarchs will be permitted to keep their ill-gotten gains as long as they do not challenge President Putin politically. Khodorkovsky, who controlled Yukos, one of Russia's largest oil firms, attempted such a challenge and languishes in jail at the time of this writing (summer 2004) as a consequence. See, for example, "Putin's Game" (*Business Week*, 6/7/04: 54–58).

5 An extensive literature on the living wage movement and its impact has begun to emerge. See, for example, Robert Pollin and Stephanie Luce (1998) *The Living Wage: Building a Fair Economy* (New York: New Press, 1998), and the January 2005 issue of *Industrial Relations*, which is edited by David Fairris and Michael Reich and is devoted in its entirety to living wage research.

6 The Republican Party of course also represents other interests, including the Christian fundamentalists or social conservatives. With only two major parties, it is inevitable that each incorporates a range of interests.

7 Capitalism and the environment

1 See, for example, Mishan (1967). The book is a sophisticated essay critical of the continued obsession with economic growth in the industrialized countries—and of the failure of economic policy to take proper account of externalities. I mean no pejorative implication when I present it as an example of concern with pollution writ small, but simply to indicate that its focus tends to be more on disamenities than on the larger threats to human existence that later became prominent in the environmental literature.

2 Other gases generated by human activity also contribute to the greenhouse effect, but carbon dioxide is the most significant.

3 A rather full discussion of the potential hazards associated with the increased use of hydrogen gas as an energy source appears on the BBC radio program, "Costing the Earth," December 18, 2003 (http://db.bbc.co.uk/radio4/science/costingtheearth_20031218.shtml).

4 Kenneth Boulding (1996), in his classic essay "The Economics of the Coming

Spaceship Earth," takes the economics profession to task for focusing almost exclusively on the benefits of economic growth, while ignoring the possible benefits of maximizing the condition of the capital stock, including human capital. This issue is pursued in greater depth later in this chapter.

5 See, for example, Lane (2000) and Scitovsky (1992).

6 As Lane (2000) indicates, levels of happiness actually appear to be decreasing over time in market economies.

7 The article originally appeared in *Science*, vol. 162, pp. 1243–1268, and has been reprinted many times. My source is Daly (1973).

8 Under the headline "EPA Rejects Cap on Carbon Dioxide," an article in *The Wall Street Journal* (8/29/03: A3) states: "The Bush administration declared that carbon dioxide and other 'greenhouse gases' aren't pollutants, rejecting calls by environmentalists to have the Environmental Protection Agency cap emissions of the gases thought to contribute to global warming."

9 Pollution rights can be marketed too. This makes regulation more efficient (by lowering compliance costs), but assumes a given amount of pollution is acceptable and sustainable.

10 See, for example, *The Wall Street Journal* (7/31/03: A3 and 8/29/03: A3). The vast majority of the scientific community is in agreement on the dangers posed by global warming, however. A study published by nineteen scientists in the *Proceedings of the National Academy of Sciences*, for example, found that "Global warming could raise average temperatures as much as 10 degrees in California by the end of the century—sharply curtailing water supplies, causing a rise in heat-related deaths and reducing crop yields—if the world does not dramatically cut its dependence on fossil fuels" (*Los Angeles Times*, 8/17/04: B1).

11 The Food and Agriculture Organization (FAO) estimates that 53,000 square miles of tropical forests were destroyed each year during the 1980s (http://earthobservatory.nasa.gov). During the 1990s, the rate of deforestation may have declined as much as 10 percent, according to the FAO, a pace of deforestation that would still eliminate much of the world's forest cover by the end of the twenty-first century (http://www.cnn.com/2000/Nature/08/09/forest.recovery.reut/).

8 The future of capitalism

1 A World Bank study entitled "Doing Business in 2005" places special emphasis on the potential for regulatory reform to improve development potential; regulatory institutions can be some of the primary impediments to development. According to the World Bank study (cited in *The Economist*, 9/11/04: 71), it takes two days to register a new company in Australia, compared to 203 days in Haiti; to do so "in Sierra Leone, it costs 1,268% of average annual income per person, compared with nothing in Denmark. To register in Ethiopia, a would-be entrepreneur must deposit 18 years' average income in a bank account, which is then frozen. That such capital requirements are unnecessary has been amply proven in the 42 mostly rich countries that have abolished them."

2 Calculated at purchasing power parity, Brazil's gross national income per capita in 2002 was US$7,250, Mexico's was $5,910, and Argentina's $9,930 (World Bank, 2004: 252).

3 My focus here is on the structural forces that appear likely to buoy the world economy in the coming decades, especially the positive impact of China's emergence on Japan, and of the growing common market the European Union can be expected to create (which also should diminish cross-border transaction costs

and provide, among other benefits, a relatively uniform regulatory environment). I do not mean to deny the possibility of severe shocks to the world economy, and in fact have mentioned in Chapter 4 that increased financial fragility especially characterizes the capitalist world economy in the era of globalization and technological change. In an article in *The Economist* (9/11/04: 63–65), Fred Bergsten cites five major risks to the contemporary world economy: "Three center on the United States: renewed sharp increases in the current-account deficit leading to a crash of the dollar; a budget profile that is out of control (and could lead to sharply higher interest rates); and an outbreak of trade protectionism. A fourth relates to China, which faces a possible hard landing from its recent overheating. The fifth is that oil prices could rise to $60–70 per barrel even without a major political or terrorist disruption, and much higher with one." While any of these factors could bring about a severe shock to the capitalist world economy, how serious and prolonged the problem would be would depend on the adequacy of policy responses. The possibility of such shocks notwithstanding, the emergence of China and the growth of the European Union represent structural forces that can be expected to strengthen the capitalist world economy in the long run and increase its capacity to recover from any shocks it may encounter in the short run.

4 The basic mechanism for this possible current change is associated with the melting of the Arctic ice brought on by global warming. At present the great conveyor current, originating in the South Atlantic, is driven by dense salty water that sinks in the North Atlantic, drawing additional warm water northward. As the polar ice caps melt, fresh water is added to the North Atlantic, reducing the salinity of the current and making it less dense. That in turn could prevent the current from sinking in the North Atlantic, stopping its ability to draw "new" water from the South Atlantic and therefore its flow. A large part of Europe and North America would become colder and drier if that were to happen. Scientists now believe that changes of this type could take place in a period as short as a decade (see David Stipp, "The Pentagon's Weather Nightmare," *Fortune*, 2/9/04, pp. 100–107).

5 In *Making Peace with the Planet*, Barry Commoner (1990: 38–39) observes that the Clean Air Act of 1970 mandated strong improvements in air quality by 1977 through 90 percent reductions in urban carbon, monoxide, hydrocarbon, and ozone levels. In 1971, the Environmental Planning Agency (EPA) set clear rules on automotive emissions to be achieved by the target year 1977. Those localities that failed to comply were to be subject to the loss of federal funding for development projects. Despite the presence of clear targets, enabling legislation and severe sanctions for noncompliance, the targets were never approached. In 1977, the deadline was moved to 1982, in 1982 it was moved to 1987, after which the three most polluted cities (Houston, Los Angeles, and New York) were given twenty more years, until 2009, to comply. There seems little reason to doubt that when 2009 arrives the target dates for clean air will once again be moved back.

6 On September 26, 2004, for example, California regulators approved a rule that would require a reduction in automobile greenhouse gas emissions starting in 2009 and reaching a peak 30 percent reduction by 2016. Much of this gain would be offset, of course, by the increased number of vehicles in use, as well as by the increase in greenhouse gas emissions from other sources. Nevertheless, the new rule appears unlikely to be implemented. Claiming that the new rule would require so much technology that it would raise car prices by an average of $3,000 (triple the regulators' estimate), "The Alliance of Automobile Manufacturers, the industry's trade group in Washington, said it would urge the California legislature and California Gov. Arnold Schwarzenegger to block the rule ...

The industry also said it is considering suing California to block the rule" (*Wall Street Journal*, 9/27/04: A2).

7 Companies that produce fuel cells or those that produce water purification equipment are obvious examples, but it is not difficult to envision a far broader array of environmental industries.

8 I am not asserting here that there is a general lack of regard for others in capitalist countries. Rather, the principle of pursuing one's own benefit is subject to obvious constraints, both legal and ethical, such as not harming others in the process. Many individuals, moreover, have a strong sense of obligation to help others, and most countries—most notably in continental Europe—provide some degree of assistance to individuals unable to fend for themselves. The fact remains, nevertheless, that the logic of the system requires individuals to pursue their own benefit on the assumption that no one else will do so. And individuals who fail to succeed in the system, and those who are in effect victimized by it—because they lack the proper skills, because there is an inadequate demand for labor, because they are aged or suffer a disability, because firms find it cheaper to dispose of toxic wastes in local waterways, or for any of numerous other reasons—as well as those who empathize with the victims, may readily develop a sense of social injustice.

Select bibliography

Amsden, Alice H. (1989) *Asia's Next Giant: South Korea and Late Industrialization*. New York: Oxford University Press.

Anderson, Perry (1974) *Passages from Antiquity to Feudalism*. London: Verso.

Angresano, James (1996) *Comparative Economics*, 2nd edn. Upper Saddle River, N.J.: Prentice-Hall.

Ashton, T. S. (1962) *The Industrial Revolution: 1760–1830*. London: Oxford University Press.

Baran, Paul A. (1957) *The Political Economy of Growth*. New York: Monthly Review Press.

—— and Paul M. Sweezy (1966) *Monopoly Capital*. New York: Monthly Review Press.

Baumol, William J., and Alan S. Blinder (2003) *Macroeconomics: Principles and Policy*, 9th edn. Mason, Ohio: Thomson/South-Western.

Beaud, Michel (1983) *A History of Capitalism 1500–1980*. New York: Monthly Review Press.

Becker, Gary S. (2003) "The Productivity Boom Is Just Warming Up," *Business Week*, October 20, p. 29.

—— (2004) "How the Skeptics Missed the Power of Productivity," *Business Week*, January 12, p. 26.

Blackburn, Robin (ed.) (1991) *After the Fall: The Failure of Communism and the Future of Socialism*. London: Verso.

Bluestone, Barry and Bennett Harrison (1982) *The Deindustrialization of America*. New York: Basic Books.

Bottomore, Tom, Laurence Harris, V. G. Kiernan, and Ralph Miliband (eds) (1983) *A Dictionary of Marxist Thought*. Cambridge, Mass.: Harvard University Press.

Boulding, Kenneth E. (1996) "The Economics of the Coming Spaceship Earth," in V. Lippit (ed.) *Radical Political Economy*.

Braudel, Fernand (1975) *Capitalism and Material Life: 1400–1800*. New York: Harper and Row.

Brenner, Robert (1977) "The Origins of Capitalist Development: A Critique of Neo-Smithian Marxism," *New Left Review*, no. 104 (July/August).

Bungo, Greg (2004) "Human Population Expansion = Oceanic Dead Zones," http://www.seashepherd.org/editorials/editorial10.shtml.

Bureau of Economic Analysis, US Dept. of Commerce (2004) "National Economic Accounts, Table 1.1.10. Percentage Shares of GDP," July 30, 2004 (www.bea.doc.gov/beahome.html).

Carlile, Lonny E. and Mark C. Tilton (eds) (1998) *Is Japan Really Changing Its Ways? Regulatory Reform and the Japanese Economy*. Washington, D.C.: Brookings.

Carter, Susan B., *et al.* (eds) (2005) *Historical Statistics of the United States: Millennial Edition*. New York: Cambridge University Press.

Cherry, Robert, *et al.* (eds) (1987) *The Imperiled Economy, Book 1: Macroeconomics from a Left Perspective*. New York: Union for Radical Political Economics.

—— (1988) *The Imperiled Economy, Book 2: Through the Safety Net*. New York: Union for Radical Political Economics.

Commoner, Barry (1971) *The Closing Circle*. New York: Knopf.

—— (1990) *Making Peace with the Planet*. New York: Pantheon.

Daly, Herman E. (ed.) (1973) *Toward a Steady-State Economy*. San Francisco: Freeman.

—— (1991) *Steady-State Economics*. Washington, D.C.: Island Press.

—— and Kenneth Townsend (eds) (1993) *Valuing the Earth*. Cambridge, Mass.: MIT Press.

Davis, John B. (ed.) (1992) *The Economic Surplus in Advanced Economies*. Aldershot, UK: Edward Elgar.

Dillard, Dudley (1984) "Capitalism," In C. K. Wilber (ed.) *The Political Economy of Development and Underdevelopment*, 3rd edn.

Dobb, Maurice (1963) *Studies in the Development of Capitalism*, revised edn. New York: International Publishers.

Dorfman, Robert and Nancy Dorfman (eds) (1972) *Economics of the Environment: Selected Readings*. New York: Norton.

Economic Report of the President: 2003 (2003) Prepared by the Council of Economic Advisors to the President. Washington, D.C.: US Government Printing Office.

Fairris, David (1997) *Shopfloor Matters: Labor–Management Relations in Twentieth-Century American Manufacturing*. New York: Routledge.

Ferrera, Maurizio and Martin Rhodes (eds) (2000) *Recasting European Welfare States*. London: Frank Cass.

Flath, David (2000) *The Japanese Economy*. Oxford: Oxford University Press.

Foster, John Bellamy (1986) *The Theory of Monopoly Capitalism*. New York: Monthly Review Press.

—— (2002) *Ecology Against Capitalism*. New York: Monthly Review Press.

—— and Henryk Szlajfer (eds) (1984) *The Faltering Economy: The Problem of Accumulation Under Monopoly Capitalism*. New York: Monthly Review Press.

Freeman, Christopher (ed.) (1984) *Long Waves in the World Economy*. London: Pinter.

Galbraith, John Kenneth (1952) *American Capitalism: The Concept of Countervailing Power*. Boston: Houghton Mifflin.

—— (1967) *The New Industrial State*. New York: Signet Books.

—— (1984) *The Affluent Society*, 4th edn. Boston, Mass.: Houghton Mifflin.

Gilbert, Neil (1983) *Capitalism and the Welfare State.* New Haven: Yale Univ. Press.

—— (2002) *Transformation of the Welfare State*. Oxford: Oxford University Press.

Gillis, Justin (2004) "Genetically Modified Organisms Not Easily Contained," January 20, washingtonpost.com.

Gilpin, Robert (2000) *The Challenge of Global Capitalism*. Princeton, N.J.: Princeton University Press.

Goodin, Robert E., Bruce Headey, Ruud Muffels, and Henk-Jen Dirven (1999) *The Real Worlds of Welfare Capitalism*. Cambridge: Cambridge University Press.

Goodman, Paul (1956) *Growing Up Absurd*. New York: Random House.

Goodman, Roger, Gordon White, and Huck-ju Kwon (eds) (1998) *The East Asian Welfare Model*. New York: Routledge.

Gordon, David (1978) "Up and Down the Long Roller Coaster," in Union for Radical Political Economics, *US Capitalism in Crisis*. New York: Union for Radical Political Economics.

—— (1980) "Stages of Accumulation and Long Economic Cycles," in Terence K. Hopkins and Immanuel Wallerstein, (eds) *Processes of the World System*. Beverly Hills, Calif.: Sage.

——, Richard Edwards and Michael Reich (1994) "Long Swings and Stages of Capitalism," in Kotz *et al.* (eds) *Social Structures of Accumulation*.

——, Richard Edwards and Michael Reich (1982) *Segmented Work: Divided Workers: The Historical Transformation of Labor in the United States*. Cambridge: Cambridge University Press.

——, Thomas E. Weisskopf and Samuel Bowles (1996) "Power, Accumulation and Crisis: The Rise and Demise of the Postwar Social Structure of Accumulation," in V. Lippit (ed.) *Radical Political Economy*.

Gregory, Paul R. and Robert C. Stuart (1995) *Comparative Economic Systems*, 5th edn. Boston, Mass.: Houghton Mifflin.

Greve, Bent (ed.) (1996) *Comparative Welfare Systems*. New York: St Martin's Press.

Hall, Peter A. and David Soskice (eds) (2001) *Varieties of Capitalism: The Institutional Foundations of Comparative Advantage*. Oxford: Oxford University Press.

Hanes, Christopher (2005) "Prices and Price Indexes," in S. B. Carter *et al.* (eds) *Historical Statistics of the United States, Millennial Edition.*

Hardin, Garrett (1973) "The Tragedy of the Commons," in H. E. Daly (ed.) *Toward a Steady-State Economy.*

Heilbroner, Robert (1985) *The Nature and Logic of Capitalism*. New York: Norton.

—— (1986) *The Worldly Philosophers*, 6th edn. New York: Simon and Schuster.

—— (1991) *An Inquiry Into the Human Prospect*. New York: Norton.

Hindess, Barry (1987) *Politics and Class Analysis*. Oxford: Basil Blackwell.

Hirata, Junichi (1995) "Economic Changes and Macroeconomic Policy in Japan Since 1955," *Japanese Economic Studies*, vol. 23, no. 3 (May–June).

Hobsbawm, Eric (1996) *The Age of Extremes: A History of the World, 1914–1991*. New York: Vintage Books.

Ito, Takatoshi (1992) *The Japanese Economy*. Cambridge, Mass.: MIT Press.

Joint Economic Committee, US Congress (1997) *China's Economic Future*. Armonk, N.Y.: M. E. Sharpe.

Kardevani, Hashem (1996) "Regulation Theory and Its Critique." Ph.D. Dissertation, University of California, Riverside.

Kautto, Mikko *et al.* (eds) (1999) *Nordic Social Policy*. New York: Routledge.

Keynes, John Maynard (1970) "Economic Possibilities for Our Grandchildren," in Romano and Leiman (eds) *Views on Capitalism*.

Kim, Eun Mee (1997) *Big Business, Strong State: Collusion and Conflict in South Korean Development, 1960–1990*. Albany: State University of New York Press.

—— (ed.) (1998) *The Four Asian Tigers: Economic Development and the Global Political Economy*. San Diego, Calif.: Academic Press.

Kirby, Alex (2004) *BBC News Online*, March 29, "Sea 'Dead Zones' Threaten Fish," (http://news.bbc.co.uk/1/hi/sci/tech/3577711.stm).

Kitschelt, Herbert *et al.* (eds) (1999) *Continuity and Change in Contemporary Capitalism*. Cambridge: Cambridge University Press.

Kochan, Thomas A., Russell D. Lansbury, and John Paul MacDuffie (eds) (1997) *After Lean Production: Evolving Employment Practices in the World Auto Industry*. Ithaca, N.Y.: Cornell University Press.

Kotz, David (with Fred Weir) (1997) *Revolution from Above: The Demise of the Soviet System*. New York: Routledge.

——, Terrence McDonough, and Michael Reich (eds) (1994) *Social Structures of Accumulation: The Political Economy of Growth and Crisis*. Cambridge: Cambridge University Press.

Krishnan, Rajaram, Jonathan M. Harris, and Neva R. Goodwin (eds) (1995) *A Survey of Ecological Economics*. Washington, D.C.: Island Press.

Kuttner, Robert (1992) *The End of Laissez-Faire*. New York: Knopf.

—— (1999) *Everything for Sale: the Virtues and Limits of Markets*. Chicago: University of Chicago Press.

Lane, Robert (2000) *The Loss of Happiness in Market Democracies*. New Haven, Conn.: Yale University Press.

Lecomber, Richard (1975) *Economic Growth Versus the Environment*. New York: Halsted Press.

Leiss, William (1976) *The Limits to Satisfaction: An Essay on the Problem of Needs and Commodities*. Toronto: University of Toronto Press.

Lipietz, Alain (1992) *Towards a New Economic Order: Postfordism, Ecology and Democracy*. New York: Oxford University Press.

Lippit, Victor D. (1985) "The Concept of the Surplus in Economic Development," *Review of Radical Political Economics*, vol. 17, nos. 1 and 2 (Spring and Summer). Reprinted in Lippit (ed.) *Radical Political Economy*.

—— (1992) "Reevaluating the Concept of the Surplus," in Davis (ed.) *The Economic Surplus in Advanced Economies.*

—— (1996) *Radical Political Economy: Explorations in Alternative Economic Analysis*. Armonk, N.Y.: M. E. Sharpe.

—— (1997) "The Reconstruction of a Social Structure of Accumulation in the United States," *Review of Radical Political Economics*, vol. 29, no. 3 (September). Reprinted in Bob Jessop (ed.) (2001) *Regulation Theory and the Crisis of Capitalism*, vol. 4. Cheltenham, UK: Edward Elgar.

—— (2004) "Class Struggles and the Reinvention of American Capitalism in the Second Half of the Twentieth Century," *Review of Radical Political Economics*, vol. 36, no. 3 (Summer).

—— and Haider Khan (1993) "The Surplus Approach and the Environment," *Review of Radical Political Economics*, vol. 25, no. 3.

MacEwan, Arthur and William Tabb (eds) (1989) *Instability and Change in the World Economy*. New York: Monthly Review Press.

Maddison, Angus (1991) *Dynamic Forces in Capitalist Development: A Long-Run Comparative View*. New York: Oxford University Press.

Mandel, Ernest (1978) *Late Capitalism*. London: Verso.

Mantoux, Paul (1961) *The Industrial Revolution in the Eighteenth Century*. New York: Harper.

Marglin, Stephen A. (1996) "What Do Bosses Do? The Origins and Functions of Hierarchy in Capitalist Production," in V. Lippit (ed.) *Radical Political Economy*.

—— and Juliet Schor (eds) (1990) *The Golden Age of Capitalism: Reinterpreting the Postwar Experience*. New York: Oxford University Press.

Marx, Karl (1961–62) *Capital*, vols. I, II and III. Moscow: Foreign Languages Publishing House.

—— (1973) *Grundrisse: Foundations of the Critique of Political Economy*. New York: Vintage Books.

—— and Friedrich Engels (1958) *Selected Works*, vols. I and II. Moscow: Foreign Languages Publishing House.

Meadows, Donella H. *et al.* (1972) *The Limits to Growth: A Report for the Club of Rome's Project on the Predicament of Mankind*. New York: Universe Books.

Miliband, Ralph (1969) *The State in Capitalist Society*. New York: Basic Books.

Minsky, Hyman (1986) *Stabilizing an Unstable Economy*. New Haven, Conn.: Yale University Press.

Mishan, E. J. (1967) *The Costs of Economic Growth*. Harmonsdsworth, UK: Penguin Books.

Mishel, Lawrence, Jared Bernstein, and John Schmitt (1999) *The State of Working America 1998–99*. Ithaca, N.Y.: Cornell University Press.

Mishra, Ramesh (1999) *Globalization and the Welfare State*. Cheltenham, UK: Edward Elgar.

Moore, Jr., Barrington (1998) *Moral Aspects of Economic Growth and Other Essays*. Ithaca, N.Y.: Cornell University Press.

Muller, Jerry Z. (2002) *The Mind and the Market: Capitalism in Modern European Thought*. New York: Knopf.

Norgaard, Richard B. (1994) *Development Betrayed: The End of Progress and a Coevolutionary Revisioning of the Future*. London: Routledge.

North, Douglass C. (1981) *Structure and Change in Economic History*. New York: Norton.

—— (1990) *Institutions, Institutional Change and Economic Performance*. Cambridge: Cambridge University Press.

Nove, Alec (1986) *The Soviet Economic System*, 3rd edn. Boston, Mass.: Allen Unwin.

—— (1991) *The Economics of Feasible Socialism Revisited*. London: HarperCollins.

Nussbaum, Martha C. and Amartya Sen (eds) (1993) *The Quality of Life*. Oxford: Oxford University Press.

O'Connor, Martin (ed.) (1994) *Is Capitalism Sustainable? Political Economy and the Politics of Ecology*. New York: Guilford Press.

O'Hara, Phillip Anthony (ed.) (1999) *Encyclopedia of Political Economy*. London: Routledge.

Ozaki, Robert (1991) *Human Capitalism: The Japanese Enterprise System as World Model*. New York: Kodansha International.

Perelman, Michael (2000) *The Invention of Capitalism: Classical Political Economy and the Secret History of Primitive Accumulation*. Durham, N.C.: Duke University Press.

Polanyi, Karl (1957) *The Great Transformation: The Political and Economic Origins of Our Time*. Boston, Mass.: Beacon Press.

Pollin, Robert (2003) *Contours of Descent: U.S. Economic Fractures and the Landscape of Global Austerity*. London: Verso.

Poulantzas, Nicos (1978) *Classes in Contemporary Capitalism*. London: Verso.

Reich, Michael (1997) "Social Structure of Accumulation Theory: Retrospect and Prospect," *Review of Radical Political Economics*, vol. 29, no. 3 (September).

Resnick, Stephen A. and Richard D. Wolff (1987) *Knowledge and Class: A Marxian Critique of Political Economy*. Chicago, Ill.: University of Chicago Press.

—— (1996) "Power, Property and Class," in V. Lippit (ed.) *Radical Political Economy*.

—— (2002) *Class Theory and History: Capitalism and Communism in the U.S.S.R.* New York: Routledge.

Romano, Richard and Melvin Leiman (eds) (1970) *Views on Capitalism*. Beverly Hills, Calif.: Glencoe Press.

Ryner, J. Magnus (2002) *Capitalist Restructuring, Globalisation and the Third Way: Lessons from the Swedish Model*. New York: Routledge.

Schmidt, Vivien A. (2002) *The Futures of European Capitalism*. Oxford: Oxford University Press.

Schor, Juliet and Jong-Il You (eds) (1995) *Capital, the State and Labour: A Global Perspective*. Aldershot UK: Edward Elgar.

Schumpeter, Joseph A. (1934) *The Theory of Economic Development*. Oxford: Oxford University Press.

—— (1950) *Capitalism, Socialism and Democracy*, 3rd edn. New York: Harper.

Scitovsky, Tibor (1986) *Human Desires and Economic Satisfaction: Essays on the Frontiers of Economics*. New York: New York University Press.

—— (1992) *The Joyless Economy: The Psychology of Human Satisfaction*, revised edn. New York: Oxford University Press.

Shonfield, Andrew (1965) *Modern Capitalism: The Changing Balance of Public and Private Power*. Oxford: Oxford University Press.

Smith, Adam (1937) *An Inquiry into the Nature and Causes of the Wealth of Nations*. New York: The Modern Library.

Sraffa, Pierro (ed.) (1951) *Works of David Ricardo*. London: Cambridge University Press.

Statistics Bureau, Ministry of Internal Affairs and Communications (2004) *Japan Statistical Yearbook 2004*. Tokyo.

Stiglitz, Joseph E. (2002) *Globalization and Its Discontents*. New York: Norton.

Sutch, Richard (2005) "National Income and Product Accounts," in S. B. Carter *et al.* (eds) *Historical Statistics of the United States: Millennial Edition*.

Sweezy, Paul *et al.* (1978) *The Transition from Feudalism to Capitalism*. London: Verso.

Swenson, Peter A. (2002) *Capitalists Against Markets: The Making of Labor Markets and Welfare States in the United States and Sweden*. New York: Oxford University Press.

Thurow, Lester (1996) *The Future of Capitalism*. New York: William Morrow and Co.

Tigar, Michael E. and Madeleine R. Levy (1977) *Law and the Rise of Capitalism*. New York: Monthly Review Press.

Tsuru, Shigeto (1993) *Japan's Capitalism*. Cambridge: Cambridge University Press.

Union for Radical Political Economy (1978) *US Capitalism in Crisis*. New York: Union for Radical Political Economics.

US Department of Commerce, Bureau of the Census (1996) *Statistical Abstract of the United States 1996*. Washington, D.C.: US Government Printing Office.

—— (2001) *Statistical Abstract of the United States: 2001*. Washington, D.C.: US Government Printing Office.

—— (2002) *Statistical Abstract of the United States: 2002*. Washington, D.C.: US Government Printing Office.

—— (2003) *Poverty in the United States: 2002* (online).

Wade, Robert (1990) *Governing the Market: Economic Theory and the Role of Government in East Asian Industrialization*. Princeton, N.J.: Princeton University Press.

Wallerstein, Immanuel (1976) *The Modern World System: Capitalist Agriculture and the Origins of the European World-Economy in the Sixteenth Century*. New York: Academic Press.

—— (1979) *The Capitalist World-Economy*. Cambridge: Cambridge University Press.

—— (1980) *The Modern World System II: Mercantilism and the Consolidation of the European World-Economy, 1600–1750*. New York: Academic Press.

—— (1989) *The Modern World System III: The Second Era of the Great Expansion of the Capitalist World-Economy, 1730–1840s*. San Diego, Calif.: Academic Press.

—— and Etienne Balibar (1991) *Race, Nation, Class*. London: Verso.

Weber, Max (1958) *The Protestant Ethic and the Spirit of Capitalism*. New York: Scribner's.

Weisskopf, Thomas E. (1996) "Marxian Crisis Theory and the Contradictions of Late Twentieth-Century Capitalism," in V. Lippit (ed.) *Radical Political Economy*.

Wilber, Charles K. (ed.) (1984) *The Political Economy of Development and Underdevelopment*, 3rd edn. New York: Random House.

Wolfson, Martin H. (1994) "The Financial System and the Social Structure of Accumulation," in D. Kotz *et al.* (eds.) *Social Structures of Accumulation*.

Womack, James P., Daniel T. Jones, and Daniel Roos (1991) *The Machine that Changed the World: The Story of Lean Production*. New York: HarperCollins.

Woo-Cumings, Meredith (ed.) (1999) *The Developmental State*. Ithaca, N.Y.: Cornell University Press.

The World Bank (1993) *The East Asian Miracle: Economic Growth and Public Policy*. New York: Oxford University Press.

—— (2003) *Urban Poverty in East Asia*. Working Paper No. 11, Urban Sector Development Unit, East Asia Infrastructure Dept.

—— (2004) *World Development Report 2004*. New York: Oxford University Press.

Wright, Erik Olin (1989) "A General Framework for the Analysis of Class Structure," in Erik Olin Wright *et al.*, *The Debate on Classes*. New York: Verso.

—— (1997) "Rethinking, Once Again, the Concept of Class Structure," in John R. Hall (ed.) *Reworking Class*. Ithaca, N.Y.: Cornell University Press.

Zedillo, Ernesto (2004) "On China's Rise," *Forbes*, May 24, p. 43.

Zweig, Michael (2000) *The Working Class Majority*. Ithaca, N.Y.: Cornell University Press.

Index